You Can't Do That, Governor!

Wallace Glenn Wilkinson

Library of Congress Catalog Number: 95-90635
ISBN 0-9648058-0-4

Printed in the United States of America

Wallace's Publishing Company
Lexington, Kentucky

Dedication

Throughout my many years in business and in the public arena, I have been blessed with the support and friendship of thousands of fellow Kentuckians and even a few non-Kentuckians. Old friends and new share liberally in the experiences recounted in this book. I remember them all and dedicate this book to them. Some for their wisdom and counsel. Some for their faith and loyalty. All for their friendship and support.

As a partner in business and a partner in life, no one has provided me with more advice, support, and loyalty throughout our many years together than Martha Stafford Wilkinson. While others said "you can't do that," Martha was one who thought I could. As Kentucky's first lady, her tireless efforts to promote literacy in Kentucky will always be a source of great pride for me.

Wallace Glenn Wilkinson

Acknowledgments

This book is the result of efforts of countless individuals who contributed in various ways to the Wilkinson administration. Largely unsung throughout any administration is the governor's personal staff. Nothing would ever get done without the tireless efforts of those working closest to the governor. The goals we tried to achieve and the effort this required put extraordinary demands on everyone. It is a pleasure to hear so many people comment, even to this day, on the friendliness and helpfulness of my staff. I am very proud of them all.

My special thanks are extended to Jack Foster and Doug Alexander, without whom this book would not have been possible. Though he has never received the public recognition he deserves, Jack Foster is without a doubt the intellectual father of education reform in Kentucky. His book *If I Could Make a School* should be required reading for everyone who has a serious interest in improving public education in America.

Table of Contents

Introduction

The greatest impediment to effective government is resistance to change and innovation. While creativity, innovation, and determination are generally considered the hallmarks for success in most areas of life, government is not one of those areas.

I probably came to public life with one of the worst possible characteristics for a politician—an unwillingness to take "no" for an answer. Repeatedly, I have refused to accept what I was told I *could not do or be.* Some thought I could never escape my rural background. Forget trying to attend college, I was advised. Others didn't think I could succeed in business. And, of course, there were those who thought I could never be elected governor. Even after winning the election in record fashion, I was told that many of the ideas I had been talking about during the campaign, particularly those relating to education, simply couldn't or wouldn't be done.

Thoughout the campaign I talked about changing the way we educate children and the way we do business. What I generally heard from the bureaucracy and entrenched special interests was a resounding "You can't do that, Governor!" Having had to come from behind all my life, I didn't find the barriers to success in politics particularly formidable as I entered public life. Slowly but surely, however, I learned just how much I had underestimated the strength and depth of institutional and political resistance to new ideas, particularly ideas coming from outside the traditional political mainstream.

This book is about what I wanted to accomplish as governor and how I went about doing it. It is about how we managed to overcome most barriers to change and accomplish most of the things we set out to do. It also is about the price one pays for challenging the *status quo.*

You Can't Do That, Governor! is not intended to be a chronicle of the Wilkinson administration or a catalogue of what I consider its achievements. Throughout the book I have tried to candidly recount the significant events of my administration: its successes and failures, triumphs and disappointments, strengths and weaknesses. I would like this book to provide insight into the ideas and issues which I hoped would have a positive and lasting effect on real people with real problems.

Regardless of the reader's opinion of me or my administration, it is my hope that this account will provide insight and perspective into the joys and frustrations of public service and perhaps even some practical experience which might be helpful to others who seek public office.

Wallace Glenn Wilkinson

December 7, 1987

Governor Wilkinson:

Kentucky now looks to you as it looks to no one else on this earth.

My prayer for you is that the blessings of governing will outweigh the burdens, and that your triumphs will overshadow any defeats.

My prayer for Kentucky is that our advances might continue, and that your vision of a better future shall come to pass.

Together, may you and our people enjoy a journey of progress.

Sincerely,

Martha Layne

Personal letter from Governor Martha Layne Collins to her successor Governor Wallace Wilkinson and left in the governor's desk according to tradition.

I. WHO IS
WALLACE WILKINSON?

As the Democratic primary campaign entered its last weekend in May of 1987, it began to dawn on the media and political observers that I might actually win the nomination. In our last planning session, my political strategist James Carville predicted that the front runner in the campaign would now attack me, asserting that I am an unknown quantity. "They will try to raise doubts about you," said James.

He was dead right. The only attack ads directed at me during the entire campaign began just a few days before the primary election. Exactly as James had predicted, the ads asked the rhetorical question "What do we really know about Wallace Wilkinson?" The ads summed up the feeling of many of the political observers and editorial writers who had basically ignored my candidacy. This upstart from Casey County is about to snatch the reins of power from the insiders. Who is he, and what kind of governor would he make?

As is true with all political candidates, I brought with me to public office certain perspectives about how and what I thought government can and should do. In order to understand some of the positions I took both as a candidate and later as governor, I want to begin this book by explaining how my life experiences have had a profound influence on my political views.

Rural Political Conservatism

Although I have spent nearly all of my adult life in urban Lexington, and it is there I had my financial success, I never forgot what it was like to be born and grow up in a place like rural Casey County, Kentucky. It was there I experienced both the blessings and curses of being isolated and poor. It was there I came to understand first hand what it means to be overlooked by those more fortunate or powerful.

I confess that coming from a poor, rural upbringing and having to fight adversity to gain what I sought out of life influenced my ideas of where Kentucky's priorities needed to be changed. Although I had found my way out of poverty, thousands of others were left behind with little or no hope for a better future.

In recalling my rural heritage, I once told a reporter that "I have always felt that growing up in Casey County was very beneficial to me. I learned the virtues of a small-town community, where people helped and trusted each other. It taught me how to trust people and how to recognize those who could not be trusted."

Instilled deep within me was the belief that, if given the opportunity, anyone could obtain almost any desired goal if he or she were willing to work hard to get it. As an extension of that personal philosophy, I entered public life believing that Kentucky could do the same. It was this belief in myself and in Kentucky which inspired me to seek the state's highest public office, even though I was a political unknown and lacked the backing of the political establishment.

The political philosophy which guided me into politics was not traditional democratic dogma. There is no question that my rural upbringing influenced many of my political opinions later in life. My parents were among the few Democrats living in Casey County. I once asked my father why all my friends were Republicans and we were not. He told me how he thought Herbert Hoover, a Republican president, had just about wiped out our family financially, and he made me promise never to be a Republican! I kept my promise but retained much of the rural conservatism with which I grew up.

Rural people are very distrustful of politicians and government. What went on in the state capitol just didn't seem to be of much concern to most Casey Countians. Family conversation tended to focus on matters more relevant to our daily lives than "politics." Much of my attitude toward government was influenced by a deep distrust of government inherited from my parents. On the other hand, I came to realize over the years that government had a profound effect on our lives, for good or ill. It seemed to me that government held the potential to make things better if those in office could just relate to what people really needed from it.

In my youth there were few political role models to interest me in a career in public service. Living in a rural, Republican county before the advent of widespread television coverage of politics meant that few Kentucky governors, most of whom were Democrats, ever visited Casey County or were otherwise seen by any of us. If one did visit, it was a big deal.

One of my most vivid childhood memories is of being let out of school to watch Governor "Happy" Chandler's motorcade pass through town. Standing on the sidewalk that day, I saw more car than governor as Happy sped by us. But to a child in rural Kentucky, it was as if all I had ever imagined about success and importance had revealed itself to me in those fleeting seconds. It never occurred to me then that some day in the future this same Governor Chandler would stand at the base of the Lincoln statue in the rotunda of the state Capitol to endorse *my* candidacy for governor. All other accomplishments aside, that day was for me a vivid reminder of how far I had come since those childhood days in Casey County.

More than political symbolism was involved, therefore, when I chose to announce formally my intention to seek the Democratic nomination for governor in Liberty, the county seat of Casey County. It was the best place I could think of to set forth clearly my political concerns and priorities. I intended to run as a rural Kentuckian, and I intended to stress the values of a close family living in a close community.

Business and Politics

What Casey County lacked in political role models it more than made up for in other influences. The work ethic, determination, and independence I developed was pure rural America. Ironically, when later applied to politics, these same qualities were interpreted by some as a "my way or no way" stubbornness and inflexibility.

I didn't start selling popcorn and shining shoes on the public square in Liberty because I had a childhood dream of becoming a successful businessman. I did it because it was the only way to have any money. As a matter of fact, despite the rags to riches, Horatio Alger-type story that has sometimes been used to describe my success, I did not grow up with ambitions of becoming a business entrepreneur. Electrical engineering was my original occupational interest.

My business experience had at least as great an influence on my political philosophy as my rural upbringing. If growing up in Casey County taught me the value of hard work and discipline, struggling to succeed in business taught me the value of persistence and resolve. "We must never forget our heritage," I said in my inaugural address. "We must continually remind ourselves that our primary mission is to foster and nurture that most basic of all Kentucky principles, the principle of achievement as a result of hard work. And it is state government's role to provide an environment that allows all of our people to realize their full potential."

Had I not had to struggle just to reach the bottom rung of the ladder of success, perhaps I would not have believed so deeply in the importance of individual commitment and responsibility. Clearly my personal experiences greatly influenced my belief that the best work government can do is not to try to solve people's problems for them, but to give them the tools with which to solve them on their own. My approach to education and economic development, two of the mainstays of government, was deeply rooted in the belief that for years Kentucky had been going about it the wrong way.

The primary focus of most government agencies and special interests is to find ways to perpetuate themselves and expand their scope of influence. Here I was saying we were not going to do that anymore. We were going to tell people how to figure out how to solve their own problems and then ask them how we could help. I was not trying to be governor to find ways to invest in more government. I wasn't the first person to approach the job with that attitude, but few had been more determined to make it work or had been more outspoken in their criticism of the status quo. And few of them had been more maligned for it.

There is a perception that businesspeople have difficulty in the political arena because they are unwilling to compromise. There might be an element of truth in this view-point. Compromise is not expected in business; but tough negotiation is. I found in politics that compromise means both sides must be willing to "give in" on something of importance. Often this means the result is something less than is needed to deal properly with the issue. In business you learn to walk away from a deal if it isn't right. Curiously, in politics this is interpreted as stubbornness and an unwillingness to compromise.

While my pursuit of what I thought was important was relentless, it was not ruthless. I had the toughness and determination needed to succeed in business, and it often showed when I was faced with a political challenge. Every time I was told I couldn't do something, I became more determined to prove it could be done. I didn't enjoy fighting the legislature, bureaucracy, and special interests, but I am convinced that often no real progress can be made without a fight.

Some political observers have suggested that businesspeople who enter politics are often ineffective because they have a hard time adapting to the way things are done in the public sector. While it probably is accurate to say that some of the practices of business are not readily embraced in government, I believe that the problem may be more with government than with business.

I have very little tolerance for the slow pace of decision making that characterizes government. I remember an incident that occurred during my first few days in office. I wanted something done that day and was told it would take five days. I was curious about why it took so long. I was told it required five signatures before it could be done! That translated into one day per signature. I personally walked the paperwork through the bureaucracy to get each signature. What I learned that day was exactly why government cannot respond to the public demand for efficiency and responsiveness. I certainly cannot claim to have conquered this problem, but it helps explain why business people who enter public service fight the government bureaucracy from the day they take office.

A Tale of Two Kentuckys

Years of neglect of the public infrastructure, particularly in rural Kentucky, gave most rural Kentuckians little hope of attracting and retaining the jobs that come with new or expanding business and industry. I considered it appalling that some areas of Kentucky did not have access to safe and clean water, not to mention fiber optics. Bridges and sewage treatment facilities needed to be built. Jails and other public facilities were either nonexistent or in disrepair all across Kentucky. Important highway improvements needed to be completed after many years of neglect or only partial construction.

The larger cities are quite sophisticated in securing needed government support—both state and federal—

to invest in their communities. Lexington and Louisville in particular are well represented in the legislature and generally receive at least their fair share of the public largesse with little effort. By contrast, the rest of the state has had to fight for everything it has gotten, and it benefited primarily from road construction but little else. Even these roads are built in a crazy quilt fashion, with some major highways still unfinished.

I was firmly convinced that Kentucky could never successfully compete economically with the rest of the nation unless there was prosperity throughout the commonwealth. We could not continue to have "two Kentuckys." One third of the state cannot carry the economic burden of the other two thirds. Or, as I often said on the campaign trail, "Fifteen counties can't continue to support the other 105." If I were fortunate enough to get elected governor, it was my intention to rectify this neglect by ensuring that rural Kentucky, including many of its smaller cities, would be the focus of job creation and public infrastructure investment. The influence of my rural upbringing was most profoundly illustrated in my determination to enhance educational and economic opportunities across the commonwealth.

Although economic issues were paramount with me because of my business background, I also had a deep concern over the inadequate education Kentucky's children were receiving. Like many other southern states, Kentucky suffered from many years of educational neglect. Clearly, rural and small schools were at both a social and economic disadvantage. The absence of a growing tax base together with a declining population doomed many schools to mediocrity. Such inequities contributed further to the distance between the "two Kentuckys."

Once again, I felt strongly that urban-rural inequality was a major reason for the continued decline in the quality of life in many areas of Kentucky. But in my case, this issue had personal significance. I was a product of this neglect and knew first hand what an inferior education would mean to future generations of Kentucky children.

As a school child in Casey County, I had many well intentioned teachers who no doubt gave me the best they had to offer, but I found it wasn't good enough. When the absence of certain high school courses prevented my acceptance into the electrical engineering program at the University of Kentucky, I was both frustrated and angry. I was forced to attend Campbellsville College to get the mathematics and science courses I didn't get in high school. Even for a conservative politician, this experience made me determined as a political leader to see that no other Kentucky child would ever have to suffer such disappointment. Public education had to be radically changed in Kentucky.

The inequality of educational opportunity in Kentucky was blatantly obvious. Sixty-two school districts had sued the governor, general assembly and superintendent of public instruction alleging that the public schools in Kentucky were unconstitutional because of inequities in funding. But the problem was more than an unequal distribution of money and wealth. It was also a problem of unequal expectations.

It seemed to me that Frankfort's politicians had written off certain areas of the commonwealth as too backward ever to offer a quality education. The approach being pursued by Frankfort policy makers was simply to hand down more regulations and continually to raise school taxes. In my view, it was time to do more than just pour more money into education. It was time to rethink what all children learn and how they learn it. There had to be equality in expectations as well as in funding.

Taxes and Fiscal Policy

Economic development and education seemed natural allies. Both were at the top of my concerns for Kentucky. They later became cornerstone issues of my administration. Still, there were other things I had to consider. Kentucky's problems were deep-rooted and of long duration. Public funding of an ambitious education and public infrastructure program would be very difficult unless tax revenues were significantly increased. This situation posed a special problem for me, since I am essentially a fiscal conservative.

It was my view that Kentucky's political leaders had badly mismanaged the tax and fiscal policy of the commonwealth. On the one hand, they had employed every tax conceivable in their effort to spread the tax burden equitably. On the other hand, the tax base had been steadily eroded through extensive use of tax exemptions for special interests. The practical effect was that the existing tax system was yielding much less revenue than it was capable of producing under current tax rates.

Another problem was the penchant in the General Assembly to enact budgets based on overly optimistic revenue projections. When revenues consistently fell below projections each year, both the present and previous governors had to make budget cutbacks, which greatly frustrated the affected agencies in state and local government. I was seeing the worst of all worlds in Frankfort. Revenue shortfalls were overcome by enacting small but steady increases in taxes required to balance the budget.

One of my first acts as governor was to move revenue forecasting from the Revenue to Finance and Administration Cabinet. My goal was to put an end to the practice of writing the budget and then working to make revenue match the wish list of the legislature and bureaucracy. I chose Dr. James Ramsey, a career economist in Kentucky state government, to assume the forecasting responsibility. He was given clear instructions to be conservative and stick to his estimates. We developed the most accurate forecasts in recent memory.

Irresponsible budgeting was combined with passage of programs which promised much but delivered little because they were never properly funded. The public had concluded, quite accurately I might add, that their taxes were continually rising, yet it seemed things weren't getting any better. It was like paying for a dead horse! In their view, government just continued to cost more without delivering more.

Some of the fiscal problems facing state and local governments could be solved through better management of available revenues, building budgets on more accurate revenue projections, and changing some spending priorities. Still, something had to be done to raise the revenues required to make the changes Kentucky desperately needed. Furthermore, it didn't appear that the revenue situation would get much better in the near term.

Antitax sentiment runs deep among Kentucky voters, and particularly so in rural areas of the state. Governors who significantly raise taxes are long remembered in Kentucky! I fully understood any increase in taxes would be politically unpopular, and it also could be a drag on an already sluggish economy. On the other hand, if taxes had to be increased, I believed the increase should yield enough revenue to have a significant impact on the needs of the commonwealth. The political pain would be the same for a small increase as for a large one.

The Office of Governor

In the late 1970s the General Assembly sharply curtailed the ability of a governor directly to influence such matters as the appointment of legislative leadership and committee chairs and the movement of legislation. These changes also gave the legislature greater control of the state budget. The intent was to make the general assembly a more equal partner in the governance of the commonwealth.

Over the following decade, I watched two governors allow the legislature to take unto itself ever greater control of matters which I thought should remain the prerogative of the executive branch of government. I was greatly disturbed by this gradual erosion of the authority of the office of the governor. In fact, I vowed that if I ever became governor, I would put an end to this encroachment on the constitutional authority of the executive branch of government.

In my view, the legislature was made up of individuals whose primary loyalty was to their own community or region of the state, which often took precedence over the general welfare of the commonwealth. I also thought many of them had become captives of special interests which used the legislative committee structure to control the passage or rejection of legislation favorable or unfavorable to their interests. I was convinced many of them were more concerned about keeping their office than making the best decisions for the people of Kentucky.

As history now will record, my relationship with the General Assembly was at best an uncomfortable one. My critics say it was unnecessarily a contentious and unfortunate one. On a personal level, I feel I was able to develop many good friends among legislators during my administration. However, given my views on legislative independence and the processes it uses to shape state policy, I suppose my confrontation with the legislature was inevitable. My attitude toward the legislature was not based on a personal dislike for *individual legislators* who made up the General Assembly. Rather, it was my concern about the collective behavior of the legislature *as an institution of government.*

The Importance of Succession

Newly elected governors in Kentucky generally have the best opportunity to get significant legislation passed during their first legislative session, because in the second session they are considered "lame ducks." The legislative process is politically awkward for any governor, but in my case even more so because of the deviousness of the leadership, especially in the Senate. Governors must find legislators willing to sponsor legislation on their behalf, and then this legislation must compete with all the legislation developed by legislators in the months preceding the first legislative session. Although legislative leadership usually will offer to secure sponsors for bills proposed by a new governor, this is more a matter of courtesy than a commitment to support its passage.

A strong political leader is needed to set the policy agenda for the state and to oversee its proper implementation. I had little confidence then, and even less now, in a government run by committee and special interest. Only the governor is elected statewide and accountable to the state at large. In the name of legislative independence, Kentucky had seriously crippled the ability of governors to lead and effect change. While governors were limited to a single four year term, legislators could make a career of elected office. The ability to remain in office for a long period of time gave them a great political advantage.

I managed to stem the tide of legislative encroachment on the executive for the time I was there, but my efforts subsequently proved to be only a temporary inconvenience in the General Assembly's drive to wrest power from the executive branch. It was my belief that the only way to redress the growing imbalance between the legislative and executive branches of government was to give governors an opportunity to succeed themselves. Although I failed to get a succession amendment on the ballot during my administration, voters did finally approve one in 1992 along with several other electoral changes.

Changing the Behavior of Government

The bureaucracy of the executive branch can be just as formidable an obstacle for a governor as the General Assembly. The budget is the ultimate policy statement and the most powerful tool for influencing state policy. I believe I spent more time and effort on the budget, and probably knew and understood it better, than any governor in recent memory. Although much of the budget is considered the "base" on which any increase in revenues projected over the coming biennium can be added, it was my belief that a strong governor could influence funding priorities by carefully looking for things to increase, reduce, or eliminate.

The political reality is that every major spending program of government has a public constituency to support and defend it. Efforts to shift priorities in government inevitably mean raising the ire of the beneficiaries of programs which might be reduced or eliminated to make way for new initiatives. The political cost of such actions leads most politicians to leave things alone and just keep increasing government to accommodate new priorities. In fact, many of these programs were originally created by legislators for the benefit of some constituents they represent (and upon whom they depend for reelection). However, once a program survives more than one budget cycle, it becomes part of the repertoire of government services and will continue whether or not the original sponsor remains in the legislature to promote and protect it.

Programs also have their advocates within the executive branch - the bureaucrats whose job it is to administer these programs. Bureaucrats typically seek to expand the programs they oversee. They are closely allied with the beneficiaries of these programs and can on a moment's notice marshal the "troops" to come to the rescue of their program if it appears in danger of a budget cut or is targeted for elimination. A governor who earnestly wants to cut back on big government often finds his own agencies at odds with this objective. I knew these obstacles lay ahead, yet I felt it was the responsibility of a governor to rein in the bureaucracy and counter the influence of those state employees whose jobs were directly tied to specific programs and constituencies.

I also had concerns about the extent to which policy is made by bureaucrats rather than by elected leaders. For a large number of government workers, their sole activity is either to make or enforce regulations rather than deliver services. Unless the regulatory process is carried out under the watchful eye of a governor, state agencies sometimes go beyond what is required to implement properly the law. The regulatory process is a powerful tool of government and should be used prudently and with great restraint.

Regulations also were (and still are) of great interest to legislators. In recent years they had attempted to overrule executive agencies through hearings to attach (ratify) every new regulation. Although oversight of executive action might be appropriate for a legislature, I considered approving regulations by legislative interim committees as just one more assault on the authority of the executive branch of government. Although I shared the legislature's concern about the over-zealous use of regulations, I believed it was the sole responsibility of the governor to ensure strong but fair implementation of the laws enacted by the legislature. Interim legislative approval of regulations clearly constituted a violation of the separation of powers embodied in the Constitution of the Commonwealth of Kentucky.

Without question, the independent spirit and skepticism of government I grew up with in rural Kentucky, together with a competitive spirit and determination to succeed, influenced my approach to the campaign and ultimately to public service. I knew I could win if I could communicate these qualities to voters, address the issues they felt were important, and get a few breaks along the way. After all, I had fought against the odds throughout my life, so why should a political campaign or public service be different?

II. THE LONG
ROAD TO FRANKFORT

Before seeking public office, Martha Wilkinson and I were totally absorbed in our businesses. I personally found business a fascinating challenge. Beginning with a used textbook business in Lexington, Martha and I expanded our business interests to include coal, real estate, farming, and banking. As the years passed, these enterprises consumed all our time and energy. Having achieved success in these areas, we felt it was time for us to consider public service.

Winning the governorship of Kentucky began in 1983 when Martha and I made the decision to commit ourselves to that goal. I recall sitting around election headquarters watching the returns come in on Harvey Sloane's ill fated campaign for governor when a few people started showing up with Wilkinson in '87 bumper stickers. At first I thought it was strange, but by the time Martha Layne Collins was inaugurated Governor, I had pretty much made up my mind to run.

Upon learning of my interest in the governorship, John Ed Pearce of the Louisville *Courier-Journal* newspaper asked why I was willing to give up a very successful business career in an effort to become Governor. I said at the time that I had always been interested in government. I told him I remembered my father working for Adlai Stevenson against Dwight Eisenhower, and when I became able to spare some time, I jumped at the chance to become more active in politics. I had a deep interest in the future of Kentucky and was committed to making it better. I was convinced I could make a difference if given the chance.

I was not the first successful businessman and Frankfort outsider to seek the state's highest political office. John Y. Brown, a multimillionaire business man who had never before held public office, was elected to the governor's office in 1979. Eight years later, another multimillionaire business man named Wallace Glenn Wilkinson seemed determined to repeat John Y. Brown's feat. Naturally, comparisons were made between the two of us. There were some significant differences, however, which I believe made my race for governor different and more difficult than Brown's in 1979.

For one thing, Brown entered his first race with much greater name recognition than I had. John was well known for building the Kentucky Fried Chicken fast food business into a national chain and earning a personal fortune along the way. His wife was a well-known celebrity. Additionally, John's father had been active in Kentucky politics for many years, having been a candidate for numerous statewide offices, including a run for governor in 1939. John Y. had high name recognition with voters even though that was his first run for public office. I also had to face two former governors, an incumbent lt. governor, and a former candidate and cabinet secretary, all of whom had high statewide name recognition compared to my own.

Another difference between the two of us was the kind of campaign we would run. I had a great interest in addressing issues facing government. In his first campaign, John took a stand on very few issues. His was a campaign of slogans, particularly his pledge to "run government like a business." In contrast to this style of campaigning, I was very outspoken on virtually every issue facing Kentucky, but particularly on the need for education reform and my support for a statewide lottery. These differences became more obvious as the campaign progressed, so the comparisons ended shortly after Brown entered the 1987 race for governor.

Lacking the name recognition of the other aspirants to the governor's office, Martha and I knew it would be a long, hard campaign. However, it was a challenge both of us were prepared to meet. We spent many days pouring over county maps and thinking through how we could build political support from the bottom up. We knew winning a general election would take persistence and money.

The most immediate challenge was to convince people we could make a difference and that *we could win*. Only then would people be willing to invest their time and money in our campaign. Wanting to be governor and demonstrating the ability to win are miles apart. The election was more than three years away. There was plenty of time to build support, but we were starting from ground zero. We had to pursue a strategic course if we were to be successful.

Campaigning for political office was not entirely new to me. I had been involved in Terry McBrayer's campaign against John Y. Brown for governor in 1979; I was campaign finance chairman for Harvey Sloane in his run for governor in 1983; and I was John Y. Brown's campaign chairman when he ran against Dee Huddleston for the U.S. Senate the next year. Even so, I was considered by the news media and political observers to be a political novice because this would be *my* first attempt to win public office.

Every political campaign is unique, and so was mine. However, the "come from way behind" campaign I waged will be almost impossible to repeat in the future. Recent changes in campaign finance laws will give an even greater advantage to incumbent officials and political activists who are willing to use their Frankfort connections to gain higher office. Much fun has been made over the years of the "revolving chairs" in Frankfort—the practice of an office holder running for a different statewide office every four years. Clearly, recent election reform has done little to diminish the influence being in Frankfort has on winning another statewide office.

Perhaps some people actually believe it's wrong for outsiders to gain public office on their first tries. Somehow it isn't right for a person to be governor who hasn't "paid his dues" by working his way up the political ladder. Maybe I am placing more importance on name recognition than it deserves, but clearly a lack of name recognition was responsible in large part for my remaining so far behind the other candidates in the voter preference polls for such a long time.

The Task of Defining Myself to the Public

With each successive election since the advent of television, political campaigns have made increasingly greater use of the electronic media. I certainly attempted to make effective use of the media in all its forms. However, I blended the media aspect of the campaign with traditional political techniques. Old style one-on-one, hand-to-hand, county-by-county campaigning was a major part of my campaign.

Over nearly four years, Martha and I walked, drove, flew, and bused our way across Kentucky from Ashland to Fulton and Covington to Somerset. From early in the morning until late at night, day after day, month after month, we took our message county by county to build a broad base of support. We did it literally one voter at a time. Campaigning in a state almost 500 miles long with 120 counties is a formidable challenge to any candidate, but especially one whose name recognition can be measured in single digits.

I remember early in the campaign being introduced as a gubernatorial candidate named Wallace Wilkerson. I thought to myself, "How in the world can you get elected when people can't even get your name right!" Still I thought people could be persuaded to support me if they got to know me personally, even if they couldn't get my name exactly right.

I believe my rural Kentucky roots and values turned out to be my greatest asset during this part of the campaign. The pleasure I got out of meeting people and talking about their problems was sincere, and they instinctively knew it. I could easily relate to their sense of isolation from the political process, the feeling that what happens in Frankfort has little impact on the real world in which they lived. I could talk comfortably about all aspects of their lives because I had grown up in the same environment, learned some of the same values, and believed in most of the same things.

In some cases the sheer determination and persistence with which we approached voters was enough to win them over. Red and Katheryn Saltsman had been having a barbecue in Sorgho for a number of years before I attended for the first time in 1986. Like many similar businesses across Kentucky, Red's Place is not simply a restaurant. It is a community, cultural, and information center. One of Red's regulars was Ulysses G. "Britches" Embry. Until his retirement in 1992, Britches was chief of the Owensboro Police Department and a strong political influence in his own right.

The day I attended Red's Barbecue, I quickly seized my first opportunity to corner Chief Embry. I gripped his arm firmly while expounding on the reasons he should support me for governor. I sensed as we talked that he was anxious to get away. Knowing this might be my best and only chance to have his ear to myself, I plunged ahead in great detail and at some length, using all my persuasive abilities. I dared not let go of his arm for fear of losing him. Finally, I asked him, "What do I have to do to get your commitment?"

"Wallace," he said, "I don't know you, but I've heard you can be very persuasive, and a lot of good people in Daviess County tell me you're going to be our next governor. But I don't care about any of that. I really have to go to the men's room, so if you will let go of my arm, you've got it!"

Week after week, Martha and I went from county to county and town to town, meeting people and talking with them one on one. I told them of my background. I listened to their hopes and dreams for a better future. I spoke of new ideas and more jobs. I promised to use my business experience to bring small and medium size businesses and industries to small Kentucky towns which desperately needed jobs to be viable communities. I did my best to convince them I would bring a fresh perspective to Frankfort.

After eighteen months on the campaign trail, I felt I had put to rest the question of my tenacity and durability. It no longer was a question of whether I would stay in the race; the question now was whether or not I could win. Political watchers in both parties acknowledged that my pursuit of individual commitments, my success in raising money, and my willingness to spend my own money made me a factor in a field of five Democratic aspirants for the governor's office. Still, I remained at the bottom of the opinion polls in name recognition for all candidates. So I continued to meet with people in all 120 counties of the commonwealth. Interviews, personal appearances, and television commercials were my front line attack.

As we neared the primary election, Jim Jordan of the *Lexington Herald-Leader* newspaper asked me where I thought my campaign stood about three months before the election. I replied that "we have been out here working our butts off, not only on name recognition but on organization—making sure we had the horses in place to pull the wagon when it came time to move the wagon." As for my low standing in the opinion polls (which were showing me with only 10 percent of the vote at the time), I responded that "80 percent of the people . . . can't even tell you who is in the race. They are going to say the first name that comes into their mind. I can't say we are going to win, but we see very clearly that we *can* win."

Establishing the Message

Personality contests are generally won by the best known candidate. I knew we had to make the election about something more than simply who is the best-known. As I crisscrossed the state I carried a simple message about jobs and a brighter economic future for rural Kentucky. When the time came to announce my candidacy formally, I knew it was time to lay down the platform of change on which I would seek election. In my announcement speech in the fall of 1986 I said:

Kentuckians are proud. They're winners. The people here can do anything, but their leadership has failed them. We can't continue to watch our kids leave Kentucky for better opportunities. They do not go because they want to, but because they have to. We owe them more than that. We're better than that. On our worst day, we're better than that!

Most of our counties are ignored by Frankfort. They are not making it economically. Their jobs are drying up. Small and medium businesses–the businesses that account for 89% of the new jobs–are struggling.

It's just business as usual in Kentucky politics, business as always in Frankfort. There are commissions and panels and task forces all the time, but the same old problems continue to plague us year after year. It's the same tired old faces, with the same tired old solutions, playing the same old political tune they've played for twenty years. But we're not going to dance to it any more!

The call for change was clear. Right from the beginning I laid the blame for Kentucky's economic woes on political neglect. I contended the first solution to Kentucky's problems is simple: "Business 101. You fire the management! You don't solve problems with the people who created them." I also wanted to make it clear that I was the only candidate who was a nonpolitician with the ideas and energy to revive the state's stagnated economy.

The economic prosperity enjoyed in a few regions of the state had missed most of rural Kentucky, and I wanted to make sure I got that message across at every opportunity. People living outside the urbanized northern Kentucky, Louisville and Lexington "golden triangle" area of the state had suffered severe economic hardship, particularly after the oil embargo ended in the late 1970s. Unemployment had remained high over a long period of time. Incomes were going backward for many Kentucky families. Job creation was as paramount in my mind as I believed it was in the minds of voters.

Throughout the campaign, I contended that we needed new ideas. "We can't be competitive following leaders who've never known how to compete," I said. Of course, I too was embarking on the greatest competitive challenge of *my* life—the goal of being governor of the Commonwealth of Kentucky. Unless I could win what most people considered an improbable political victory, I could not possibly pursue the vision I had of a better Kentucky for all—especially for those who had not tasted the economic prosperity enjoyed by those living in the golden triangle.

As I took aim on the political insiders in Frankfort, I was quickly labeled by the news media and political pundits as "antiestablishment." A political outsider. A populist. A novice in government. Over time all of these terms were used to define me and my candidacy for governor. But I believe my call for change contributed in large measure to the ultimate success of my campaign. I built my case for being governor upon a deep rooted feeling of economic and political alienation throughout rural Kentucky. I wanted to underscore that message by announcing my candidacy for governor in my hometown of Liberty.

A candidate's formal announcement is generally planned to generate the biggest splash possible. Liberty was not the first choice of some of my advisors. It was not the most accessible place in the world to hold the most important public event of the campaign up to that point. Before deciding to announce formally in Liberty during the weekend of the annual Apple Festival, I asked my campaign press secretary Doug Alexander what suggestions he had for getting the most media out of the story. Doug was pretty blunt in his assessment. "Whatever you do," he said, "don't announce in Liberty on a

Saturday." In other words, Doug was saying, "You can't do that, Governor."

Working My Way Up the Opinion Polls

As we entered the last six months of the primary campaign, I still had only about 5 percent of the Democrat vote. The *Courier-Journal* showed me at 4 percent in their poll reported on December 7, 1986. Brown was at 20 percent, with other candidates all about 10 percent. The undecided vote was 31 percent. My staff maintained that voters would not begin to focus on the election until Kentucky Derby weekend. Nevertheless, it was getting more difficult to generate enthusiasm and momentum for "fifth place Wilkinson."

It was obvious my campaign was in trouble. News articles relegated coverage of my campaign speeches and appearances to the "also are running" comments at the end of the lead article. Although television ads helped improve my name recognition, they were not bringing me votes. It also was especially evident in fund raising. I had never raised the kind of money the better known candidates raised, but the "horse race" opinion polls published regularly in the *Courier-Journal* and John Y. Brown's entry in the race combined to dry up even those relatively small sources. Later on, when I was criticized for accepting campaign contributions, I reminded the media that a fund raiser for the Wilkinson '87 Campaign was me writing the check to my own campaign.

I realized we needed to do something to get the media to pay attention to me. My campaign manager, Danny Briscoe, suggested that I add a political advisor to my staff. At first I was cool to the idea. Danny had good experience running political campaigns in Kentucky. I also had good people handling various aspects of the campaign. And besides that, I found it difficult to understand how an outsider could improve on what we already knew. Nonetheless, I consented to interview a few people Danny had identified as successful consultants.

It was then I hired James Carville, who over time came to be one of my most trusted advisors. James, as is now well known, went on to become the principal architect and "crisis control" manager for Bill Clinton's campaign for U.S. President in 1992. But when I first met him, he was just beginning to make a name for himself, particularly as a specialist in helping "come from behind" candidates.

Every consultant I talked to about working for the campaign made a point of stressing the variety of services they offered and the size and experience of their rather extensive staffs. James was different! In many ways he probably was the most unlikely prospect in the group of consultants Danny had contacted. James not only didn't talk like the other consultants, he didn't look like them either. Tall, lanky, poorly dressed, speaking with the heavy twang of his native Cajun Louisiana, James did not fit the image most people have of political consultants. Richard Gere in the movie "*Power*" he was not. He didn't even have an office, much less a staff.

At the end of my last interview with James, I finally asked him why I should hire him instead of someone else with a bigger reputation and plenty of staff support. "Guv'nor," James replied, "the sheriff of a small Texas town once called on the Texas Rangers for help to put down a riot. Anxiously waiting at the depot for the promised reinforcements, the sheriff was shocked when only one Ranger got off the train. 'Where's everybody else,' cried the sheriff. 'I've got a major riot on my hands.' The Ranger's response was short and to the point. 'One riot, one Ranger.' That's me, Guv'nor." The more I worked with James, the more I learned to appreciate his skill in getting right to the heart of an issue with just the right message.

Carville immediately identified several problems facing the campaign. First of all, we needed better coverage by the "free media"—what is reported daily by the working press who cover politics in Kentucky. The worst possible position for a candidate is to be ignored by the press. Somehow I had to involve myself in issues which would put me at the top of the story rather than in a paragraph at the end. I needed to take advantage of issues which were handed to me on a daily basis rather than try to create my own.

Second, we had to find a way to get the working press and editorial boards to view me as a serious contender. The news media had long characterized the Democratic primary election as a two-person race between John Y. Brown and Steve Beshear. The other three candidates, including myself, were given no chance to win. Such characterizations by the news media have a way of being self-fulfilling. It was imperative that such images of my candidacy be reversed.

Third, I had to broaden my message beyond being a political outsider who would turn the economy around and improve education. It was very unlikely that I would get endorsements from statewide elected officials, organized labor, or other high profile groups. Most endorsements would go to the more familiar and front-running candidates. Primarily through the efforts of northern Kentucky physician Floyd Poore, we did manage to garner two important endorsements. The only statewide group to endorse me as a candidate was the Kentucky Firefighters Association. Floyd also put together a group of over eighty northern Kentucky elected officials in an unprecedented show of support for any gubernatorial candidate, but particularly one considered to be a long shot. No one worked longer or harder for me than Floyd Poore in this campaign.

It was obvious I had to win the unaffiliated voter if I was to win without the support of traditional Democrat interest groups. I had to find their political "hot buttons" and get them to consider me as a viable alternative. Otherwise, many of them would vote for the front runner or simply would not vote at all. It was Carville's opinion that I needed to link myself more closely with issues that were on the minds of voters who were not enamored with either of the front runners.

Turning the Campaign Around

It is difficult to know, even in retrospect, what turns a campaign into a victory. As noted earlier, a key objective at this point was to get more attention from the working press. One issue I tried to use was my belief that Governor Collins had offered too much to attract Toyota Motor Company to Kentucky. A year earlier I had taken issue with the incentive package offered Toyota Motor Company. I supported the deal but thought Kentucky had paid too much to get it. I said at the time that "the Japanese are very patient, very skillful negotiators and business people. I think they just simply out-negotiated us."

The point I tried to make was that a businessman like myself could have brought Toyota to Kentucky for much less money. The euphoria of the Lexington news media over winning this economic prize resulted in editorials and stories designed to discredit my views. At the time, I seemed to be the only person expressing concerns about Kentucky's negotiating position. In the end, I was characterized in the news media as engaging in Japan bashing and failing to realize what a boon this would be to central Kentucky. It is interesting to note that the *Lexington Herald-Leader* has since then devoted quite a lot of editorial space to criticizing the use of state incentives of *any* kind in economic development. What a difference a little time makes.

My concerns for Kentucky's negotiating position were far more sincere than the media portrayed them at the time. I was aware of one particular aspect of the deal which involved the use of suites at the Capital Plaza Hotel, which I owned. The first inquiry we received simply sought the rate for leasing one of the suites. Pretty soon we were asked what it would cost to lease all of the suites on both floors. Then a request was made about furnishing and decorating the suites. Finally, someone admitted that cost wasn't an issue since the state was going to pay for it anyway. It was obvious that

Kentucky was upping the ante as each day passed without a decision by Toyota.

I tried to make it clear at the time that my criticism was not directed at Toyota. Had I been in their position, I would have done exactly the same thing as a businessman. If Toyota had not been astute enough to stop negotiations when it started looking like they might get too much, we might still be upping the ante. Regardless of the controversy, however, it did result in some talk about my campaign. All of a sudden, Wilkinson was now on the front page a few times rather than buried in the back.

The Toyota issue surfaced again during the final stretch of the primary campaign. A staff economist for the Legislative Research Commission (LRC), the staff arm of the General Assembly, testified at a legislative hearing in Wisconsin that he thought Kentucky had paid too much to get Toyota. He testified that the deal would cost more than it would bring to Kentucky, a statement that ultimately led to his dismissal.

When this story broke, we decided to run a TV spot on the Toyota deal in an attempt to take advantage of this renewed interest in the issue. Our opinion polls indicated the public still had mixed views on the deal, but it turned out the issue didn't have the political punch we thought it might have. This time the TV ads appeared not to gain us much, so we dropped them after a brief showing.

Capitalizing on the Lottery Issue

The idea of a statewide lottery had been around for some time. Several efforts by legislators to put a constitutional amendment before the voters to remove the restriction on lotteries from the state constitution had failed in the General Assembly. By 1987 every state bordering Kentucky except Indiana, Missouri, and Tennessee had a state lottery, and

Indiana already had a constitutional amendment headed for voter approval.

As we neared the first televised forum for the candidates in April 1987, the idea emerged of pushing the lottery to the forefront as a means of generating revenue for education. The forum was sponsored by the Prichard Committee for Academic Excellence and the League of Women Voters to deal exclusively with education. It presented a great opportunity to drop the lottery issue into the campaign. During my remarks at the forum, I proposed a state lottery as a way to increase funding for education. The public seemed to have had little interest in what I said that night about education, but the idea of a lottery "hit the jackpot" in a political sense.

The day after the forum was not a travel day. We had scheduled it as a day of rest and an opportunity to work on issues. Late in the day, as my meeting was breaking up, Martha, her sister Katherine Rubarts, and Wanda Terry returned from campaigning in Winchester. James Carville, Danny Briscoe, Doug Alexander, and I were standing in the driveway when they literally jumped out of the car at us. While I was holed up at the house, out of contact with the real world, they had experienced a virtual turnaround overnight in recognition of Wallace Wilkinson. All day long people had been coming up to them to talk about the lottery. "It was unbelievable," Martha said. "It was like electricity in the air."

We had become accustomed to the polite but noncommittal response we were getting from people who attended our political rallies. But on this day, people were coming forward to express their support for the lottery and for me. We definitely had hit the hot button James had been looking for. He instinctively knew we were on to something very big. Within five minutes he was on the telephone discussing a television commercial on the lottery. By the next day, we were looking at a rough cut of a new television spot. It was on the air in forty-eight hours!

Even though the vast majority of voters supported the lottery, it had vocal opposition from conservative church groups and a few others. Their opposition had always scared off most politicians, including all of my political opponents. The news media sensed a new dimension had been introduced into the campaign and immediately seized it. The effect on my campaign was immediate and dramatic. It moved me from the end of the news story to the headlines, a position I had been working hard to achieve without success. From that moment on, the lottery was a key talking point in every speech I gave.

Certainly the lottery proved to be much more politically potent than even I had considered it to be early in the campaign. It turned out to be the grass roots issue we needed to ignite voter interest in our campaign. All our opinion polls indicated sufficient support for a lottery to assure passage of the needed constitutional amendment, so I was confident in pursuing it. I felt the lottery was something people wanted, and I could use it to deflect some of the criticism I was receiving for not acknowledging the need for new sources of revenue. I can't say that it won the election for me, but clearly the working press acknowledged that it had made headlines for me.

Some Good Things Just Happen

Several things happened over which I had no control but which I believe directly influenced the outcome of the election. As I noted earlier, we were very concerned about the view that this was a two-person race. Something had to happen to break the lead Brown and Beshear had in the opinion polls. We had to show some movement in order to remain viable in the race. The first opening came when John Y. Brown made an offhand remark in the education forum that "HB 44"—the property tax restraint law —should be repealed to raise more money for public schools. The second came when Steve Beshear launched a series of negative advertisements assailing Brown's personal character and fitness to be governor again, and Brown decided to respond.

Although John Y. Brown repeatedly tried to clarify his statement on House Bill 44, he never fully recovered from the political damage it did to his campaign. As a matter of fact, campaigning in Henderson the next day, he confirmed his statement of the previous night. House Bill 44 had long been the litmus test for candidates on the tax issue. Repealing it would lift the restrictions on the amount of increase in property taxes local governments could levy without going to the voters for approval. To this day I'm not sure John realized what a significant impact advocating its repeal would have on his effort to return to Frankfort.

Steve Beshear, seeking to attract the pro-education vote, said he was willing to support higher taxes if they were dedicated to education. However, this equivocation on the tax issue made my proposal for a lottery to raise money for education even more attractive. It also gave me an opening to distinguish myself from the others on the basic issue of raising taxes.

These were not the only critical errors the Brown and Beshear campaigns would make. By virtue of his second place position in the opinion polls, Beshear was stuck with having to decide whether or not to go on the attack. Even though the number of undecided voters gave every candidate some reason to be optimistic, Beshear clearly thought time was running out for him to make a move on Brown. The decision to "go negative" backfired on Steve, but not necessarily for the reasons one might think.

Throughout the campaign, I felt I had the best group of advisors of all the candidates. Among them were two young men doing our research and polling—Mark Mellman and Ed Lazarus. Like James Carville, Mark and Ed were just beginning to make names for themselves and since then have gone on to considerable success. Mark and Ed analyzed every aspect of the campaign for me.

Conventional wisdom held that voters were put off by Brown's lifestyle and didn't think he had been a very effective governor. Mark and Ed had a slightly different but critically important assessment of Brown. Mark and Ed contended that Brown was not as vulnerable on his lifestyle and his political record as he was on his motivation. Generally, people thought Brown had earned the right to live his life pretty much as he pleased. They did not think he was a particularly bad governor. The celebrity status of John Y. and Phyllis, and its attendant lifestyle, interested the media and generally played well with ordinary Kentuckians. However, they didn't think he worked particularly hard at being governor.

It was our opinion that attacking Brown's lifestyle, and to a lesser extent his record as governor, would not be effective. Beshear did and missed the target. He ran a television spot based on a parody of the popular television program "Lifestyles of the Rich and Famous" to raise questions about Brown's fitness to be governor again. The message in the TV spot quickly got lost in a debate in the media about the fairness of the attack. The decision to "go negative" got more media attention than the personal character issues Beshear tried to raise.

An attack on Brown's character was a desperate effort to cut into his lead. The negative nature of the attack may have cost Brown a few percentage points, but it clearly cost Beshear much more. Brown probably would have been well-advised to have just ignored the attack and leave Beshear with yet another difficult decision: continue to pursue the issue or drop it altogether. It was our hope that at some point in the campaign these two opponents would so muddy themselves that voters would reject both of them. Once Steve Beshear launched his negative advertising, we felt we had the opening we were looking for. Then Brown made the mistake of responding to the attack, which gave me the opportunity to characterize myself as the alternative to both.

I took full advantage of the opportunity when it came. I pointed to the dirty fight between Brown and Beshear as a reason for voters to consider me as the only candidate who could beat both of them. In a closing speech in Florence, Kentucky, I said "the voters are tired of hearing about cocaine pushers, lawsuits, and baseball bats. They don't want to hear new charges; they want new ideas."

The long awaited movement in the opinion polls began to show up as predicted about Kentucky Derby weekend. The *Courier-Journal* poll released on Derby Day showed John Y. Brown at 36 percent, Steve Beshear at 20 percent, Julian Carroll and myself at 9 percent, and Grady Stumbo at 8 percent. Boosted by the lottery proposal and the negative Brown and Beshear exchange, we experienced a move up in the voter preference polls.

Not many candidates have held a news conference to announce opinion poll results which showed they were still behind the front-runner by double digits, but that is exactly what we did soon after the Derby. I despise the "horse race" opinion polls, and the media generally give them far more importance than they deserve. Nonetheless, we decided to play the poll game ourselves. I announced on May 14 that our tracking polls had me ahead of Beshear by one percentage point (15 to 14 percent) and Brown falling to 29 percent. Having started with a solid base, but little potential beyond it, Brown's percentages could only decline in the opinion polls when the relatively large number of undecided voters started to move into his opponents' camps. Brown really had no where to go but down in the opinion polls.

The point we wanted to make with the voters was not that Brown was losing support. We wanted to make the point that I was the only candidate with *upward* momentum. The strategy was risky because much of the gain was attributable to the "bounce" we were getting from the media focus on the lottery issue. But we were successful in using this effect to convey the perception that this was no longer a race between

Beshear and Brown. Nonetheless, in spite of this upward movement in the opinion polls, we still were the only ones who believed I could overtake Brown in the time that remained.

Obviously, the frequency of our paid media increased as we closed in on election day. I had been working since early in the campaign with David Sawyer and Scott Miller of the Sawyer-Miller Group in New York, and their efforts intensified with each passing day. They assigned Mandy Grunwald to work with the campaign virtually fulltime in the final week as we kept pounding the airwaves with our message.

As the primary election drew near, I increased the pace of my campaign, crisscrossing the state, making speeches from morning until late at night. Although I was losing my voice and getting bored with making the same speech over and over again, the prospect of finally reaching my goal of being elected governor kept the adrenaline rushing through my body. It was clear that I was the only candidate entering the final critical two weeks of the primary election on the upswing. Victory now was within reach!

The Stretch Drive

The three weeks between the Kentucky Derby and election day were as exciting as any candidate could possibly enjoy. With each passing day you could feel the enthusiasm growing, and with it the energy level of everyone involved in the campaign. Ironically, just as we reached the point where the campaign was really getting noticed, we faced yet another unusual challenge: fatigue.

Most candidates save themselves for the stretch run at the end. You may recall that John Y. Brown didn't even enter the 1979 race until February, only four months before the primary election. In this election, Brown had campaigned so little the *Courier-Journal* suggested in an editorial that he "stop laying low." Steve Beshear had the benefit of visibility and name recognition afforded every incumbent statewide official. Having comparatively little money with which to sustain a long campaign, Julian Carroll and Grady Stumbo had saved their meager resources for the last four weeks before election day. As a result, my opponents came to Derby Day relatively fresh for the stretch drive.

My situation was much different. I had already expended as much energy getting to this point as my opponents would spend from this point on. I had no choice as a come from behind candidate. I had to press hard from the very beginning. Yet in many ways, my campaign was just now beginning, for it was only now that my candidacy was being given serious consideration by voters and the media. This was no time to "run out of gas."

Day after day, dawn to dusk campaigning is physically and mentally grueling. In keeping with our tradi-tional, one-on-one style, we had conducted two to three day "whistle stop" type bus tours early in the campaign. By Derby Day we had already completed two tours of the fifth congres-sional district in November and January, a ten county tour of the seventh district in late January, a first district tour in February, and a sixth district tour in April.

During the stretch drive, we moved from bus tours to two day helicopter "fly arounds." These trips were largely designed as media events. We would begin one day in Frankfort with the capitol press corps before stopping in Owensboro, Paducah, Hopkinsville, and Bowling Green. The next day generally included stops in northern Kentucky, Hazard, Pikeville, Somerset, and Ashland. At each location we would hold a press conference and address at least one new issue, but I always included the lottery, jobs, and education themes that were the trademark of my campaign.

On a normal day on the campaign trail it was not unusual to make at least seven or eight appearances in several counties. It is hard to keep a campaign fresh for the media with that kind of schedule, so we were constantly looking for new ways to do the same old thing. What kept me going the last few days was the incredible wave of excitement and enthusiasm I felt in the crowds. In any endeavor, coming from behind is always an exciting way to win. With each passing day, we realized that the seemingly improbable, maybe even impossible, just might become reality. As I neared election day, I used the energy coming from the crowds to keep me going.

The stretch run was the most grueling thing I had ever experienced in my entire life. In the twenty-three days between Derby Day and Primary Election Day, I was in forty-two counties at least once, many of them more than once. I made almost eighty campaign appearances, participated in two candidate forums, and lost my voice and fifteen pounds. Election day couldn't come too soon. Just when it seemed there was no way to squeeze any more effort out of anyone, James Carville came up with one of the ploys that are his trademark.

James kept asking in the waning days of the campaign what we could do to introduce a new twist to wring just a little more out of the "free" media. I sat in silence as he presented an outrageous idea as we flew between stops on our last fly around. "Guv-nor," he said, "we need to do a twenty-four-hour campaign day. Cover the state from end to end and stay up all night!" After the initial shock faded, I looked him in the eye and said "James, you're going to kill me!"

As usual, James had more than shock value in his idea. We knew from our research that voters questioned Brown's work ethic. "He wants the job; I want to *do* the job" had been one of the slogans of the campaign. What better way to call attention to this issue than to dramatically demonstrate our resolve to win. The idea worked better than even James had hoped it would. As we expected, the media was hungry for a fresh story in this last week of the campaign. We chose the Wednesday of the week before the election to spring the idea. WHAS television in Louisville decided to follow each candidate for one day during the last week. As luck would have it, they chose Wednesday to chronicle my activities.

We began the twenty-four-hour campaign day the same way we had started the campaign—in Liberty, Kentucky. After stops in Radcliff and Fulton, WHAS caught up with us in Maysville for live coverage of our rally. By 11 o'clock that night we were in Louisville for another live shot from an all-night bowling alley. A middle of the night stop at UPS for the shift change and an early morning stop at Southern Screenprint gave them another story for the morning news. From Louisville, we traveled to Lexington where we greeted the Lextran drivers as they arrived for work at 6 o'clock in the morning. Tired, but with adrenaline flowing, the trip ended in Frankfort with a wrap-up session with the capitol press corp.

To top off this bizarre trip, Terry Meiners of WHAS radio satirized it by spending much of his afternoon program calling bowling alleys all across the state asking if Wallace Wilkinson was there. It was a public relations bonanza. The twenty-four-hour day turned into three or four days of solid coverage in all the major television markets in Kentucky.

The last significant strategic decision I had to make came when we decided not to respond to Brown's "What do we really know about Wallace Wilkinson?" television spots. As I just mentioned, I had undertaken one of the most grueling campaigns conducted by any candidate in recent memory, involving almost two years of statewide travel, numerous candidate forums and several debates, hundreds of media interviews, and the release of comprehensive position papers. I felt the "Who is Wallace Wilkinson?" issue raised by Brown's campaign was too little too late.

In my opinion, Brown had made a mistake by responding too quickly to Beshear's attack ads, but these are the frustrating decisions that face the front runner. I thought Beshear had attacked Brown on the wrong issue. As I said earlier our research indicated that Brown was more vulnerable on his motivation for wanting to be governor than on his personal lifestyle or his record as governor. Beshear had taken aim on the two issues least likely to benefit him in the election. Had Brown chosen not to respond, I believe Beshear's attacks probably would have fizzled in a few days. We risked making the same mistake when Brown focused on my fitness for public office.

Instinctively, when your character is attacked you want to respond in kind. Instead, I stayed with the refrain which I felt was most on the point. At every opportunity, I stressed that "He (Brown) wants the job. I want to *do* the job." Even though we had shot a television response, I was so physically drained at the time we probably would not have used it anyway. I must admit that it felt strange in those last few days deciding strategy from a position of strength for a change.

If the twenty-four-hour day was my best day in the final stages of the Wilkinson primary election, the last two days of the campaign had to be the worst for the Brown campaign. Brown's schedule for the last two days did nothing but draw attention to his motivation. On Sunday he attended a Cincinnati Reds baseball game while I held a rally in Elizabethtown. On Monday, election eve and Memorial Day, Brown played golf in a celebrity tournament while I participated in a parade in Lexington with a group of veterans in the morning. Later in the day I worked the crowd at Heritage Days in downtown Louisville.

The coverage on the evening news was devastating for Brown. On television statewide there were shots of John playing golf and me shaking hands and still looking for votes. For everyone to see, John had decided to take off the last two days of the campaign. The media image was one of total indifference or arrogant overconfidence. I will never know how many voters may have been influenced by these events, so I cannot assess how critical they might have been to my victory at this late date. I am certain that his personal conduct on those two days did not serve him well, and it certainly was in stark contrast to my conduct in those critical last days.

The First Glimpse of Victory

Once we started to move up in the opinion polls, hardly a day went by that I didn't ask Mellman and Lazarus how close we were to Brown. Mark and Ed, the professionals they are, were scrupulous about the integrity of their research. To their credit, they always gave me an honest appraisal. At one point, probably growing impatient with my continual questioning, Mark said I should quit asking. He promised to tell me the minute he could confidently say he thought I was going to win. In fact, he put it this way: "You'll know you have taken the lead when I ask for Derby tickets."

Our nightly tracking polls had clearly shown we were steadily gaining momentum. On the Friday before election day, I was awakened by the telephone about 3 o'clock in the morning. We had just completed the two-day fly around and the 24 hour campaign day. I was absolutely bushed. It was my first good night to rest. I wondered who in the world was calling me in the middle of the night! Well, it was Mark Mellman asking me to put him down for those Derby tickets! What great news. With four days to go, it truly looked like we were going to make it. Mellman had called that Friday morning to report that we were within two percentage points of Brown in Thursday's results. Mark was the first to suggest to me that our momentum was going to carry us through election day. The only thing left to do was to keep working and avoid any last minute mistakes.

Despite the early morning hour, Mellman's report eased the fatigue that had weighed me down on Thursday. I was fresh for Friday's fly around which started with a news conference in Louisville. Few in the media still gave me any chance of winning. About the best any of them were prepared to say at that point was that we had run a good campaign and would be in a position to run again in 1991. Given the momentum we had, I figured that if we were only two percentage points behind on Thursday, we probably would be ahead by that much on Friday. So to the surprise of my staff, I told the media that morning we had taken the lead over Brown by two percentage points. When pressed for confirmation, my staff reminded me that I was two points *behind*, not two points ahead, thinking I had misspoken.

When Mellman and Lazarus were asked by the media to confirm my statement, they obviously could not. The resulting story in the media tried to correct the error. One headline read "Poll mix-up incorrectly put Wilkinson ahead of Brown." Of course, the real message to the public was that the polling results were within the margin of error and it now seemed feasible that I could win the election after all.

The use of voter preference polls by the media is an important element in any campaign. No one wants to waste a vote on a loser, so the front-runner in the opinion polls is given an edge throughout the race. I knew the major contenders were using opinion research firms just as I was. I don't know what they learned from them or how accurate they were. I do know that the company used by the media were far off the mark right down to election eve. At 6 o'clock that night, the media announced that their polls had shown Brown *winning* by a 5 percent margin! It wasn't "Dewey Defeats Truman" but it was close.

How badly did the media and political experts miss the election? Other than my supporters and a handful of reporters who covered my campaign for months, no one thought I had even a slim chance of winning the nomination. Throughout the campaign I thought our tracking polls were considerably better than the ones conducted by the media. But the constant reporting of our poor showing in the media's "horse race" polls was troublesome in the closing days of the campaign. Even though we knew we were doing better than the media was indicating, we were not about to get into a public dispute about numbers.

When the primary election votes were counted, I had pulled ahead of John Y. Brown by almost 58,000 votes and won the Democratic nomination for governor in a tough five-person race in which I started out dead last. A large rural vote for me helped offset Brown's urban lead in Jefferson and Fayette Counties. This victory demonstrated the appeal my message had to those who were not among the urban power-brokers who had controlled Frankfort in recent years.

Assuring Election in November

I was looking forward to some much-needed rest before the start of the general election campaign. It made no sense for me to start campaigning in July for election in November. The primary election had proven once again that the electorate doesn't focus on the race until the last three weeks. Besides that, my upset victory had given me great press coverage and momentum. There was little to be gained from continuing to campaign so soon after such a major victory. Therefore, I publicly announced my intention to take the summer off and resume campaigning after Labor Day. Having pushed the limits of my endurance as far as I could, I felt a two month campaign in the fall was in both my personal and political interest.

The media had other ideas. Since my Republican opponent John Harper wasn't considered a serious opponent, the media started immediately to make me my own opponent. The newspapers used this opportunity to "investigate" me to determine my fitness for office. Relatively little background work had been done before the primary election because I was not considered a serious contender. The two major newspapers apparently had decided there was little reason to spend their resources on someone whom they thought had no chance of winning the election. Recognizing now that, barring some form of divine intervention, I was going to be

Kentucky's next governor, they were obligated do what they could to inform the public about my fitness for the state's highest elected office.

Media coverage of my primary election campaign focused on things like my stand on the lottery and Toyota, but comparatively little was written about me as a person other than what was obvious to everyone. Now the media would turn mean-spirited. The "chewing" started soon after the *Courier-Journal* published a Bluegrass State Poll showing me with a 71 percent to 12 percent lead over John Harper. Not many days passed before the *Kentucky Post* ran this banner headline: "A Shadow Could Cloud Wilkinson Campaign." The "shadow" to which they referred was my well- publicized kidnapping in 1984 by a former business associate.

Articles of this type are typical of the self-created controversy that so many people find disturbing about the media these days. There was no "shadow" until the media created one by recounting events surrounding the kidnapping. The provocative headline was reinforced by speculation. The article said "there remains an unresolved matter in Wilkinson's past that *has the potential* [emphasis added] to detract from his well-oiled campaign machine." The potential referred to was fulfilled when the media which first raised the specter of a shadow *pursued* the alleged "unresolved issues."

For example, in the *Kentucky Post* article this statement appeared: "Three years ago, Wilkinson —*by his account* [emphasis added] —was abducted at gun point by a former business partner, Jerome Jernigan." Without seeming to be overly sensitive, isn't it rather obvious that this wording was designed to suggest that there was some *other* account than my own which was more reliable? The implication of this statement was that a more accurate account existed somewhere, even though the journalist who wrote the article had no idea that such an account did in fact exist anywhere.

Nothing new was revealed in the article, but the journalistic rehashing of the event would lead the reader to believe that a conspiracy lurked behind the facts which, once revealed, would surely show that I was unfit for public office. Of course, the *Post* did not, and could not, prove that such a conspiracy existed or might ever be proven at some later date. It was sufficient to plant the doubt and then leave the rest to the imagination of the reader. The presumption of my culpability is so obvious in these stories that there is little question that the editorial position of the paper was that I *was guilty* of something which they could not yet determine, but they were convinced *could* be proven if they looked into it enough.

There is no way a person can defend against accusations which take the form of "when did you stop beating your wife?" The question implies the beating, and only asks when you stopped. The circumstances of my kidnapping had been investigated by various law enforcement agencies, including the FBI. At no point did any of these agencies conclude, or even suspect, that I had staged my own kidnapping at gun point. My account of the events was never disputed. Unfortunately, the perpetrator died while awaiting trial, so the evidence was not made public through the trial process.

I made a decision not to respond publicly to this and other articles alleging one thing or another. The kidnapping situation had been resolved to the satisfaction of every independent and objective observer, at least until I won the primary election. Perhaps I should have gone on the offensive, but it seemed futile. The facts had already been deemed an inadequate defense, so what more could I offer? Facts don't seem to be of great interest to investigative reporters who begin their work believing there is more to a story than has been told. The shadow referred to by the *Kentucky Post* writer was the unknown story yet to be written about things yet to be discovered. So the search went on for the cover-up that the media believed must exist if it could only be uncovered. "Shadows" begin with speculation and soon take on a life of their own.

There were other stories covering my business investments, international connections, and the World Coal Center project which did not prove feasible after the end of the oil embargo. Each story was a recounting of old news with nothing damaging revealed. However, each story was written in a manner designed to lead the reader to believe there is something unknown and sinister about me which should give them reason to go to the polls and vote for John Harper.

What I find curious about all this is the double standard used by the press. When Steve Beshear went "negative" on John Y. Brown, their endorsed candidate, the media scorched him for engaging in a personal attack on his opposition. They urged Beshear to stick to the "issues" and leave Brown's personal lifestyle and character out of the campaign. But when I became the nominee, the media immediately raised questions about *my* personal lifestyle and character. If personal lifestyle and character were not relevant to Brown's candidacy, why were they so important for mine?

Many people, both in and out of public life, have commented on how negative the media have become in recent years. Ever since the Watergate fiasco, every newspaper is out to get a Pulitzer Prize for uncovering the next political scandal. At the national level we have had Irangate and now the Whitewater affair within the span of one decade. Enormous resources are spent by the media to cast a shadow over the character of every person who seeks high public office. It has nothing to do with politics or the national interest. It is driven by intense competition between the various news networks and media forms.

Debunking public figures is not new, of course. We have had long periods in American political history when the media turned negative. I certainly am not contending that what I experienced was unique. Everyone who makes the decision to seek public office recognizes the right of the public to know everything they need to know to assess the character and fitness for office of an aspiring political leader. Whatever our sensitivity might be to having our private lives put under such scrutiny, we recognize the role the media must play in informing the public about the qualifications any candidate brings to public office.

What I and others object to is the unbridled use of speculation, rumor, innuendo, and insinuation by the media to besmirch the personal character and reputation of those who are willing to commit themselves to public service. When something factual is reported, we have no reason to object. However, during the summer of 1987 I was the target of one of the most vicious attempts in recent times to prevent someone from gaining office by publishing malicious and purely speculative statements designed to personally discredit a candidate for public office.

In the end I weathered the storm. The media assault during the summer of 1987, though very distracting and distressful for my family and me, seemed not to have had a serious effect on my campaign. Once I got on the campaign trail, I discovered that much of the media focus on my personal life had little if any negative impact on my supporters. In fact, the record will show that I won the election in November by a landslide. I lost to the Republican candidate in only five counties, making this the largest sweep ever.

III. CAMPAIGNS HAVE CONSEQUENCES

There is a widely held belief that candidates don't take specific stands on issues because they fear alienating segments of voters. The broader the position one takes, the harder it is to criticize. But that's not the only reason. Anyone qualified to be governor knows it's harder to deliver on promises than to make them.

Historian Garry Wills very succinctly illustrated one of the many ironies of politics in a May 1992 syndicated column. "We force our politicians to grovel their way up, then despise them for accepting the ordeal," he wrote. "If they want the prize that much, then they must be unworthy of it. The voters have to conjure up a candidate who does nothing so crass as asking to become one." Such is the environment of politics in which a candidate is expected to have answers for all of the problems of concern to the public, but is often criticized for having the temerity to suggest he can actually solve them.

Most responsible candidates make an effort to satisfactorily address the issues on the minds of voters. Through the course of weeks and months of campaigning, the candidate will discuss dozens of issues with hundreds of voters. Despite the many miles of travel and constant interaction with voters, when all is said and done, a candidate's stand on the issues is invariably reduced to a few generalities. Why is there such an aversion to taking a strong stand on an issue of great importance?

At least part of the answer lies in the complexity of most problems and their solutions. In an age of thirty-second "sound bites," one finds it very difficult to articulate in thirty words or less a position which requires some background information for an uninformed person to understand it. A candidate soon learns it is much easier to come up with a slogan like "discipline in and drugs out" than to explain why it is necessary to restructure the institution of public education totally and how to go about doing it.

There is more to it than just communication, however. There is a political price to be paid for candor. It is my nature to speak my mind without thinking how what I am saying might be interpreted or used against me at some later time. James Carville and Doug Alexander used to cringe when in a press conference I started to drift into an area they thought I should avoid. I never was very good at obfuscation. Being so outspoken can sometimes cause serious political problems later on. In my case, there were several instances where I created problems for myself by being candid during the campaign.

Comments I made during the summer of 1987 on three issues in particular had lasting impact on my ability to address these issues later when I was governor. The first was my statement to the Prichard Committee for Academic Excellence that I would not assure funding for the education reforms enacted in 1986. Another was my opposition to a special legislative session to raise more money by bringing the state tax code into conformity with revisions in the newly enacted federal tax code, leading to the perception that I *never* would raise taxes. The third was statements I made that gave the impression that I would not seek to be included in any succession amendment which might be put on the ballot during my administration.

Although the news media often make more of campaign statements than voters do, my positions in these particular instances later adversely affected my ability to get support for some of the policy objectives of my administration. I am not suggesting that I should have hidden my real views on these matters to avoid offending important constituencies during the campaign. Rather, I am suggesting that today's campaign rhetoric may very well become tomorrow's policy statement.

Funding the Education Reforms of 1985-86

The Collins administration was under great pressure from the newspapers in the state to push for major reforms in public education. Educators who saw school funding sharply curtailed during the Brown administration were calling for a large increase in taxes to restore lost funds and to bring teacher salaries closer to the Southeast average. University presidents also wanted full funding of the formula recently adopted by the Council on Higher Education. During her first legislative session in 1984, Governor Collins offered various proposals for improving schools. The newly elected superintendent of public instruction, Alice McDonald, also campaigned on a platform that called for major education reform and offered her own agenda for legislative consideration.

The 1984 regular legislative session was very contentious. Most of the education initiatives enacted were those which did not require much financial support. The revenue required to meet the call for higher expenditures on education was not available. Furthermore, neither the legislature nor the governor was prepared to enact a major tax increase while the commonwealth was still mired in a deep economic recession. Pressure for major education reform escalated after this fruitless legislative session.

Governor Collins agreed to call the legislature into special session in 1985 to enact a reform bill if there was agreement ahead of time that it would be passed. Under the direction of Secretary of the Cabinet Larry Hayes, the governor negotiated a reform bill known as HB 6 passed in a special session held in the summer of 1985. However, no revenue measure was passed at the time to support the legislation. The Legislative Research Commission, in a memo to the Appropriations and Revenue Interim Joint Committee dated Sept. 25,

1985, wrote that the 1985 reforms would cost $792 million in additional biennial expenditures through fiscal year (FY) 1990. The leadership of the General Assembly wanted to deal with revenue measures during the regular legislative session in 1986 rather than in the special session.

When the legislature met in regular session in 1986, it failed to pass a revenue measure large enough to finance the education package it had approved in the 1985 special session. Educators were angered at what they considered a betrayal by the political leadership in Frankfort, and sixty-six school districts proceeded to file a law suit asking the court to declare the method of funding public schools in Kentucky unconstitutional.

In an appearance before the Prichard Committee for Academic Excellence in August 1987, I laid out the broad philosophy of how I would improve education. My call for fundamental change in the way we educate children was a part of every speech I made during the campaign. Among other things, I told the Prichard Committee I would commit $70 million a year to an incentive program which would reward schools which had improved student test scores, reduced dropouts, and made other gains in student performance. I did not mention the earlier reforms in my remarks.

Suspecting a reluctance to commit to fund fully the 1985-86 reforms, I was asked in a question and answer period following my prepared remarks if I intended to fund these reforms if elected governor. I responded, "I am committed only to the reform package I'm presenting today." A storm of protest from editors and legislators followed, which eventually led to a standoff between myself and key legislators over how to improve schools.

My position on the earlier reforms alarmed many in the education community and angered the legislators who had taken great pride in what was done in 1985-86. Reporters covering the story sought out supporters of the earlier reforms who revealed the position they were going to take on this matter. Senator Michael Moloney, chairman of the powerful Senate Appropriations and Revenue (A & R) Committee, was reported as saying I would have a fight on my hands if I tried to cut funds for the 1985-86 education packages. Representative Roger Noe, chairman of the House Education Committee and a strong supporter of the earlier reform legislation, was quoted by the Louisville *Courier-Journal* the next day (August 12) as follows:

> *I would have to look very seriously at any attempt to dismantle the* [1985-86] *programs. Just to walk into the General Assembly and say, "Hey, I've got this new idea and I want $150 million for it," —generally, historically, someone with these ideas has not been successful the first time without convincing evidence.*

The remarks of these two key legislators were echoed by others. It was clear they perceived my unwillingness to promise to fully implement the earlier reforms as an implied threat to *defund* what they already had put in place. Thereafter, the press characterized my position as one of wanting to *substitute* my programs for the earlier reforms to which these leading legislators were deeply committed. The perception grew that I was "throwing out of the window" the earlier reforms. This was particularly troubling to many educators who were tired of having politicians begin something only to abandon it a few years later. Educators wanted a long-term commitment to change, and they viewed my position as just one more example of a politician using education for personal political gain.

The school finance lawsuit was still pending at the time I was campaigning for governor. It was obvious to me that I would have to deal with this issue at some point in my administration if I was elected governor. I estimated that it would take at least $150 to $200 million annually in additional appropriations just to bring about equity in school funding *before* funding of the more expensive elements of the 1985-86 legislation could be considered. In addition, the state already had a significant revenue shortfall during the current 1988 fiscal year and faced budget cuts as a result.

It was my view that we should wait for the lawsuit to make its way through the courts and significantly increase the funding for education at that time. Furthermore, I didn't believe many of these earlier "reforms" would make much difference in the education of Kentucky children. Whatever new funds would be available I wanted to use to implement my incentive plan. Therefore, knowing the lawsuit loomed ahead, it would have been foolhardy to commit such a large amount of money to past reforms *before* dealing with the equity issue, which certainly would require a large infusion of money into education.

Education advocates and editorial writers grew concerned that education reform in Kentucky would come to a screeching halt if I became governor. My own ideas for reform were completely overshadowed by the debate about funding the 1985-86 reforms. Even when we managed to get the message through the uproar, my ideas were described as radical. You can imagine how ironic it seems to me now that some of the most outspoken critics of my ideas on school incentives, local school accountability, site-based management, and other ideas we proposed then are now traveling the country to explain how they helped Kentucky pave the way in school reform. Instead of provoking a constructive debate about various reform options, my coolness toward the 1985-86 measures was characterized as anti-education. I greatly underestimated the extent to which this controversy would later become a serious obstacle to enacting my own reforms into law.

To counter the mounting criticism, I accepted an invitation to appear before the Council on Higher Education to try to clarify my views on education funding. Although I had serious reservations about the formula used to fund higher education, I said I would *seek* full funding of the formula but could not promise it in light of the very tight revenue situation.

I also pledged that during my administration there would be no cuts once the budget was enacted by the legislature. As for the reforms of 1985-86, I said I would not *defund* anything in place, but at the same time I would not commit myself to fund fully those programs for which insufficient revenues were provided at the time they were enacted. While I knew this would not satisfy the call for *increased* funding for these initiatives, I hoped at least this would dispel the notion that I was going to take money already appropriated to these programs to fund my own.

At the urging of some of my advisors I had Jack Foster, then a consultant to the campaign, meet with key members of the House Education Committee often referred to as "the Turks" to see if we could find a way to alleviate their concerns. He also met with Speaker Donald Blandford's staff for the same purpose. These talks always came down to this: "We will support Wilkinson's programs *only* if he first will commit to fully funding the reforms of 1985-86." Obviously, I was unable to make that commitment, so I became "public enemy number one" in the eyes of these legislators. We went into the 1988 session headed for a bitter fight over funding priorities.

Money, Money, Money!

The dispute over education priorities gradually was over- shadowed by the fiscal crisis facing the commonwealth. While all this discussion about funding the education reforms of a previous administration was going on, attention was turning more and more to the revenue shortfall for the current year and the impact this would have on the 1988 legislative session.

The issue of taxes was a constant theme throughout the campaign. My position was clear: *No new taxes!* As the education debate heated up, it also was clear that the issue was money, not education policy. As a writer for the *Lexington Herald-Leader* put it:

*Money, as always, is the biggest issue facing
education as the legislature prepares to convene. But more is at stake than usual. The $300
million education improvement package of 1985
and 1986 is threatened by severe money shortages. The stage seems set for what could be a
tense tug of war between the new governor, as
he pushes his education agenda, and the legislature, as it defends existing programs.*

*All this is being played out against the backdrop
of a predicted shortfall that some say will be
$400 million in the next two years if existing
programs are maintained. With more money,
both branches could have their way. Without it,
some hard choices appear unavoidable.*
(Monday, December 21, 1987)

As mentioned earlier, Kentucky had experienced a prolonged recession following the end of the oil
embargo in the late 1970s. Each year revenues failed to meet
projections, so governors regularly faced the unpleasant task of
calling for cutbacks in state expenditures. Even though the
General Assembly passed a small tax increase in 1986 to
support in part the education reforms enacted in the 1985
special session, budget analysts cautioned at the time that it
might not yield even the modest $70 million on which the
budget was based. Indeed, their concerns were well founded.

The General Assembly had embarked on a
major education reform costing many millions of dollars. Now
it faced a large revenue shortfall in spite of the modest tax
increase it had passed the year before. The fiscal situation was
further clouded when a massive unfunded liability was discovered in the special fund in the workers' compensation program
which awards benefits to injured workers beyond an employer's responsibilities. The fiscal condition of the commonwealth was in such a poor state that the editorial boards and

education advocates concluded the *only* solution was a large increase in taxes. Obviously, my "no new taxes" stand put me in the camp with those who wanted a different solution.

Throughout 1987 there was talk of a special legislative session to deal with workers' compensation. However, money was at the heart of every solution. Since the U.S. Congress had passed the Tax Reform Act of 1986 the year before, Senator Moloney and Representative Joseph Clarke, the two budget experts in the legislature, proposed that Kentucky conform its tax code to the revisions in the federal code and reap a windfall of about $130 million over the biennium. The idea was endorsed quickly by the major newspapers, and pressure was applied for Governor Collins to call a special session to address these issues.

I openly opposed the conformity proposal, saying I would do whatever it took to prevent it from occurring before I became governor. I argued that we were acting too quickly with conformity since some parts of the federal code were still under fire and were likely to be changed. Once again I was sharply criticized by key legislators, education advocates, and editorial writers, this time for being so arrogant as to try to tell a sitting governor what to do about taxes. Realizing budget cutbacks were imminent, these people saw conformity of the tax code as a window of opportunity to alleviate some of the pain.

Of course, had I chosen not to respond to the persistent questioning from the media about my position on this matter, I probably would have been accused of trying to duck the issue. I am certain I would not have been considered nearly so arrogant if I had been telling the sitting governor to do what the editorial writers wanted done. In other words, sometimes you lose no matter what you do.

Conventional wisdom said I should keep quiet and let Governor Collins take the heat for raising taxes—something I vowed I would not do—and reap the benefit from it when I became governor. However, I had a much different view of the situation. Obviously, it would be in my political interest to have the workers' compensation problem resolved before I took office. On the other hand, I was greatly concerned about the talk of conforming the tax code at this time.

Past performance of the legislature indicated there was little likelihood revenues gained from conformity would be used for anything other than balancing the present budget. The new revenues from conformity would merely pay for the sins of omission made in the past. From my point of view, this was just another example of the wrong-headed thinking that had prevailed in Frankfort over the years. New taxes are passed, but nothing new happens for the taxpayer, and the old problems remain.

As mentioned earlier, it was highly probable the Kentucky Supreme Court would declare unconstitutional the school finance program during my term in office. I was in sympathy with the plaintiffs' case and wanted to be in a position to respond with the necessary funds when the time came. We would need to use every means available to us to raise the additional revenue needed to satisfy the court decision. Although dealing responsibly with the workers' compensation problem was important to me, conforming to the federal code at this time would have denied me access to a major source of new revenue later on.

As it turned out, my decision during the campaign to oppose conformity made my first budget as governor much more onerous than I had expected. When I came into office, I found we were going to be short another $54 million, even after the budget cuts made by Governor Collins. Since I was determined not to raise taxes during my first legislative session, I had to make some very tough decisions and use what the press later called "creative budgeting" to get us through my first biennial budget.

Particularly rough politically was my decision not to increase funding to the universities and to give state employees and public school teachers only a seven percent salary increase over the next two years instead of the ten percent they expected and I had hoped to provide. I also had to deal with a state employee health care insurance crisis which resulted in these same people paying more for their health insurance.

Had conformity occurred without my intervention, the public would have perceived that taxes had been raised, and *none* of the significant revenue problems would have been addressed. There would have been no meaningful increase in funding for education reform, for example. On the other hand, I probably would not have had to make such severe cuts in the expected salary increases. In any event, my decision to intervene was characterized as having made worse an already bad situation and cost me a significant amount of political capital with legislators, public employees, and the education community in the early months of my administration.

No New Taxes

Political advisors contend the public knows that all politicians will do whatever they have to about taxes *once they are elected.* Therefore, there is no compelling reason to signal ahead of time the conditions under which they might find it necessary to do so. Let the circumstances take care of themselves later. My strident rhetoric against new taxes, combined with my quick rebuff of the idea of using tax conformity to balance the budget, certainly galvanized the perception that I was unalterably opposed to increasing taxes under *any* circumstances.

Not raising taxes at that time was more than just a matter of good politics. It was good fiscal policy in the long run. For reasons already mentioned, it was essential that I take a firm stand against any interim tax increase, no matter how much pain this position might inflict on those affected in the near term. On the other hand, I hoped to articulate my position in such a manner as not to appear later on to have reneged on my "no new taxes" pledge.

My proposal of a lottery was taken by many people to be my alternative to new taxes. My critics point to my campaign TV commercials which said "New Taxes or a Lottery—It's Your Choice" as evidence that it *was* my alternative. I never claimed the lottery would solve all of Kentucky's problems, but I did offer the lottery as an alternative to new taxes *under present circumstances.* From the time I first proposed the lottery, I suggested that it would bring about $70 million to the state treasury. A majority of Kentuckians wanted the lottery and saw it as an acceptable way to raise additional revenues. They certainly thought the lottery was preferable to a plain vanilla tax increase. I saw no good reason not to pursue it.

Trying to straddle the fence between keeping the tax message simple while not appearing later to have changed positions was not easy. I was careful in interviews with the news media to note that I thought it was unfair to ask Kentuckians to pay more in taxes until they saw more in their paychecks. However, if incomes improved and more people were working, then I would be more inclined to consider additional revenue measures in the second half of my term in office.

Speaking to reporters after a meeting with the Council on Higher Education in Lexington, September 3, 1987, I said "The only way I would ever consider a tax increase would be after people's personal incomes had risen. I would consider it at that point if there was a need for it." Let people *make* more before they are asked to *pay* more. This was a position I restated on various occasions later, always making it clear that *under present conditions* I was unalterably opposed to a tax increase.

The reason this issue is relevant to the discussion here is the extent to which my firm stand during the campaign resulted in my being characterized repeatedly in the news media as the one person who stood between progress and total disaster in Kentucky. If I would only agree to raise taxes *now*, so the argument went, I would go down in history as a great statesman. The editorial writers, and education advocates in particular, never could see beyond the immediate fiscal need. Consequently, I was constantly vilified as being unresponsive, committed only to the backward thinking of "Bubba," as they liked to put it.

When the time did come for me to do what they had chided me to do throughout my first two years in office, in their view I did it only because I was forced into it by the Supreme Court decision on education funding. My contribution to education reform was to get out of the way of a court-mandated tax increase even though the decision never contained such a mandate. The reality was much different. I saw the court's education decision as giving us the opportunity of a lifetime to do more than just pass more taxes. I saw it as an opportunity to *expand* the existing tax base before raising tax *rates*. In addition to bringing more revenue into the state coffers now, broadening the tax base would ensure that revenues would grow more consistently with the economy in the future.

Many times I said to myself, "If they only knew now what I was prepared to do when the time was right, would they still view me with such disdain?" Of course, I will never know the answer to that question. In fact, I probably will be accused now of trying to put myself in a better light after the fact. Nonetheless, I am as convinced today as I was then that the opportunity to do what we did in 1990 would have been severely diminished had I yielded to the pressure to raise taxes in the first legislative session.

The moment I agreed to increase revenues without achieving significant changes in the existing education system would have been the moment when we lost any opportunity to enact major reforms. Furthermore, there was no way I could have gone back to the public two years later and told them we were too shortsighted to see what was clearly on the horizon, so we must hit them with a tax increase one more time. Kentuckians had seen enough of that kind of thinking to last them a lifetime!

Succession in Office

On the issue of succession, I am probably vulnerable to criticism for appearing to change my position after winning the election. Early in the campaign I never gave the issue much thought. "One office, one time" was my response whenever asked about the opportunity to succeed myself. On the other hand, I had long felt that depriving a governor of the opportunity to put his record before the voters deprived him or her of an important aspect of the "checks and balances" system of government.

A governor needs more than two legislative sessions to sustain a political agenda long enough to have permanent impact. Without succession, members of the General Assembly and many career state employees take the attitude that they will be here long after the governor is gone, so just wait him out. "This too shall pass" was their motto. I felt at times that legislators were so accustomed to changes in governor, they had come to believe only they could bring continuity to government.

Given that many legislators had made a career of serving in the legislature, their long tenure clearly gave them a feeling they could just wait for the next governor if they didn't get along with this one. Such attitudes do little to promote a feeling of cooperation and mutual obligation to work together to get good things to happen for the people who elected them. My personal views aside, succession is one of those issues of far more importance to the insiders at Frankfort than to the electorate. I did not sense the public was clamoring for succession, although I did hear supporters say from time to time they hoped I might have the chance to be governor for more than four years.

I soon learned that capitol reporters liked to raise this issue with each new governor. They knew what a loaded issue it was to those who spend their days walking the halls of the Capitol. After being asked the question several times, I realized that I had to be more prudent in how I answered it. I *did* favor succession, and I *did* want to serve more than four years if I could. But it was not the kind of obsession that the media made it out to be. As I sought to clarify my position, I tried to say the governor's office was the only one of interest to me, but I might consider a second term if the opportunity presented itself. However, in retrospect, I can see that my clarification came too late to alter the impression I had created, at least in the minds of the reporters who make up the political press corp.

When the results of the general election were analyzed, it was clear that I had received a very strong popular vote in the rural areas of the state where a succession amendment had been defeated in the past. I thought I could carry such an amendment if it were voted on early enough in my term. It would make it possible for me to return if I fulfilled the expectations of those who saw in me the alternative to politics as usual in Frankfort. The editorial writers quickly took issue with my logic and reminded me of my previous statements on the subject. The *Lexington Herald-Leader* wrote the following in an editorial titled "Wilkinson and succession: His original idea was better":

> *What a difference a year makes. Last January, candidate Wallace Wilkinson told the Lexington Kiwanis Club that Kentucky governors should be allowed to seek a second successive term. But if such an amendment were proposed while he was governor, Wilkinson said, he would urge legislators to word the amendment so that it did not apply to him. "I'm going to run for one office, one time," he said at the time.*

*A year later, Gov. Wallace Wilkinson still sup-
ports the idea of gubernatorial succession. But
now, just a month into his term, he wants to be
allowed to succeed himself.*

*It would be better—for the state, for the
amendment and perhaps for himself—if the governor would revert to his original position.*
(*Lexington Herald-Leader*, January 7, 1988)

Once I was in office actively pursuing my
agenda, succession was raised again by the capitol press corp.
The issue hit a real hot button in the General Assembly. I
naively believed that letting the general public decide whether
or not to retain a governor could be discussed in a rational
manner. The discussion quickly got out of hand when my
efforts to get the General Assembly to put the issue on the
ballot was considered a grab for power and a "clear and present
danger" to legislative independence. Characterized in the press
as a power-hungry tyrant for holding my ground on taxes and
education reform, I could say nothing now about the subject to
abate the storm.

As the legislative leadership tried to fight off
my desire for a constitutional amendment, the press started
stylizing my interest in succession as an "obsession." Wanting
something and being willing to put up a fight for it surely don't
qualify as an obsession. Nonetheless, those who preferred that
the voters not be given the choice about my succession in
office found it convenient to recount the position I had taken
early in the campaign. It seemed to be a continuation of the
media's effort to wrap me in a mantle of mystery and intrigue. I
certainly learned something I should have realized all along—
everything you say during a campaign can come back to haunt
you later, no matter how innocuous it may have seemed at the
time.

IV. FROM PROMISES
TO PERFORMANCE

I campaigned on the idea that Kentucky had to change its priorities and pursue different policies if we were to enjoy the prosperity experienced by people living elsewhere in the United States. I had great hopes of bringing "new ideas" into government—ideas which would leave the commonwealth a much better place to live and work. In my inaugural address I said:

> *My mission today is not to take the ship of state over the murky and foggy waters of the old order and status quo, but to feel the strong breeze of change in ourselves and move resolutely ahead to the favorable seas of the new order and change. Our agenda will be new and our agenda will be challenging.*

During the primary campaign, I released a series of papers outlining the policy objectives of my administration. In fact, my original education plan was released April 16, 1987, as the Kentucky First Plan for Education. These position papers were redrafted after the primary election and reissued under the title *Kentucky First*, suggesting that it was time to make Kentucky first in the nation. While my public speeches during the campaign focused on the handful of issues of political importance, the *Kentucky First* booklet represented a comprehensive policy and program agenda I intended to pursue as governor.

Kentucky First was a unique document in that no other candidate for governor in my memory had ever released for public review *before being elected* such a thorough outline of proposals on so many issues. Perhaps these

---

statements were considered at the time to be just campaign rhetoric, but in my case they were in fact the policy and program agenda for my administration. Perhaps to the surprise of some of my critics, with the election campaign over, I began to move forward on this agenda.

An Agenda to Make Kentucky First

In *Kentucky First* I proposed a plan for action in six major areas: economic and infrastructure development, education, health, criminal justice and corrections, agriculture, and the environment. Although I eventually expanded most aspects of *Kentucky First*, it did represent the priorities of my administration. Here are some of the key elements of the six-part Kentucky First plan.

I. Actions for Jobs and Economic Development at Home

Most job creation in Kentucky and elsewhere over the previous decade was coming from small and medium-sized businesses. While I would obviously work to secure and retain larger corporate investments in Kentucky, I wanted to use the resources of the state to create and expand existing small and medium-sized businesses within Kentucky. Among my ideas was a plan to: (a) work with the universities to identify promising technologies with commercial possibilities; (b) create a $300 million venture capital fund ($100 million in state funds and $200 million in private funds) to help existing businesses and new enterprises develop commercial technologies, with repayment tied to royalties or participation; and (3) create a Kentucky Enterprise Development Corporation (KEDC) to provide seed capital to help people with innovative ideas develop new products and processes. This new entity would be capitalized by the private sector through a tax exemption against Kentucky income tax.

To be competitive in economic development, Kentucky needed to make a significant investment in its workforce. A massive campaign was needed to erase adult illiteracy. I wanted to restructure public job training and vocational education programs to make them more responsive to the training needs of small and medium-sized businesses. I also wanted the state to provide training certificates to people who had been unemployed for more than sixty days so they could acquire the skills needed to reenter the workplace, and to encourage the private sector, vocational and technical schools, and public colleges to provide more marketable training. I also wanted to make more customized job training available to growing businesses located in Kentucky.

Growth in small and medium-sized businesses could be stimulated through better use of foreign sales corporations and business industrial development corporations, and by providing venture capital for exporters. The state also could help Kentucky businesses identify potential foreign markets, find distributors, get export licenses, and even customize their products for foreign markets. We also could help by changing the mission of Kentucky's foreign offices from seeking reverse investment to export promotion and sponsorship of international trade fairs.

Many of our communities are not in a position for economic development because of inadequate or deteriorated public services. Community infrastructure needs would be addressed by using a $500 million bond infrastructure program to create 50-50 matching grants for a $1 billion program to provide water and other needed public facilities in areas of high growth potential in Kentucky.

Finally, I wanted to reorganize our way of doing the public's business so as to promote greater economic growth within the commonwealth. I wanted to use state capital investments to foster economic growth by basing capital construction decisions on economic development criteria rather than simply politically-driven need. I also wanted greater involvement of local officials in the planning and justification of these capital projects so they could be more closely tied to local economic development activities.

II. Actions to Improve Kentucky Schools

A major centerpiece of my agenda was to reshape the classrooms of Kentucky schools. The restructuring would replace a state curriculum and instructional mandates with a set of learning objectives or "outcomes" which all students should attain. Educators would be free to use their expertise to determine how best to achieve these objectives, but they would be held accountable for results. Educators who were successful in improving the performance of their students would receive cash bonuses.

Schools would be granted exemptions from any state laws or regulations that impeded their ability to succeed. I pledged to seek more flexible use of state funds to help schools meet their improvement goals. "Benchmark schools" would be created to demonstrate effective ways to achieve the desired learning objectives. I also wanted to work with school officials and educators to improve their ability to control disruptive students and substance abuse. Programs for early childhood education throughout the commonwealth also were goals.

It should be noted here that I was aware of the need to restructure the way schools were funded, even though this issue was not addressed in the *Kentucky First* plan. It was my judgment that the courts ultimately would define what constituted an appropriate remedy, so it would be inappropriate for me to propose a solution at this time. However, as I will discuss later on, I did address the equity issue in a modest way during the first legislative session, even though I made no mention of it in my policy document.

To higher education I made a commitment to invest in the human resources of the system by raising faculty salaries to a competitive level. I was less committal about fully funding the "benchmark" formula because I had serious misgivings about using the spending of other states as a criteria for how much to pay for higher education in Kentucky. Nonetheless, I pledged to work toward full funding of the formula. I also wanted to guarantee access to the first two years of post-secondary education for students from lower income families.

III. Actions to Guarantee a Healthy People

The agenda for health had three objectives: reduce infant mortality, maximize the independence of our senior citizens, and extend health care coverage to indigent families and the working poor not currently covered. These were the populations—both rural and urban—whose health problems were burdening the health care and welfare systems of the commonwealth.

I thought we could expand prenatal and child health care services with only a modest increase in state expenditures through better leveraging of federal funds available through Medicaid, WIC, and other federal family health care programs. I also wanted to expand the availability of home health care and homemaker services to families caring for elderly persons whose medical condition didn't require nursing home care. Every dollar invested in caring for the elderly at home would save many dollars in nursing home bills.

IV. Actions in Criminal Justice and Corrections

The corrections system was seriously over-crowded at both the state and local levels. New prison beds had to be constructed as soon as possible to accommodate the many state prisoners being held in local jails. It was time to put in place a strategic plan for corrections to guide new legislation which has an impact on correctional facilities and to guide the construction and location of new facilities. I also wanted to see better compliance with victims' rights laws, and I pledged to sign death penalty orders after an appropriate review of any capital punishment cases which might come before me.

V. Actions for Agriculture

Agriculture is a major contributor to the Kentucky economy. Agricultural policy in Kentucky is vested in the elected commissioner of agriculture, but as governor I, too, would be in a position to directly influence this sector of the economy. Since many Kentuckians are farmers, it was important not to ignore their concerns. Essentially, I pledged to support expansion of markets for major agricultural products raised in Kentucky such as feed grains, tobacco, livestock, horses, dairy products, poultry, and horticulture.

Furthermore, I felt I could work to encourage vegetable marketing cooperatives; help establish a statewide system for cash hay production and marketing; and support greater home consumption of Kentucky's agricultural products. We also had to do more to help small farmers' transition from tobacco to some other cash crop. In short, we would do whatever could be done to keep our farmers on the land and in production.

VI. Actions to Restore our Land and Water

Part of Kentucky's great heritage is its natural beauty—its mountains, forests, lakes, and streams. People in Kentucky are concerned about their environment and want it protected. Beneath these mountains, forests, lakes, and streams lie rich veins of minerals which over the years have contributed greatly to the economic prosperity of our people. However, many years of pollution from a variety of sources had spoiled many of these streams and poisoned or depleted our precious water resources.

As governor, it was my intention to enforce both state and federal laws and regulations affecting ground water contamination. I also wanted the various public agencies to cooperate and act with vigor to reverse the decline in our waterways. I also envisioned working with our hunters and fishermen, ecologists, conservationists, and tourism and parks officials to develop scenic easements, wild and scenic river designations, and expanded recreational and economic development opportunities.

Finally, I wanted to eliminate politics from environmental regulation and maintain an appropriate balance between economic growth in the natural resource sector of the economy and protection of our natural environment.

Facing the Realities

Having ruled out an immediate tax increase, I planned to move my agenda forward by reallocating existing resources to support new priorities. I was mindful that Kentucky was facing the most austere fiscal situation in recent memory. As bad as the budget news had been throughout the summer, I had assumed it was probably even worse. In fact, it was worse than even I had expected. Walking in the door, I faced a budget deficit of over $50 million that had to be made up by July 1, 1988, and very anemic revenue projections for the coming year.

Even though I tried to put the best face possible on the situation in which I found myself, this was hardly the scenario one would choose as the backdrop for launching an agenda as ambitious as was envisioned in *Kentucky First*. I had to begin my administration deferring every expenditure I could in order to balance the budget I inherited. To make matters even worse, the bond rating agencies were threatening to lower Kentucky's credit rating, which had the potential to cost the state even more money.

In my first message on the State of the Commonwealth, I tried to prepare the legislature and the public for what was to be a very harsh and controversial budget. I also tried to convey a message of hope, even though I knew this would be a tough sell at best.

Busted! Broke! Tapped Out!

In my State of the Commonwealth message delivered to a joint session of the General Assembly on January 21, 1988, I described the situation like this:

> *The financial state of the Commonwealth is miserable. No amount of rhetoric can change that simple fact. . . . I say in plain talk that we're broke. Busted. Tapped out.*

I contended that Kentucky suffered from an eroding economic base caused by a mass transfer of assets out of the commonwealth in the last decade which had occurred because we were producing less and less and being paid less and less for it. These factors were further complicated by what I called a "credit card" mentality and irresponsible fiscal policies which had prevailed in state government.

I spoke of actions I had taken during the initial weeks of the administration to deal responsibly with the fiscal problems facing the state. I had moved revenue forecasting out of the Revenue Cabinet and instructed the staff to prepare a conservative but accurate picture of the revenue stream the state could expect during my first budget. I pledged to continue my tough stand against new taxes in spite of the problems this created in advancing my own agenda. I said:

> *We are in the process of putting together an austere, tough, budget which continues to provide and deliver . . . necessary state services without the burden of additional taxation on our people. Make no mistake about it, the budget will be controversial in many quarters. But we cannot tax our way out of our problems. We must work our way out of our problems with a vibrant and growing economy that provides jobs for those who want and need them. . . .*

*We are going to prove to the people of this Com-
monwealth that we are spending properly what
we do have before we ask them to give us more.
We are initiating a new era of common sense with
a year of common sacrifice.*

In spite of the gloomy fiscal picture, I wanted to communicate
my optimism about the future. Something good was going to
happen in government in spite of hard times. I said:

*Over the first weeks of my Administration, we
have taken the initial steps towards a new Kentucky. I wish they could be bigger steps because
we have some big problems. I wish we could
make the changes Kentuckians are demanding
faster than we are able to. But make no mistake
about one thing. We are going to live up to our
commitment to the people to change the way we
do business in Kentucky. . . . We are getting our
house in order.*

Having made clear how I intended to deal with
the fiscal crisis, I then gave a brief overview of the key things I
would push for in the first two years of my administration. I
talked about new initiatives in education, job training, rural
economic development, infrastructure improvement, early
childhood health programs, and the lottery. Although it would
be a time of belt tightening, I was determined to move forward
on the things I thought were important to the revitalization of
Kentucky.

The response to my call for fiscal responsibility
was mixed. Groups with an interest in protecting their special
programs expressed concern that I would cut spending on their
programs to make room for my own. Some members of the
General Assembly were offended at my blaming much of the
state's fiscal problems on the credit card mentality of the past.
Some thought I was referring to the use of bonds, but I actually
was referring to the practice of enacting programs which are

under-funded or not funded at all. I was specifically criticizing the habit of passing expensive programs (like the education reforms of 1985-86) and leaving it to someone else to figure out how to pay for them later.

The editors of the two major newspapers were outraged. Basically they believed it was unrealistic to think Kentucky could improve itself without a significant increase in revenue. It was obvious that, in their view, only a tax increase would make me a true political leader. In an editorial titled "Grim vision for Kentucky," the *Courier-Journal* wrote:

> *What was most disappointing about Gov. Wilkinson's State of the Commonwealth address was that he evidently means what he's been saying about taxes. He acknowledges Kentucky's critical needs, but he won't consider raising the required revenues.*
>
> *This is from a governor who was shocked to find the cupboard bare when he took office. This from a governor who lambasted his predecessors for not confronting chronic problems. This from a self-styled visionary. It's disheartening.*
>
> *Gov. Wilkinson says he isn't going to do things the "old way," meaning raising taxes. ... If Gov. Wilkinson were serious about doing things differently, he would raise taxes. Squeaking by on inadequate revenue is the old way, not the new.*
>
> *Some of the governor's criticism is on the mark. ... We hoped that when he took office, other facts of life would become clear and that he would be persuaded to tackle them not only with ingenuity, but with money. So much for wishful thinking.*
> (January 24, 1988)

The *Lexington Herald-Leader* was equally dedicated to the proposition that raising taxes was the *only* way out of our problems. In its editorial response to my State of the Commonwealth speech, the paper wrote the following:

> *Wallace Wilkinson claimed in his State of the Commonwealth Message that Kentucky's problem is its "credit card mentality." That's Wilkinomics for you: It sounds good to say that Kentucky has been crucifying itself on a cross of plastic. It's dramatic. It's catchy. Trouble is, it is irrelevant to the state's needs.*
>
> *Kentucky is not overly in debt; the state's constitution keeps that from happening. The state does have the ability to raise taxes; conforming to the federal tax code would accomplish that easily.*
>
> *No, the problem is that Kentucky simply lacks the will to invest in a better future. So there is a bitter irony when Wilkinson asks Kentuckians to sacrifice today for the future, while stubbornly sticking to his opposition to new taxes.* (January 24, 1988)

The fiscal situation gave me little room to move forward with even my highest priority programs. Even so, I remained convinced that any call for more revenue had to wait, regardless of the pressure I knew I would receive to raise taxes once the executive budget proposal was made public.

The Other Shoe Drops

In my first budget speech to the General Assembly I called for "a budget that reorders our priorities and directs our resources where they are needed the most." Although I felt we had done a reasonably good job within the limits of available revenue, it seemed like *deja vu*. As I noted in my speech,

*All my life I've watched Kentucky struggle. I've
watched as one Governor after another came to
Frankfort with high hopes. We've seen those hope
dimmed by the fiscal realities of a state whose
economic base is unable to support our needs. It
is an economic base that is continuing to erode
day by day, year by year. It's frustrating to watch.
It's frustrating to know we can be better. To know
we must be better.*

Although the budget would cast a dark shadow over the first
two years of my administration, I felt we were making a good
beginning. My first priority was to get state government back
on sound footing and at the same time to make as much progress on my agenda as possible.

*My priorities for the budget are clear: (1) to
bring spending into line with revenue; (2) to continue good programs without additional taxes;
and (3) to advance new programs and priorities
within our existing resources.*

Nonetheless, my first Executive Budget proposal was destined
to be controversial. It was indeed a budget with no "frills, no
luxuries, no conveniences, no extras." The net increase in
spending for the first year of the biennium was only 0.6 percent
over the previous fiscal year. It only increased 4.9 percent the
second year.

The budget was balanced by using a mix of
tactics. On the expenditure side I reduced pay raises for state
employees and teachers from 5 percent to 2 percent the first
year; made major shifts in spending; held most state agency
budget increases to 3 percent or less; discontinued part of the
over match to state pension funds; kept spending for higher
education essentially flat for the first year; and reduced funding
for some of my own programs. On the revenue side I proposed
a one-time tax amnesty program; accelerated collection of sales

and use taxes; and transferred some money from the road fund and several agencies with surplus funds. Although I called for creation of a state lottery, I did not include expected lottery receipts in the budget because I wanted these funds earmarked for special purposes.

I knew some of these decisions would be controversial and politically difficult to sustain in the General Assembly, but I was determined to present a balanced budget and stay within the revenue projections I had been given. At the same time, I felt it was necessary to do more than just "tighten the belt" on government spending. I needed to move forward in each of the areas I considered critical to achieving my vision of a better Kentucky. One-half of my administration was tied up in this budget, so a delay in implementing high priority programs was not an option. In that regard I was pleased with the budget because it contained at least some money for all the high priority initiatives I had proposed in *Kentucky First.*

My Budget Priorities Made Clear

The first steps to implement my education plan took relatively little money. Most of the program involved structural or policy changes. The most costly item was the cash bonus teachers in successful schools were to receive; this could be deferred since the bonuses could not be paid until the next biennium, anyway. It wasn't necessary to appropriate $70 million for this purpose in the current biennium. I asked for just $10 million to begin the process of establishing the learner outcomes and to launch the Benchmark School program.

I felt it was important from a political perspective not to abandon or dismantle key elements of the education reforms enacted in 1985 and 1986, so no cutbacks were made in programs *already funded.* Some programs like the Parent and Child Education program (PACE) received additional funds in the budget. On the other hand, I thought some elements of the earlier reform, such as continuing to lower class size, were of doubtful value. I considered it inappropriate to *increase* the level of funding for these programs under the circumstances.

Funds for basic elementary and secondary education—the minimum foundation and power equalization programs—were increased. I also proposed that an additional $12 million be awarded to the most disadvantaged school districts in the commonwealth. I funded adult literacy and dropout prevention programs as I said I would in *Kentucky First*. Funds were proposed for the Job Training Certificate Program and I fulfilled job training commitments made to two Kentucky corporations. One education campaign promise I could not keep was to fund higher education at 88 percent of the benchmark formula at least the first year. This goal had to wait until the 1990 session. On the other hand, I did propose funding a number of capital construction projects that the universities wanted.

Economic development funds were significantly increased, especially in the money appropriated to various economic development loan programs. New funds were requested for the public infrastructure program I promised. I also requested money for school construction and renovation, new and better vocational education facilities, new prisons, state park improvements and expansions, and several state government facility projects, some of which had been approved but not funded by the previous General Assembly. I also requested an additional $1.75 million to support the surface mining primacy program, which would attract an additional $9 million in federal funds.

I proposed a significant increase in funds for various human service programs for children, the elderly, and the medically indigent—areas in which I proposed improvement in *Kentucky First*. No new programs were needed, but previous funding levels were not meeting the need. Federal funds are available for these programs, but they are directly tied to the level of state funding. Increased spending in these areas has a greater multiplier than in any other sector of the budget. I thought it was good fiscal policy to obtain as much federal assistance as possible for these programs.

As with the State of the Commonwealth message, my budget proposal was met with an outcry by legislative leaders and critical reviews from newspaper editors. Of particular concern to legislators was my dipping into politically sensitive funds like the road fund and the fish and wildlife agency fund to balance the budget. They also complained it would be difficult to explain to teachers and public employees that suspending the extra payments into their pension funds would not jeopardize the future safety of their pensions. Criticism also was leveled at my $303 million capital construction bond request at a time when money was tight for ongoing programs. Editorials basically said I had turned my back on Kentucky's needs instead of moving the state forward as I had promised to do. Their response came as no surprise, since they saw no alternative to an immediate tax increase.

The Peril of Raised Expectations

The need for a government program is always justified in terms of what someone *wants* from government. I believe there is a practical limit to what government can and should attempt to do. A public expenditure cannot be justified simply on the argument of human need. Kentucky is a relatively poor state. Government can ill afford to try to meet every human need presented to it. Something more than need has to be taken into account in the equation, especially when resources are scarce.

Reordering priorities means by definition some things are more important than others. Making decisions when there are competing interests is what politics is all about. The General Assembly must do it in the end since it determines the appropriation for each program. Someone must prioritize these needs. Hard choices must be made. Central to this process is the ability to just say "No!" However, all the rhetoric about cutting back on government and reordering priorities generally is lost on most legislators.

The source of government's reluctance to eliminate or cut funding for programs can be found in the legislative process itself. The legislative committee structure gives small groups of legislators, who often act on behalf of special interests, great power to move legislation and programs through the legislature. These special interests heavily lobby legislators for money and legislation that address their concerns. Legislators want to be helpful and will generally agree at least to submit legislation for consideration by the committee.

Along the way legislators develop a personal commitment to protect and expand programs they have personally sponsored. Therefore, among legislators there always is a constituency for every program and item in the budget. Almost never will they step forward and say, "I don't think we need to do this anymore." We just keep on trying to do more and more. A typical approach of legislators is to get enabling legislation enacted into law and then seek funding "to get the program started." Now there is one more program that seeks expansion in future budgets.

We have an ever growing number of programs that are not funded at a level sufficient to have a meaningful impact and that have little likelihood that of ever being funded at such a level. Programs of this sort just leech away the resources of the state without ever really dealing effectively with the problems these programs were designed to address. Yet the programs are continued in the hope (or expectation) that they will be properly funded at some future time. In my view we should either make the program a priority and fund it at a level sufficient to have the intended impact, or stop funding it until such time as enough money is available to make it effective.

Financial overcommitment, especially in education, was a serious political problem for both the General

Assembly and me. More had been promised for education in 1986 than could be delivered. When politicians raise expectations, they had better follow through or be prepared to face the wrath of those whose hopes were raised. Legislators who fought for the education reforms of 1986 were feeling tremendous pressure not to let this "regressive, antitax governor" turn back the clock of progress. These legislators took the position that we should complete implementation of one reform before beginning another. "Stay the course" with the reforms of 1986 became their motto.

My problem was just as serious. I, too, had raised expectations for which there were limited resources. Although I had not made the earlier commitments in education, I was under great political pressure to honor them. At the same time, I wanted to do something in education, but also in human services, corrections, the environment, and economic development. The bottom line was this: there just wasn't enough money to satisfy both the legislature and myself, so a struggle was inevitable. In the end nobody liked the budget.

Some Success in the Midst of Turmoil

Although my first legislative session turned out to be more contentious than I would have liked, I felt I got most of what I wanted out of it. We took the first step toward keeping my promise to give voters a chance to approve a state lottery when the General Assembly voted to put the constitutional amendment on the November ballot. The 1988 General Assembly appropriated money for nearly all of my high priority programs, our tax amnesty program was adopted, and new economic development tools were put in place that would prove to be of tremendous benefit in the coming months. My only major defeats were in education and job training.

Probably the most significant thing about the 1988 legislative session was what I *didn't* do. I didn't raise taxes. No new sources of revenue (read that "taxes") were approved even though talk about it continued right up to the end of the session. In the end, the General Assembly refused to use the $3 million fish and wildlife agency funds and restored $40 million of the $80 million pension fund overmatch I had suspended. The money diverted from the road fund was left alone. The tax amnesty program I sought was approved, even though the amount of money I said it would yield was disputed. Skeptical of my amnesty revenue projections, the General Assembly put only $10 million in the budget. Amnesty eventually raised $63 million.

When the 1988-90 biennial budget was finally approved by the Senate and House of Representatives conference committee, it was so onerous to Joe Clarke, chairman of the House budget committee, that he refused to vote for it. As one editorial writer put it, there was something in it for everyone to *dis*like. I wasn't exactly thrilled with it either, but nearly everything I wanted remained in the budget, although in many cases at a lower level of funding than I had requested.

The Credit Crunch

While the budget debate was raging, an unexpected but not surprising crisis arose. A few legislators expressed concern over my seeking such a large increase in the state's debt at a time when we could hardly balance the budget. Their concern had some merit in terms of the state bond rating, which was about to be lowered. When I looked into the issue, it was clear the threat was real. However, the problem was not one of debt *capacity*. The rating companies were concerned because of the lack of a sizable reserve and repeated failure to meet revenue targets. The problem was exacerbated by the revenue shortfall in the present budget.

Since bond ratings directly affect the cost of money, I knew I had to deal with this issue before we negotiated a new round of bonds. My strategy was to try to buy time, since I knew the present fiscal condition of the state probably would justify a lower rating. During the legislative session, I invited representatives of Standard & Poore and Moody's, national credit rating companies, to meet with me to determine what needed to be done to maintain the state's good rating. After lengthy discussions, I convinced them to give me a year in which to get the fiscal house in order.

In a way it was good that the General Assembly was so skeptical of my revenue projections from the tax amnesty program. Had they taken my figures, they would have appropriated the money for other purposes than the reserve I had asked for. I felt confident that we would satisfy the bond market concerns once the money from the amnesty program came in. These funds would create the budget surplus the bond rating companies wanted to see (but the legislature did not have the business sense to provide in the budget). In spite of the tight money budget problems in the first year of the biennium, we were able to maintain our high rating without further question for the rest of my term in office.

Funding for My Priority Programs

On the expenditure side, several economic development, health care, and education programs were of specific interest to me. In economic development, I wanted an overall increase of 64 percent in spending for economic development. The amount I requested for certain programs was reduced, but we still ended up with an increase of more than 30 percent over the previous budget. The largest single amount requested was $56 million in economic development bonds. The final appropriation reduced the amount to $46 million, which still was more than four times the amount currently available excluding the Toyota deal. On the other hand, a $10 million bond issue requested for the Kentucky Development Finance Authority (KDFA) to finance additional job creation was eliminated from the budget.

My economic development strategy called for a significant increase in training funds available through the Blue Grass State Skills Corporation, which provides customized job training for business and industry in Kentucky. The request was cut by almost 50 percent. The funds I requested for the job training certificate program were eliminated entirely since the enabling legislation never made it out of committee. Finally, I had sought to streamline the state vocational education system by eliminating ninety positions I felt were unnecessary. All ninety positions were fully restored in the final budget.

Infrastructure investment, particularly in rural Kentucky, was a high priority. I supported two bills designed to improve the position of rural communities to attract business investment: the Kentucky Public Works Act (HB 217), which funneled federal and state money into waste water treatment and economic development projects; and the Rural Kentucky Jobs Act (SB 280), which provided financial incentives to businesses which located or expanded in counties with chronic high unemployment. Both measures were enacted into law and funded in the budget.

The infrastructure bill (HB 217) created a new agency within the Finance Cabinet called the Kentucky Infrastructure Authority, which replaced the Kentucky Pollution Abatement and Water Resource Finance Authority. The act created a "revolving loan" fund to finance a broad range of water and waste water projects, often related to economic development, under local government control. The loan fund is administered by the Authority and is financed by state revenue bonds issued on a project-by-project basis. Local governments repay the Authority, which in turn retires the debt.

Consolidation of financing for local infrastructure projects at the state level was intended, among other things, to lower the cost of the bonds needed to pay for them. Many of Kentucky's rural counties were bordering on bankruptcy and could never obtain on their own a favorable bond issue. Also, through its loan decisions, the Authority could more closely link state economic development initiatives with local infrastructure investment to ensure the most strategic use of state and federal expenditures on water related projects. In the past, individual local project decisions often did not take future development needs into account.

The budget contained most of the capital construction projects I had sought, along with a few I had not requested. I believe capital projects make good sense even in a period of tight money if they are directed at areas in need of economic development. Capital construction projects create high paying jobs with minimal immediate impact on the general fund because they are funded by bonds. Unlike money spent on *services* which government provides, capital construction projects stimulate the economy through a multiplier effect.

Another economic development program I wanted and got legislation for was creation of a privately funded venture capital fund (HB 19). Kentucky had the least amount of intrastate venture capital available of any state. The program was enacted into law without an appropriation. As it turned out, we found it to be much more difficult to attract private contributions to the fund than I had anticipated. However, the structure is now in place, and hopefully it will benefit future new ventures.

I also wanted to expand the scope of the Kentucky Development Finance Authority (KDFA) to include businesses other than just manufacturing. Growth in service industries was at the heart of many of Kentucky's employment and revenue problems. Like most states, job growth in manufacturing was stagnant. I felt many major business opportunities were possible in service industries currently outside the scope of KDFA. I was pleased to get this expansion through passage of HB 963.

It was in education where I suffered my most significant and personally disappointing setback. Not only was money not appropriated for my school improvement incentive program; the legislation never even got a hearing in the House of Representatives. House Education Committee members, many of whom were beholden to KEA, were committed to the education reforms of 1986. These legislators in particular felt I had killed the momentum of their efforts at school reform. They retaliated by refusing to hold a hearing on my bill, which had passed the Senate.

The Kentucky Lottery

A major victory in the 1988 legislative session was the fulfillment of my campaign promise to create a state lottery. A bill calling for a lottery had been introduced at every legislative session for almost a decade without success. The most recent attempt had been in 1986 when a lottery bill was approved by a House committee but never came to a floor vote. House Democrats decided there were not enough votes for passage, and leadership let the bill die.

This time I was certain we could get the votes needed in the General Assembly to put on the November ballot a constitutional amendment to repeal the prohibition against a lottery. Furthermore, I had brought so much attention to the issue and made it such a priority that legislative leadership would not be able to finesse it as they had in the past. This time the public was sufficiently aware that a lottery was under consideration. There would be no way the special interests who had opposed it in the past could prevent a floor vote.

Legislation to create a lottery had to await the vote on a constitutional amendment repealing the prohibition against lotteries, so the focus in the 1988 session was to get the General Assembly to approve the amendment so it could be placed on the November ballot. Leadership in both houses recognized that the time had come to let the voters decide the issue. A lottery amendment passed both houses and went to the voters that fall.

In July of 1988 I appointed an eleven-member Kentucky Lottery Commission to gain background information on lotteries in other states and to prepare enabling legislation based on experience elsewhere. I wanted our legislation to be the best possible. The commission membership included the majority leaders of both houses of the legislature, Sen. Joe Wright and Rep. Greg Stumbo. The commission presented the results of their work on October 31, just before the vote on the amendment would be held. Hopefully, the findings of this commission would answer most of the questions the public had about how the lottery would be organized and operated.

Even though our opinion polls showed overwhelming support for a lottery, I knew we could not take the amendment vote for granted. As expected, there was a strong push by church leaders and others to defeat the amendment. The only group organized specifically to oppose the lottery was Citizens Against State Lottery, which launched a public information campaign about five weeks before the election. The initial thrust of their campaign was to argue that insufficient information about how the lottery would actually work was available for the public to make an informed decision. Later in their campaign, they used the arguments that lotteries and all forms of gambling threaten the morals of the community and prey upon the poor, who can ill-afford to engage in any form of gambling.

A pro-lottery group called the Lottery Yes Committee was formed to raise money for a media campaign if necessary to counter the anti-lottery forces. We continued to monitor voter sentiment and decided not to engage in a full court press effort to get voter support. In the last week I made a flying tour of the western part of the state, where support seemed weakest. Coincidentally, the anti-lottery group also focused on that part of the state in their last effort to get the amendment defeated. We felt confident going into the election that the amendment would pass.

Experience in other states had shown that the margin gets smaller as one gets closer to the time a decision has to be made at the ballot box. When the votes were counted the amendment won by a solid but smaller margin than the early polls had indicated. Nonetheless, I was very pleased at the outcome. On November 11, three days after the election, I issued the call for a special session of the General Assembly to enact legislation to create the Kentucky Lottery.

As I approached the special session, I was determined to shake the perception that I could not work with the General Assembly. After making the call for the special session, I met with Senate and House leadership to present my views and solicit their responses. The meeting went well by everyone's account. Based on these discussions, it was clear the debate would be over four issues: (1) the business structure of the lottery; (2) legislative oversight; (3) taxation of the winnings; and (4) use of the proceeds.

The bill which the Lottery Commission drafted became the bill that was introduced in both the House and Senate. Rep. Greg Stumbo, who sponsored the House bill on my behalf, warned that it would face stiff opposition on several fronts. He also told me he could not support some provisions in the bill even though he had been a member of the Lottery Commission which drafted it. However, he pledged to help me get the intent if not the letter of each provision enacted into law. For my part, I told him I was prepared to make concessions on some things but not up front.

The most serious points of disagreement between the legislature and myself were over dedication of lottery proceeds to specific purposes, legislative oversight, and the governor's control of the lottery. In this instance there were some basic differences in objectives and fiscal policy which could not be accommodated. I said from the beginning I wanted the proceeds divided in thirds the first year to pay for a one-time bonus to Vietnam veterans, early childhood, and senior citizen programs, and then equally divided thereafter to support programs for preschool children and medical programs for senior citizens.

The Kentucky constitution limits legislation in a special session to the items specified in the call. Realizing this, I made certain that the executive order calling the special session of the General Assembly contained language regarding how the proceeds were to be used. I used this tactic to put the legislature in a position where it had to either dedicate the lottery proceeds to the programs I named in the call or not spend them at all.

Legislative leaders of both houses strongly objected to the dedication of funds for any purpose whatever, because it limits their discretion to use the money for other things which might be given greater priority in future years. Even the beneficiaries of the lottery money were skeptical about being so named. The concern was that the legislature would just use the lottery money to offset whatever they would otherwise have appropriated, and in the end the beneficiaries of these programs really wouldn't be any better off. The Kentucky Education Association objected on the grounds that people would think I was funding public schools with lottery money so no increase in taxes would be needed in the future.

While these arguments are plausible, I felt we could still dedicate the money to programs which otherwise might not be funded at all. Leadership offered to dedicate the first revenues to the veteran's bonus and thereafter split the money evenly between the other two program areas during the 1990 regular session, when the exact amount of available money would be known. Lottery proceeds would be held in trust until then. Obviously they were trying to give me some-thing without changing their basic position on not wanting to dedicate lottery funds to any specific purpose. I didn't like it, but in the end that was what they did.

At the time I was very concerned about the impact the decision to defer spending the lottery money would have on the effort to get it enacted. In researching the experi-ence of other states, I found that earmarking proceeds for specific purposes was believed to be an important element in getting voter support for a lottery. Managers of lotteries also believe that dedicating lottery proceeds for specific purposes promotes ticket sales. People like to feel their gambling is contributing to something they believe is worthwhile. My position was that a state lottery is similar in concept to gaming for charitable purposes. The proceeds should not be treated as a tax to be used for general government purposes.

The lottery has done well, exceeding the estimates I had made for the revenues it would bring to the state treasury. It is conceivable that it might be doing even better if the players knew their money had a direct benefit. In the end I was quite pleased with the legislation, even though I lost on the issue of dedicating the proceeds to specific purposes. I said at the time that "we started with a good lottery bill and we've ended with a great lottery bill." I still think so. Nevertheless, we will always have a problem answering the question "where does the money go?" as long as it disappears into the general fund.

V. A ROUGH BEGINNING

A kind of emotional darkness falls over a legislature when money is scarce. A sense of gloom prevails. Most legislators come to the state capital to take something back home. There isn't much to take home unless additional money is available. Much of the state budget is relatively untouchable, and raising taxes is highly undesirable, so both legislators and governors depend on *growth* in the state budget to finance what they want. Unfortunately, in my first two years as governor there would be little growth in revenues.

Even though legislators do not like to raise taxes, a shortage of money greatly frustrates them. The tone throughout the 1988 session was often contentious and bitter. While I surely cannot attribute the foul mood I found entirely to a shortage of money, I can see how my refusal to raise more revenue put many legislators under great pressure. Leadership didn't have anything with which to barter votes. The budget types didn't like some of the ways I balanced the budget. Others saw their programs stalled at current funding levels with no new money available to fund some of the things they wanted to do.

My stubborn refusal to ease their pain by agreeing to raise more revenue was bitterly resented. Legislators knew I was determined to fund my own priorities, and they were equally determined to restore or increase funds in areas I had cut. I knew from the outset that my plan to shift priorities in state spending was headed straight for the legislative buzz saw. We were all in for a very rough ride.

The Fight Over Taxes

As noted previously, the battle over taxes actually began before I was even elected governor. During the election campaign, there was talk about a special session of the

General Assembly to deal with the workers' compensation fund problem. Conforming the state tax code to the federal code was being touted as the way to resolve this issue and avoid further cutbacks in the state budget due to a shortfall in revenue.

I expressed my opposition to conformity to the federal tax code and was criticized for meddling before I was even elected governor. Talk of raising taxes continued throughout the fall as some legislators grew fearful that I would not fund the education reforms they enacted in 1985. House and Senate Democratic leadership were quoted in the news media as saying they might seek a tax increase on their own. Apparently they thought they could get enough votes to pass such a measure even if I were to veto it, as I threatened to do.

I responded to this idea with a pledge to oppose *any* tax increase until Kentucky's average personal income rose substantially in national ranking. I really didn't believe there were enough votes in the General Assembly to pass a tax increase, but I wasn't about to take any chances. I wanted to make my position clear before any movement might be undertaken to counter my position. Other than a proposal by House Majority Whip Kenny Rapier to put a five cent tax on soft-drink containers, there was little more done proactively by legislators to raise taxes on their own.

The whole idea that the General Assembly would raise taxes if I just got out of the way seemed curious to me. In spite of all the public talk by a handful of legislators, the idea of raising taxes was not shared by the run-of-the-mill legislator. I met many of them on the campaign trail and knew their sentiments were the same as my own. The last thing in the world they wanted to do was to come to Frankfort to pass more taxes. I was reasonably certain that few legislators would agree to more taxes without strong support from the governor.

I had publicly committed myself first to reorder how we spent the money we had before going to the public to ask for more. I firmly believed this was the right and necessary thing to do. I had to stick to my no new tax pledge during this first legislative session, no matter how tough it got or what it cost me in terms of moving my own agenda forward. If the economy improved and I demonstrated my commitment to the agenda I had put forth, then I could go to the public during the second half of my term in office with an appeal for more money, assuming the court had ruled by then on the school finance issue.

Critics of my "no new tax" pledge were very vocal. I knew as well as they that Kentucky was in exceedingly poor financial condition —both in its economy and in its ability to pay for much needed public services. However, in politics as in business, timing is everything. Anti-tax sentiment in Kentucky is historic and strong. The "old way" of politics was to get elected and then declare a crisis and raise taxes. The public no longer trusted a politician who said he would not raise taxes. It was my view that I first had to establish political credibility with the voting public.

But more was involved here than just political credibility. Clearly there existed a very deep philosophical difference between myself and the editorial writers, special interest advocates, and a few influential legislators as to the best way to move Kentucky forward. This difference in philosophy went straight to the heart of why the fight over taxes was so intense and acrimonious.

One editorial after another castigated me for turning my back on the serious problems facing Kentucky. The litany of needs was recounted over and again by various interest groups who called upon government to do something about these needs. I also recounted many of these same problems in my *Kentucky First* document. I was painfully aware of what Kentucky needed. But I saw a much different solution than simply raising taxes. The fact that a majority of legislators shared my beliefs was largely ignored.

If more revenue comes from economic growth, then it is better to stimulate the economy with strategic public investment than to raise taxes, which only places a greater burden on an unhealthy economy. When the economy prospers, government can do more without increasing the tax burden of the people. In my view Kentucky would never be able to meet its needs unless we had a sound, vibrant economy. Unless government were willing to address the economy as an integral part of the solution, there was only despair ahead. There was no way I could see us taxing our way into a better future.

Government spending can play an important role in the economy if properly directed. Any entity that spends around $20 billion a year (as Kentucky state government did at the time) certainly can have a great impact on the economy. As I looked at what government needed to do, I was convinced the answer was to make more strategic use of its public expenditures. Government fiscal policy should maintain a careful balance between public capital investment and support for those human service programs that in the long run will reduce the need for continued government intervention. It was this rationale which led me to put so much emphasis on increasing expenditures for job training, economic development, and capital construction projects in a time of tight money.

After the budget bill was passed by the House in March 1988, Rep. Joe Clarke reviewed for the news media his view of how Kentucky government came to be in such poor fiscal condition. The newspaper accounts of his remarks indicate he felt that the state had been on the wrong course for a long time. He warned "a moment of truth" was fast approaching for Kentucky. I certainly agreed with his assessment of where we were headed. Where I disagreed with Rep. Clarke, if in fact we disagreed at all, was with the time when he and others thought that "moment of truth" should be addressed with a tax increase.

I certainly don't want to characterize everyone who opposed my stand on taxes as misguided idiots. On the other hand, the people who quickly wrote off my "no new tax" position as simply old style Kentucky politics should recognize that a debate about the role of taxes in fiscal policy is a legitimate one. Not everyone who opposes tax increases is engaging in political chicanery. In any case, I don't think I deserved to be characterized in the print media as insensitive to what was best for the commonwealth because I did not share the view of the editors that raising taxes at that time was the only proper answer to the fiscal crisis facing state government.

The Price of Holding Out

From a purely political perspective, I paid a rather heavy price for my success in heading off a tax increase during this first legislative session. "The sky is falling" rhetoric which followed my budget message gave the impression that I was leading the state back into the dark ages rather than into a new era of prosperity. Instead of beginning my administration in an atmosphere of hope and optimism, I had to fight through a fog of negativism and despair.

Some of the political cost of the tax fight came from the way I tried to balance the budget rather than directly from my opposition to raising taxes. The lack of real growth in revenues extracted a price from me as well as the legislature. I kept my pledge to "reorder priorities" by redirecting funds wherever it could be justified. I captured every potential source of money I could find. Still there was not enough money to do what I felt was needed to get my own agenda moving. None of the remaining options were very desirable. In particular I was warned that touching the pension funds and denying the teachers a $300 bonus for successfully completing an evaluation mandated by the General Assembly in 1986 could have very damaging political consequences.

As predicted by some legislators, the decision to suspend the overmatch payment to the state pension funds proved to be very difficult to explain to teachers and state employees. In the late 1970s there was much concern about the unfunded liability found in many public pension funds. Some states were on a "pay-as-you-go" basis while others, like Kentucky, were counting on the investment of premiums to pay part of the cost of the pension program. Actuarial studies at the time indicated there might not be enough money available to pay the beneficiaries of these programs unless more money was put into them.

The Kentucky legislature addressed the problem by agreeing to increase the state match of employee contributions until the pension funds were able to cover their estimated liabilities. I felt that the unfunded liability no longer existed, and the additional match could now be used for other purposes. I proposed that the state suspend making the *additional* contributions, which I referred to as the *over*match, until a new actuarial study could determine the need to continue such payments. In the interim, the roughly $80 million in over match should be used to support the ongoing programs of government.

The executive director of these pension programs claimed my actions would seriously undermine the safety of the pension of every teacher and state employee. Many of the pensioners who wrote letters to protest my position clearly did not understand the difference between the state's regular match of the employee's contribution, which we were continuing to make, and the *additional* contribution, which the state agreed to make for a limited period of time to cover the alleged unfunded liability. Some of the news media kept referring to my "borrowing" from these funds which implied that I was actually taking money *out* of the employee pension funds. This uninformed use of words added to the confusion and misunderstanding.

As for the $300 bonus for a good evaluation, I conferred with several key legislators as to their interest in retaining the money for this program in the budget. One said to me that, quite candidly, he didn't feel obligated to pay it since most of the teachers were given inflated or meaningless evaluations. The legislators who sponsored this program in the first place had ample opportunity to restore it in the budget later, just as they did other elements of the 1985 reform which I chose to eliminate. Obviously, they didn't think enough of the program to restore the money when they approved the final budget for education.

The bonus issue came back to haunt me later as teachers used it to discredit my proposal for a bonus of as much as $7,000 under my school improvement incentive program. They viewed with skepticism my promise of such a large bonus when from their perspective I was too stingy to pay out the $300 bonus they had already earned. Their skepticism was fueled by KEA leadership, which would much rather have gotten a $300 bonus for virtually every teacher in the commonwealth than a much larger bonus for a smaller number whose students showed improvement from one year to the next.

Teachers were of special importance to me. I didn't expect educators to come to Frankfort in huge numbers to say they were *in favor of* my proposals for improving education. On the other hand, I certainly didn't need them to be openly hostile toward me at a time when I was trying to restructure education. All of this debate about pension funds, together with refusing the $300 bonus and reducing expected teacher salary increases the first year, all added up to a potent potion in the political cauldron.

The pressure continued to mount for me to change my position on taxes. The university presidents were vocal in their criticism, and some members of their faculties wrote me very nasty letters. Student government representatives were at my door. Then there was a march on the Capitol in February by college students and others who wanted me to increase spending on higher education. The group was orderly and modest in number but was organized to protest my stand on taxes and plead for more money. A group of student representatives met with me that day for what turned out to be a very pleasant and informative exchange of views.

About six weeks later, near the close of the legislative session, there was a much larger march on the Capitol sponsored by the Kentucky Education Association but supported by other organizations of educators and advocates for education. Various estimates placed the number of marchers between 15,000 and 20,000, including children who marched with their parents. The rally was very hostile and focused primarily on me personally. Most of the signs the marchers had made carried slogans which caricatured me or statements I had made in a very negative way. I was not even given the courtesy of an invitation to speak to the group as it gathered on the steps of KEA headquarters on Capitol Avenue.

As I sat in my office and watched the marchers pass by, I felt a deep sadness within. It was clear evidence of how many educators saw me as the worst thing that had ever happened to them. It is hard to estimate the damage these things did to my efforts to promote school reform, but I believe they were great. At every public event over the next eighteen months I was met by angry teachers and administrators.

In terms of changing my position on a tax increase, the rally had no impact whatever. However, the show of strength by these teachers and administrators did seem to strengthen the resolve of key legislators to trash my program as an act of defiance and to renew their commitment to the reforms of 1986. In that regard it was a serious setback for me in my effort to change the direction of education reform in Kentucky.

Learning What Really Matters

As I mentioned earlier, I had taken special care to retain all of what I had been told were the key elements of the 1986 reforms with one exception—further reductions in class size. Later I was told by some legislators and educators that reduction in class size was the "corner stone" of the 1986 reform and had to be continued for reform to work. I found little research to either confirm or deny that assumption. Apart from increases in teacher salaries, class size reduction was the most costly part of the underfunded 1986 reform.

I put more money into the minimum foundation and power equalization programs, school construction, and all but a few of the very small special programs like the innovation grant fund. Yet the rhetoric persisted that I had undercut school reform in Kentucky, apparently because I sustained existing class size levels but did not fund any further reductions at the present time. As it turned out, my gesture of good faith received nothing more than a sigh of relief. It certainly won no support for my own program in the legislature or from educators. The reason became very clear as the session wore on.

When all is said and done, teacher salaries and benefits were more important to them than funding school reform. A little song sung by teachers and school administrators as they marched around the Capitol seemed to capture for me what this was really all about. According to a *Courier-Journal* news reporter, the song was written by a group of Campbell County teachers while they waited for the parade to start. Here are the words:

> *School days, school days,*
> *We lost our golden-rule days.*
> *Salaries, and buildings, retirement, too.*
> *What will the cuts to our children do?*

Salaries, buildings, and retirement. That was the bottom line for those who saw me as their personal and professional enemy.

One never knows what might have happened had things been done differently. It could be argued that my first two years in office probably would have been much easier in many respects had I acceded to the call for more revenue and raised taxes at that time. Although I got most of what I wanted out of the first legislative session without doing so, the fight over money left me with political liabilities which severely diminished my image as a progressive political leader in the early years of my administration.

On the other hand, the appetite for money in government is virtually insatiable. Had I simply sought to appease the editors and others who put extreme pressure on me to raise taxes immediately, I doubt that they would have been any more satisfied with the old way I disdained—doing just enough to get a solid balanced budget for now. Once I agreed to seek a tax increase, they would then have wanted me to solve in that one act all the fiscal problems of state government. The timing was wrong from both a fiscal policy and political perspective. Action of that magnitude simply had to await the court decision on school finance.

The Budget Process is Seriously Flawed

The budget process in Kentucky leaves much to be desired. I found the whole process awkward and seriously flawed. From a constitutional standpoint, the General Assembly has sole responsibility and authority to set taxes and to appropriate money. However, the governor is required by statute to submit to the General Assembly at the beginning of each regular session an executive budget which includes requested appropriations for all three branches of government.

The budget process has become unnecessarily adversarial and hostile. I fully recognize it is the constitutional responsibility of the General Assembly to approve a budget. At one time governors expected the General Assembly to adopt the executive budget without change. I know those times are gone. No legislator today is going to agree ahead of time to an executive budget which has not been scrutinized in detail. I certainly didn't expect them to *like* my budget.

On the other hand, I reject the idea held by certain members of the legislature that a governor should have no greater influence on the budget than a lobbyist. In effect the General Assembly is saying, "You're the governor, so we'll give you the first shot. But remember that you're *just* the governor. Don't try to influence what we do. We alone will decide what is good for the commonwealth."

Much of the budget is considered the base, or that portion of the budget which is relatively fixed. Most of the debate is over any discretionary money available to create new programs or to expand existing ones. The governor's special requests are considered along with those of legislators who also are seeking funds for their own programs. Each legislative session is a protracted struggle over the way individual legislators want to spend the taxpayers' money and the way the governor wants to spend it.

During his or her term in office, a governor prepares only two budgets. A new governor has about six to eight weeks in which to review the first budget (which is prepared by the preceding governor) before it is sent to the legislature for action. Since this first budget directly affects what a new administration can accomplish in its first two years in office, a new governor must be certain the budget reflects his or her priorities. The second budget is the only one which is truly prepared "from scratch" by a sitting governor.

The budget is the most important policy document of government. It is too important to the people of the state to relegate the only person in the process elected by all the people to the role of advisor or spectator when the budget is prepared. Consultation and negotiation between the branches should be the basis for building a budget, not exclusion of one by the other. I don't think the public is well served when a governor who is elected by the people is treated like an enemy to be kept at arm's length. Perhaps this tension is built into the process and is inevitable; but, if it is, the media should recognize the institutional nature of the interchange and not blame all the fighting over a budget on the style or personality of a governor.

VI. THE GAME
WITHIN THE GAME

The political pundits and editorial writers contended that my problems with the General Assembly were due to my threatening style and my insistence that things be "Wilkinson's way or no way." In their opinion, I could have been more successful with the legislature if I had been more cooperative and willing to abandon what they considered my combative style. I disagree with that assessment. At the heart of my struggle with the General Assembly was my determination to pass my programs and protect what I believe are the prerogatives of the executive branch in the face of growing legislative erosion of executive authority.

In the mid-1970s, the General Assembly made some major organizational changes designed to give it a more equal footing with the governor. In their drive for independence from the political domination of a governor, legislative leaders steadily tried to gain control over government functions that previously were the sole prerogative of the governor. I represented a clear and present danger to that expansion.

The problems I had with the General Assembly were not mere matters of style or personality. The underlying dispute was over the proper exercise of executive and legislative power. Legislative leadership's determination not to lose ground so permeated my entire term of office it deserves special consideration. It became a game within the game.

A Struggle Over Succession

Early in the first month of the 1988 legislative session, I let it be known that I had an interest in seeing a succession amendment put before the voters. I also acknowledged that I thought the incumbent governor should be included in the amendment. I said, "If I am a good governor, then the people of this commonwealth ought to have the opportunity to reelect me."

The rural vote had historically defeated a succession amendment while it was generally favored in the urban areas. The previous attempt failed during the Brown administration. My polling of the issue indicated that the urban vote would continue to support the amendment whether or not the incumbent was included. I felt my popularity in rural Kentucky would easily give the amendment the votes it needed to pass. I also felt that having the succession amendment on the same ballot with the lottery would increase the liklihood of its passage.

Early in January 1988 I asked the House and Senate leadership for a succession amendment with incumbents in it. Both agreed to support the amendment. The Kentucky constitution permits only four amendments to be placed on the ballot at a time. Historically, the House and Senate had agreed to take two amendments each. Because "Eck" Rose said the Senate had several other amendments it wanted passed, House leadership agreed to give up its two amendment options to sponsor both the lottery and succession amendments if the Senate would agree to pass them without change. A deal was made, and I felt good about the prospects for the amendment.

Concern over the balance of power between the executive and legislative branches had been a big issue with Senate Leadership for some years. Notwithstanding the agreement, rumors persisted that the Senate would not agree to what I called a "clean" amendment, that is, a succession amendment that had no other items as part of it. I had heard from several sources that the Senate would lobby the House to include some provision in the amendment to offset the greater influence a two-term governor was presumed to have. Furthermore, Rose was quoted several times in the media as saying he was against including the incumbent in a succession amendment and he would oppose it.

These rumors concerned me, so I questioned the Senate leadership in a breakfast meeting at the Governor's Mansion regarding their commitment to passing a succession amendment. I remember in particular how offended Joe Wright was at the suggestion they would not keep their word. Wright and Rose both restated that they were committed to "work" with the Senate to pass the two amendments as submitted to them by the House.

In a meeting with Rep. Stumbo the day the succession amendment was introduced, I told him I hoped for quick action on the succession amendment so it could be before the Senate at the earliest possible date. I knew the measure faced strong opposition from Senate leadership and a fierce battle was ahead. To put pressure on House leadership to act quickly, I told Greg I wanted to see the bill passed before the February filing deadline for legislative races. When Greg said this would be very difficult to do, I insisted that he try to get it done anyway.

The capitol news reporters who covered my meeting with Rep. Stumbo got a second-hand version of our discussion and learned of the February deadline. Al Cross, a seasoned capitol news reporter for the *Courier-Journal* newspaper, knew how skittish legislators would be at the thought of having opposition and saw an opportunity to exploit the issue. In interviews with legislators to get their reaction to my discussion with Rep. Stumbo, he suggested this date might have been chosen so I could run opposition candidates against any Senators who opposed the amendment. As might be expected, this set off a political firestorm.

Realizing that the Cross article had touched a hot button, I sought to control the damage as quickly as possible. Our meeting had provoked rumors that I had called certain Senators names and vowed to see that they were defeated. Cross's second- and third-hand account of the meeting exacerbated the problem. I suppose if you were paranoid enough, it was plausible to think that I was prepared to spend time and money defeating legislators who opposed me. But the time to launch an organized campaign to unseat incumbents had already passed. Had I been serious about something like that, it would have been news long before my meeting with Stumbo.

I was indeed upset at learning it would take so long to get action on what I considered a rather simple piece of legislation, and I told Stumbo that in rather plain English. A meeting with legislative leadership had already been scheduled for the day the story appeared, so I took some time at that meeting to clear the air. I expressed to leadership my dismay that so much time had been spent by the media to promote a fight which I didn't think existed. Majority Leader Stumbo also tried to set the record straight, but it seemed to me that his recounting of our meeting to others had been embroidered somewhat the day before. The legislators in attendance seemed to accept my explanation and appeared not to be unduly concerned about the press account of what was said. However, I am sure their basic mistrust of me remained in spite of my efforts to allay their concerns.

I don't think it was the threat of my running candidates against them that sparked the fire. What really got legislative leadership so upset was the perception that I was trying to tell them when *they* should pass *my* legislation. There was a time not long ago when a governor had enough influence over the legislature to call committee chairs and tell them what bills to call up from committee—something which they thought they had put behind them. No doubt my behavior was seen as an attempt to intimidate them into passing legislation at the call of a governor. There was no way they would yield to such pressure.

Certainly I understood I could not dictate the legislative process. I did think it was acceptable to work with someone whom I considered an ally to help move legislation of importance to me in a timely fashion. Although I might be accused of not being cautious enough or politic in the way I expressed my views, I saw nothing wrong with telling the person introducing my legislation when I thought it should be passed and why it should be expedited.

After this initial skirmish, I backed off for awhile to see what would happen. Unfortunately the specter of interference in legislative races surfaced again when a family friend and supporter of mine named Joe Popplewell filed at the last minute to run for Senator Joe Wright's seat. Sen. Wright was a powerful member of the Senate and served as majority floor leader. I had nothing to do with Mr. Popplewell's decision to oppose Joe Wright in the Democratic primary election, but it confirmed for some the suspicion that I indeed intended to run opposition against Senators who disagreed with me.

To quiet this latest development, I had to call my friend and supporter to request that he drop out of a race he wanted very much to run. Popplewell did what I asked, but our relationship was never the same. Joe Wright was supposed to help raise money to repay Popplewell's contributors but never did. I doubt that Popplewell posed a serious threat to Joe Wright. Though acting completely on his own, he was to legislators a living symbol of the extent to which they thought the man in the governor's office was willing to go to get his way. Their fears seemed confirmed at last. Once again I did what I could to dispel that idea.

Succession a Test of Independence

As the legislative session rolled on I realized that my succession proposal had hit the "trip wire" of legislative insecurity. Leadership was convinced that their newfound independence would be placed in serious jeopardy if I were to be governor for more than one term. The struggle over legislative independence continued throughout my entire administration, but succession became the symbolic proving ground in this struggle with a governor committed to ending the encroachment on the executive branch of government by the legislature.

What I found was a legislature obsessed with its own independence to the point that the mere appearance of cooperation with a governor was considered *co-optation* by the governor. Independence had turned into defiance. Equality in power had come to mean being able to have the last word in a struggle with a governor. In this environment, power was *not* something legislators shared with the executive branch to achieve responsible goals. Power was the goal in itself. Rather than use power to address issues, they use issues to acquire power. The manifestation of this attitude led to a series of unfortunate events during the week the House voted on the succession amendment. What I am about to relate shows how fragile the legislature's psyche is when threatened.

Just as a crucial vote on the succession amendment was nearing in the House, a lengthy article appeared in the *Courier-Journal,* again by Al Cross, which focused on the legislative independence issue. The story line was that Speaker of the House Don Blandford was being criticized by some House members for giving in to me on certain legislation. The sources were quoted as complaining that Blandford had worked hard to get support for the lottery and succession amendments which the Governor wanted, but cut off a move by some House members to get support for a tax bill proposed by Rep. Joe Clarke which would increase revenues by $158 million. They wanted to offer the tax increase as the price for giving me a succession amendment.

The article struck a raw nerve in both the House and Senate. Blandford strongly objected to the inference that he was giving in to the governor and went out of his way to show his independence of me. I was frustrated that the story came just as negotiations were underway in the House to get support for an amendment not burdened down with other issues. But the blow was struck and echoed through the halls of the Capitol like a gunshot.

In light of the allegations made in the article, House leadership now would surely appear weak if they followed my wishes on *anything*. Once again the specter of a governor trying to impose his will on the legislature was etched in the minds of legislators already wary of this new governor. Leadership was put in a position where they could only prove their independence with a public display of resistance. Whatever strides I had made with legislative leaders were dashed by the Cross article.

What I found truly astonishing about the whole episode is that legislators working *with* the governor to get something done should warrant the headline "Legislators Pass Bill Supported by the Governor!" The story says more about editorial bias than what the public would consider news. Having repeatedly been criticized for having such a poor relationship with the General Assembly that it prevented progress, I feel it defies logic to then describe a success in working together as the House "caving in to" the governor.

On the Monday after the article appeared in the *Courier-Journal*, the Senate Democratic caucus met and notified the House leadership that they would not support the succession amendment currently under discussion in the House unless it was coupled with measures to strengthen the legislature. Undoubtedly this was meant to be a preemptive strike by the Senate membership, which saw the House was prepared to pass a constitutional amendment in the form I wanted. I thought we had enough votes in the Senate to pass a clean amendment and was not prepared to accept as final the decision announced that day.

The next morning I met with Senate and House leadership at the Executive Mansion for breakfast as I had been doing for several weeks. At this meeting I wanted to get a reading on how the succession amendment was progressing. I particularly wanted to know where the Senate stood on a "clean" amendment—one without any other issues attached. Senator's Joe Wright and Eck Rose both confirmed there was virtually no chance that the Senate would approve such an amendment, unlike the assurances they had given to the contrary at all the previous breakfasts. In a fit of impatience I abruptly left the meeting and returned to my office.

Later in the day I received a telephone call from Greg Stumbo telling me that Eck Rose had called Speaker Don

Blandford asking that House and Senate leadership meet for lunch to discuss having the House take back the succession amendment and incorporate some changes the Senate wanted included before taking action on the bill. Greg told me the meeting was held, but Blandford was offended by the Senate's change of position on the agreement with me and refused to go along. At that point, however, I could not discern if this actually was a conspiracy to have the Senate take the blame for scuttling the amendment Blandford probably no longer wanted.

After discussions with several trusted advisors, I decided to approach the one person I saw as the obstacle, Senator Rose. Later that day I placed a telephone call to Eck to see if I could reach some agreement before the House bill reached the Senate. The discussion was candid, testy at times, and not very productive. It was obvious from the conversation that Eck was not going to budge. He said the Senate simply would not pass the amendment as proposed. I reminded him of our agreement and said he could get anything passed he wanted to pass. He said he strongly resented what he considered my heavy-handed attempts to put pressure on himself and the legislature.

In closing the conversation I told a story which by analogy implied that I would find a time and place when Senate leadership would pay politically for their refusal to keep their promise. "I am reminded," I said, "of the old movies where the good guy knew the bad guys were about to shoot him and said 'I know you will get me, but before I go down I'll get one or two of you!.'" It was obvious that Eck took my story as a threat to seek the defeat of Joe Wright and himself. Senator Rose's version of this conversation circulated on the Senate floor that afternoon and the feeding frenzy began.

That same day, the House Democratic caucus met to discuss the succession issue. I requested and was granted an opportunity to appear briefly before the caucus to present my arguments for a clean amendment. In a way it was an extraordinary move, given the implication of the *Courier-Journal* article that I was already exerting too much influence in the House. But the news that came out of the meeting was mixed. The caucus decided to send the Senate a succession amendment that was clean, but it also would send another amendment that would lengthen legislators' terms to offset any advantage a two-term governor might have.

House leadership finally agreed to a clean amendment that allowed all statewide officials to succeed themselves for one term and HB630 passed the House on a 95 to 3 vote with little floor debate. Reps. Joe Barrows, Bill Lear, and Ernesto Scorcone cast the only dissenting votes. Reps. Roger Noe and Joe Meyer did not vote. A second constitutional amendment (HB1022) was also passed which among other things extended the length of House member terms to four years and Senators' terms to six years. It also moved statewide office elections to even rather than odd-numbered years, extending the terms of present officials by one year.

The balance of power issue was raised during the debate on both bills, and several amendments were offered to HB1022 which would have eliminated or combined some statewide offices, removed the limit on the number of constitutional amendments that can be presented to voters at one time, and provided for a thirty-day legislative session on odd numbered years to deal with a limited number of issues. None of the amendments were approved, and HB1022 passed the House on a 77 to 21 vote. Rep. Lear who had tried to amend the bills on the House floor, voted against both amendments saying, "I think it's important to preserve the balance of power in the state."

The Struggle Moves to the Senate

In the meantime, the Senate bottled up the lottery amendment in committee, and Senator Danny Meyer introduced a far-reaching constitutional amendment (SB296) which included succession, but not for incumbents. It also extended the terms of legislators and proposed additional changes dealing with other state and local officials. The Senate clearly wanted to hold the lottery amendment hostage to make certain no succession bill left the Senate unless it contained expanded legislative powers. Senate leadership was insistent that both changes be incorporated in the same amendment.

The concern over separate amendments was well founded. If voters approved succession without approving the changes designed to strengthen the legislature's position with the governor, then it is unlikely that voters could be persuaded to make these changes at some later date. They also knew that I would work to defeat the legislative amendment if it stood alone. House leadership was quite willing to give me the clean succession amendment I wanted because they knew the Senate would combine the two amendments and avoid an outcome such as the one I just described.

Over the next week negotiations went on between House and Senate leadership as they sought agreement on how best to balance the power of a two-term governor. Senate membership was prepared to support a succession amendment even with the incumbents in it, but there was no consensus on how to counter the perceived increase in power that succession would accord a governor. Senate leaders were of the opinion that annual legislative sessions would most directly affect the balance of power between the governor and the legislature. Eck Rose said the Senate preferred a relatively short session in the odd-numbered years in which legislators would be limited to considering the state budget and whatever the governor might want to add to the agenda.

There also was serious talk about including a runoff for primary elections in the amendment, a measure intended to make certain the winning candidate in the primary had the support of at least 50 percent of the party's voters going into the general election. I strongly opposed this amendment as making elections even more costly and discriminating against minorities, women, and regional candidates. It simply was bad public policy and should not be written into the constitution. Voters have always seemed more concerned about the number and cost of elections than the percentage of votes the winner received. Most disturbing to me is that a runoff makes it that much more difficult to successfully challenge incumbents or candidates with high name recognition.

As the deadline for floor action on a succession bill drew near, I worked hard to get a compromise from the Senate. It was clear I couldn't get a clean succession bill. Could we agree on something which I could support in November? On the last day for floor action, the Senate Democratic caucus met and approved going forward with a succession amendment with interim legislative budget sessions and runoff elections in it. I was told this was a "take it or leave it" proposal.

During the day I met with several key Senators to discuss the possibility of a compromise. I could agree to interim budget sessions since they probably would eliminate some of the need for special sessions, which had been called every year since 1983. However, I could not agree to the runoff provision. Other possibilities were discussed, but clearly the Senate was in no mood to debate the alternatives any longer. Each person I talked to said I should either accept what was on the table or forget it until the next session.

Time to negotiate had finally run out. I either had to go with something I didn't believe in or give up the fight. After much discussion with others and some personal soul searching, I decided to forego for this session the pursuit of a succession amendment rather than saddle the commonwealth with a constitutional provision which was not in the public interest. As it turned out, this would be the only opportunity I would get to have succession while in office.

Some of my supporters continued to lobby to get the Senate to act after I had given up the cause, but to no avail. By the time the next session came along, succession was overshadowed by education, tax reform, and other issues of great interest to me. Although the issue came up from time to time, I made no effort to get a succession amendment on the ballot in 1990. For reasons I will discuss later, Senate leadership was more determined then than in 1988 to resist my efforts.

From a purely personal perspective, I probably should have accepted the compromise offered by the Senate. A runoff provision was passed anyway in 1992, the first session after I left office. I find it interesting that the runoff provision was approved by statute rather than as a constitutional amendment. In other words, the general public has not yet had the opportunity to express an opinion on the issue. If voters had approved the amendment in 1988 with the runoff provision in it, this would not have kept me from running again in 1991. On the other hand, if the amendment failed at that time, then I could blame the legislature for having encumbered it to the point voters rejected it. A try for a clean amendment could be made again in 1990, with perhaps greater success.

It is difficult to assess the role Al Cross's articles played in the confrontation I had with leadership over the succession issue. He later wrote two more inaccurate stories about succession which were equally damaging. In July 1989 he reported that I was going to tie support for school reform to succession. He based his story on a statement made after a television interview of my former campaign manager Danny Briscoe. Following a taping of "Your Government" on a Lexington television station, Briscoe was asked if it were possible that succession could be tied to education reform. Briscoe said he supposed anything was possible, much like I responded to the question about using PAC money to run opposition candidates.

The subsequent story made it appear there was actual consideration of such a strategy. In a Sunday political commentary appearing in the *Courier-Journal* the fourth week of the 1990 session, Mr. Cross once again speculated that I would make succession a condition for my support of something—this time it was to be tied to my support of a tax increase. Again there was no truth to the story, nor was I asked for comment. It doesn't take a rocket scientist to understand how stories of the kind written by Mr. Cross would create tension between the legislature and myself. There was enough institutional paranoia for me to overcome without seeing in print statements which only served to inflame their passion to be independent of a governor's influence.

Both major newspapers had supported a succession amendment for years, but they always held that the incumbent governor should not be included. In this case the idea of including the incumbent was particularly reprehensible. The *Courier-Journal* made no secret of its opposition to my ever having a chance to be governor again. I am not suggesting that Mr. Cross was in each case acting on instructions from the editorial board, but he clearly understood the political impact of what he was writing and gave his editors what he knew they wanted. He also knew that controversy always made better news than simple reporting events at the Capitol. He most certainly knew how jumpy legislators were over any hint in the press that they were giving ground to *any* governor, but especially this one. If you want to see a fight, just play to the fears of one of the parties and then stand back to watch how they react.

Certainly it is unreasonable to argue that everything bad that happened during the 1988 session can be attributed to the media, but it did seem like a new story would appear every time we reached a critical point in delicate negotiations I was pursuing with legislative leaders. Al Cross, like some of his colleagues, loved to promote fights and create controversy between the legislative and executive branches. We will never fully understand the damage he and others like him have done to legislative-executive relationships over the years by spooking legislative leaders and playing to their fears. It is frustrating that the news media, whether their actions are deliberate or not, can have such a negative effect on the political process.

Usually I am very effective in one-on-one discussions, but in this situation nothing seemed to work. Perhaps I underestimated how tenacious leadership would be in protecting their turf when they felt under attack. On the other hand, I can be just as tenacious as anyone when I am pursuing something I want. This was a situation where both sides had strongly held positions. The impasse that resulted probably would have occurred even if the controversial discussions with certain legislators had not taken place or had not been publicly reported in the press.

I did learn one important thing about the legislature from all this. Legislators want more than anything else to avoid opposition at the polls. A large number of Democratic legislators run unopposed. I have to think leadership feared that a strong, popular governor with succession might at some time in the future carry out the threat to support a slate of legislators. In this scenario, the will of legislators to defy governors in their first term in office would be seriously weakened out of fear that candidates favorable to the governor might run against them. Just the thought of this was like being hit on the crazy bone. Little wonder they got so upset at the thought that I might even consider backing candidates who supported my programs.

In the end, this was not a fight over whether governors should succeed themselves. It was about how the legislature should strengthen itself, using gubernatorial succession as the cover. The myth about Kentucky governors being among the strongest in the nation continues in spite of a steady erosion of the office of governor over the last decade. Certainly I can testify that the legislature has matured enough not to be intimidated by a governor, although in my opinion it still is adolescent in the way it behaves and flaunts its independence.

It occurs to me that what has really happened as a result of all this drive for independence is that legislators have swapped domination by the governor for domination by leadership. If the choice has to be one or the other, it seems to me that legislators are better off working with a powerful governor who can act on their behalf to get what they need than to have to depend on legislative leadership, which first has to appease the political forces within the legislature from which they derive their power. Legislators generally end up going to a governor to get action anyway, especially if they are not in the political favor of leadership. At least that is what I observed on a daily basis as one legislator after another came seeking something. It is much more likely that a governor will be more inclined to help a legislator because they share a constituency—and recognize the same need to be responsive—than leadership, which may not share the legislator's constituency at all.

Keeping the Balance

While criticizing my confrontational style, the media and others have overlooked the power struggle that is going on in Kentucky and where it is leading. Obviously one cannot discount the part personalities play in government, or anywhere else for that matter. But the confrontational atmosphere during my administration was not totally the product of personal disputes between those in leadership. When power meets power, confrontation almost always results—personalities not withstanding.

The argument for increasing the power of the legislature was based on the fear that succession would give a governor too much power. What is meant by the phrase "too much power?" I believe it is time Kentuckians understand what this slogan has come to mean for the governance of the commonwealth. It seems to me that the issue has become one of primacy—which branch of government can dominate the other. Domination is not sharing power. It is supremacy. That is not what the writers of the constitution had in mind when they formed three separate but equal branches of government in Kentucky.

The refusal to support a succession amendment without at the same time increasing the power of the legislature was just the most visible of many power plays by the legislature I encountered during my four years in office. In the next few pages I will illustrate some of the ways the General Assembly tried to use its lawmaking authority to expand its power during my administration and explain why I refused to go along.

Legislative Veto of Administrative Regulations

Once the General Assembly adjourns, it is the responsibility of the executive branch to implement the law. In many instances, these statutes require implementation by an executive agency which has the authority and responsibility to promulgate any regulations (or changes in regulations) needed to enforce the law. Administrative regulations are an extension of state law and have the legal force of the laws on which they are based. Inevitably, questions arise regarding the intent or interpretation of laws that the executive branch seeks to resolve. Those who may question the executive agency's interpretation of the law can seek relief through administrative appeals and the courts.

For years legislators have wanted the power to negate regulations they feel do not accurately represent the intent of the laws they enacted before they are put into effect. While in regular session, the General Assembly can correct errors the members believe exist in current regulations by amending the relevant statute to clarify legislative intent. Since the General Assembly meets only once every two years, regulations are generally promulgated by the executive branch before the legislature can intervene. Legislators have been limited to oversight authority exercised by legislative committees which meet in the interim between regular sessions of the General Assembly.

Since the early 1980s the General Assembly has tried one way or another to gain veto authority over administrative regulations. In 1982 the General Assembly enacted statutes which empowered the Legislative Research Commission (LRC), the administrative arm of the legislature, to take various actions on behalf of the General Assembly when it is not in regular session. Among these actions was authority to veto administrative regulations. Governor John Y. Brown subsequently sued the General Assembly, contending it was unconstitutional to delegate powers it has only when convened in regular session.

In 1984 the Kentucky Supreme Court in *Brown v. L.R.C.* struck down the right of the LRC to do the following when the legislature *is not* in regular session as provided in the constitution: veto administrative regulations, approve certain gubernatorial appointments, and veto the governor's reorganization of executive departments. The court further ruled that at no time does the General Assembly have the power to appoint or nominate members of certain boards. In contrast, the *Brown v. L.R.C.* decision upheld the General Assembly's right to require all executive agencies to submit proposed regulations to an interim subcommittee created for review and comment. The executive branch might or might not change a proposed regulation based on guidance provided by this legislative oversight committee. Obviously this was not enough control to satisfy the General Assembly's ambition, so each session thereafter more legislation was passed to achieve this objective.

In the 1988 legislative session the Senate wanted this authority written into the Kentucky constitution. However, the amendment got tangled up in the debate over succession and never got out of the Senate. The General Assembly launched an all out campaign to gain control over administrative regulations in the 1990 session. This time it passed two bills (HB544 and HB855) that would have any administrative regulation found deficient by a legislative subcommittee during the regular session of the General Assembly expire upon adjournment unless the regulation was enacted into statute during that session. What this law required, in effect, was an *affirmative* action by the legislature to keep any regulation a subcommittee found "deficient." Some legislator would have to care enough about a regulation to sponsor a bill to codify it into law.

In vetoing these two bills, I took the position that once again the General Assembly was attempting to do by statute something which the Kentucky Supreme Court had ruled unconstitutional in *Brown v. L.R.C.*. Requiring the General Assembly to enact a regulation into law as the only way to override the veto of a regulation by a subcommittee is an abuse of the lawmaking power of the General Assembly. If affirmative action is not taken by a legislator, the simple objection to a regulation by a subcommittee could nullify it without further hearing. It would be nearly impossible for a governor to get any legislator to sponsor, let alone lobby for its passage, a bill to codify into law a regulation once a subcommittee had deemed it to be "deficient."

My position on the legislative veto of regulations is that the responsibility to implement statutes enacted by the legislature is vested solely in the executive branch. There is good reason for this. No law can be written well enough to anticipate every possible situation under which it might be applied. Regulations permit a rational administration of the police powers of the state to ensure the fair and just application of law without resort to the courts. Such power should not rest with lawmakers.

All administrative regulations are subject to an extensive public hearing process before they are implemented and enforced. The public and legislators have ample opportunity to object if regulations are thought to go beyond the intent of the law on which they are based. The governor, not the legislature, has the responsibility to ensure strong, consistent, and fair application of law. To give the legislature the power to veto regulations it disagrees with is unnecessarily redundant, and is an encroachment on the separation of powers under the Kentucky constitution.

Anticipating a possible court reversal on this issue, the 1990 General Assembly also passed a constitutional amendment which would give the General Assembly clear, undisputed authority to act on regulations when not in regular session. I carried the fight to the ballot box that November, lobbying the public to reject this and one other amendment designed to expand the constitutional authority of the General Assembly. Both amendments were defeated by a large margin. However, the legislature overrode my veto of the other measures, which went into law over my vocal objections.

Control of Economic Development Bonds

In the 1988 session, the legislature passed a bill which required the Commerce Cabinet, thirty days prior to the commitment of any economic development bonds, to submit the proposed project to the State Property and Building Commission and the Legislative Research Commission for review. The complaint of the legislature was that business deals were completed by the governor, and the General Assembly was expected to approve them. The leadership was particularly upset at the size of the Toyota deal, which they were expected to ratify after the fact.

In vetoing this bill I reminded the legislature of the effect newspaper *speculation* concerning the Toyota site at Georgetown had on the cost of land needed for that project. Under this bill such information would not be just a matter of speculation; it would be a matter of public record. I let stand two other bills which required among other things annual reports to the LRC on economic development projects and KDFA loans. Certainly the legislature has a right to information on how money is spent, but it should not be in a position to get involved in the day to day negotiation of economic development projects.

The General Assembly tried again in 1990 to control economic development funds. SB 331 prohibited debt-issuing authorities such as the Kentucky Development Finance Authority and the Kentucky Infrastructure Authority from issuing certain bonds unless they were for projects specifically authorized in the appropriations act. It further prevented use of revenues from the repayment of revolving funds for projects which were not specifically provided for in the appropriations act. The issue in the latter case was whether repayment of loans in a revolving fund had to be reappropriated.

In vetoing this bill, I contended that economic development funds, whether new appropriations or generated through repayment of loans, should be used at the discretion of the executive branch to meet the needs of communities and businesses on a real time basis. Neither the governor nor the General Assembly can possibly be in a position to see in advance what opportunities might develop over a period of thirty months. It is sufficient for the General Assembly to set the debt limit and give the executive branch flexibility in the specific use of such funds.

In my veto message, I cited various projects which could not have been funded if the constraints of this bill were in effect: OEM Exhaust Manufacturers in Christian County; Image Graphics in McCracken County; Whiting Manufacturing Company, Inc. in Wolfe County; Excalibur in Johnson County; Academy Broadway Corporation in McCreary County; Scott Paper Company in Owensboro; H.J. Heinz Company, which was locating one of its divisional corporate headquarters in Newport; and the Trane Company project in Fayette County. Legislative micromanagement of economic development activities would hinder the ability of Kentucky to respond rapidly to business opportunities like these.

I failed to see what the problem was. Apparently some members of the General Assembly were concerned that a governor might use this money to reward political friends and allies. Business decisions like these are not based on the desire of a governor to enhance his or her political influence. The professional staff of the Economic Development Cabinet works hard to win business for Kentucky as a whole. A governor will work with every community in which a business has an interest to secure that business for that location. But in the end the decision is up to corporate executives, not the governor or members of the Economic Development Cabinet.

No governor wants to risk alienating a community in order to award an economic development project for purely political purposes. Job creation and business development are just too critical to be used like patronage. In fact, I might argue that giving the governor some discretion over economic development funds is a useful way to balance the political whims and power struggles within the General Assembly, where trading projects is the stuff of political bartering. What was going on here was more than legislators trying to protect the investment of tax dollars. The General Assembly wanted to stamp its own imprimatur on economic development projects.

In the end the legislature finally won this one. The General Assembly in 1992, under the leadership of Rep. Bill Lear of Lexington, reorganized the Cabinet for Economic Development. The legislation placed economic development decisions in the hands of a committee and effectively removed the governor, the state's CEO, from any meaningful role. As will be seen later, there is no substitute for strong, decisive state leadership when jobs and prosperity are on the line. The rationale again was to get "politics" out of economic decisions, not a difficult task since there was little politics to be taken out. What did get taken out, though, was the one thing Kentucky needs the most and we had worked hard to attain—momentum! This was one of the most damaging policy actions in recent times. One has only to observe what has been lost in economic development momentum to understand that. Bill Lear did this state a great injustice in promoting that legislation.

Limits on a Governor's Control of State Agencies

Another area in which the General Assembly exercises power over the executive branch is through control of the way executive agencies are organized. The Kentucky constitution says the governor is the chief executive officer over the executive branch. All agencies of state government other than the immediate office of each constitutional officer are created by statute. The executive branch is a creature of the General Assembly and may be organized any way it chooses.

The General Assembly has written the executive organizational structure into law in such detail that it severely curbs the ability of a governor to effect change in the executive branch. Governors can use executive orders to make changes between legislative sessions, but under current law these changes must be ratified by the General Assembly at its next regular session. In addition to codifying the state organizational structure, the budget also places personnel caps on each state agency.

Over the years the legislature has used its organizational powers to systematically remove or place outside the control of the governor a large number of state agencies, boards, and commissions. For example, the entire higher education system and elementary, middle, and secondary schools all are outside the direct control of a governor. These education agencies alone account for about two-thirds of the general fund budget, but they are beyond the reach of a governor. The largest agencies which answer directly to the governor are in the Human Resources and Transportation Cabinets.

The argument usually made for putting so much of government out of the reach of a governor is to curb political patronage. While that probably was the case at one time, this argument is no longer relevant. Most state jobs are under the merit system and not available for patronage appointments. Ironically, far more requests for political favors come from legislators than anywhere else.

The existing level of micromanagement of the executive branch by the General Assembly is not generally understood. Positions three and four levels deep in the organization chart are named and their duties described by statute. No corporate board of directors would attempt to tell the CEO of a private corporation what positions should be created and what functions they should have.

Each governor in recent years has tried to improve the cost effectiveness of the executive bureaucracy. However, with most employees protected by the merit system and job descriptions written into law, a governor has little reorganization authority other than to move boxes around on an organizational chart. Real reorganization can only be done through a massive reorganization bill which must be approved by the General Assembly. Few governors want to expend that much energy or political capital to bring about efficiency in government.

Study after study has been conducted to improve the efficiency and effectiveness of government. In fact, the General Assembly in 1988 ordered such a study to be done during my first two years in office. It came to nothing because so much of the government is outside the management control of the governor. Little is gained from reorganizing that part of government which the governor manages unless the scope of that control extends to the large number of agencies, boards, and commissions now independent of the governor.

Once an agency is independent of a governor, it puts up strong political resistance when it anticipates this independent status might be changed. Agency administrators want out from under the control of a governor because, under the committee structure of the legislature, they can develop a much cozier relationship with legislators on the committee with oversight of their agency and can get most of what they want without ever having to deal with the governor. Independent agencies basically tell the governor they don't wish to go along and take their case directly to the General Assembly.

A governor can cut out positions in various agencies, but the legislature still has final budget authority to reinstate these positions after the affected agencies complain about what the governor has done to them. I tried to reorganize a very small agency—the Department of the Arts—and ended up with negative stories in the press for weeks. It just wasn't worth the political cost. Little wonder few governors are willing to take on the battles of reorganization. I did achieve one major reorganization when I asked the General Assembly to create the Workforce Development Cabinet, but this effort was made relatively easy because of the radical changes which were being made to the Department of Education as part of the Kentucky Education Reform Act.

Another dramatic consequence of having so much of the executive branch beyond the control of the chief executive of the state is its effect on the budget process. Regardless of the appropriations proposed for such agencies by the governor, their administrators know they can go directly to the General Assembly to make their case. Not only does that reduce a governor's influence over a large part of the budget, it often creates the spectacle of executive branch agencies making appeals to the General Assembly in direct conflict with the governor's budget request. Observers of legislative behavior believe such relationships are encouraged by the legislature so its members can get information they want directly from the agency without going through the governor. "I'll take care of you if you will take care of me."

The Dispute Over Legislative Office Expansion

In both legislative sessions I vetoed bills which expanded the office space available to legislators in the Capitol Annex building. The budget provided money to renovate and furnish the legislative offices, but no money was appropriated to relocate and lease office space for the executive agencies now occupying the space. When the issue came up again in 1990, there was enough money to accommodate the planned renovation, but the legislature chose once again to appropriate money for itself but not for the executive agencies that would be dislocated.

Every executive agency that wants to renovate, expand, or relocate must have the details approved along with cost estimates before the governor will include the project in the budget. In this case, the General Assembly appropriated a large sum of money for itself with no justification of the cost. Estimates indicated that the office suites would cost more than the average Kentuckian pays for a home. I considered the expenditure to be excessive, the process secretive, and the summary eviction of executive agencies with no appropriation to cover the cost of relocation an abuse of legislative power.

My veto of the renovation bill they passed in the first session was sustained because the Senate refused to convene itself for a veto session. In the second legislative session, the General Assembly overrode the veto, but I still refused to approve the project for the reasons stated above even though the money for the renovation and furnishings was in the budget. It might appear that I did this out of spite, but I could not finance the move of executive agencies presently in that space without an appropriation to pay for it. It was as simple as that. Later they did it anyway, and Governor Brereton Jones didn't have the stomach to stop it as I did.

The Road Bond Debate

One of the campaign promises I made was to complete many of the main state highways which had been in various stages of construction for many years, particularly in Eastern Kentucky. Everyone recognizes that a first-class land transportation system is essential to economic growth. I wanted to see the construction schedule moved up by using road bonds to pay for specific projects. The first budget didn't allow for this, but the tax increase in the second legislative session gave us the opportunity we needed.

In my 1990 budget message to the legislature, I asked for authorization of $600 million in road bonds, $300 million of which would be issued during the 1990-92 fiscal year. The chair of the Senate Appropriations and Revenue Committee, Senator Michael Moloney, strongly opposed using bonds for this purpose and fought the proposal to the end. Passage of the road bonds was one of the conditions I set for agreeing to the sales tax increase the General Assembly insisted on before they would approve the education package. Leaders of both chambers agreed to work to that end, but of course Sen. Moloney was not part of that agreement.

As my relationship with the General Assembly leadership deteriorated during that session, the road bonds became a political target. It was something the leadership knew I wanted; they also knew they could deny it to me, all private agreements to the contrary. Leadership saw an opportunity to use the road bond issue as a way to get control of another part of the executive function—the six-year road plan.

The road plan is the guidebook for state priorities for highway construction. It is revised and approved every two years by the General Assembly. Many things influence whether a road is built on the timetable proposed in the road plan. Acquisition of right-of-way, law suits, environmental and historic preservation reviews and approvals, weather, and a myriad of other things can cause delays. Due to the many variables involved in construction projects, governors have had the flexibility to move projects in the plan up and down the priority list.

There is no denying that priorities in the road plan can and do change with a change in governors. The legendary Louisiana politician Huey Long was once asked if he was building roads in order to secure support for reelection. As always, Governor Long was blunt. Not only did he confirm it, he said he would pave his way clear to Baton Rouge if he had to. All politics, but especially rural politics, has long been the politics of roads. One of the things legislators like to take home from each legislative session is "asphalt," as they refer to it. They work closely with a governor to get certain projects of interest to their supporters in the road plan, and then go home to tell their constituents that the road will be built or improved.

Roads and bridges are probably the biggest area in the budget which resembles pork barrel politics. Of all the things I was asked to do as governor, nothing approached the appeals from legislators on behalf of road projects in their legislative districts. Legislators lobby the Transportation Cabinet relentlessly for projects in their districts and continue to keep up with progress on roads being built or proposed. They want assurance from the governor that certain projects will be undertaken if they are put in the six-year road plan. Also, it is easy to understand why they feel frustrated by the road plan process when roads they have promised seem never to get built or improved.

Previous to the 1990 session, legislators used the budget memorandum to identify the specific projects in the road plan they were funding with the road fund appropriation. Governors have not regarded the memorandum as binding and have generally considered the road plan a guide rather than a statutory directive. In the 1990 session Senator Eck Rose introduced an amendment to the road bond bill which would give the legislature direct control over the road plan by statute. I strongly opposed the amendment on the grounds that the road plan would become more of a political document than it already was if 138 legislators got hold of it.

The road bond bill passed both houses with the amendment attached, giving the legislature authority to approve the first two years of the road plan and require the administration to follow it to the letter. If I vetoed the road bond bill, I would be killing one of the major goals I had for my administration. On the other hand, I realized that the legislature probably would override my veto anyway. I simply let the bill become law without my signature.

Getting the road bonds were important to me even under these onerous conditions. I had promised to address several long standing needs for road construction which had been neglected for years. The bonds were key to keeping this promise. I believed then that the projects I proposed would never get built if they were not started during my term in office. They were either too expensive or did not have the political clout behind them to see them through to completion.

During the campaign I had promised to complete or improve the two unfinished legs of the AA highway across northern Kentucky, 25E, 23, 119, 127, and 68 from Bowling Green to Cadiz. It is impossible to judge any one's motivation in opposing these projects, but it is noteworthy that they primarily serve rural Kentucky. The most vocal opposition to the road bonds came from legislators from the so-called Golden Triangle.

Just about every governor in my memory has promised road projects as part of their election campaign. Whether this is a good practice might be open to debate, but clearly the legislature was tired of hearing candidates for governor promise projects which they knew had been held up by previous governors. I guess in the end the only "good" politics is each individual's politics. In this case, the legislature thought credit for roads that are built or improved should go to it, not to the governor.

I still cannot understand why legislative leadership would want to be put in the position of having to settle fights among their membership over what road projects to fund. The way things were they could blame the governor and keep out of the fight. This was just one more place where a governor still had some discretion which they thought had to be reined in by the legislature. Once more I saw government made more inflexible because of the legislature's insistence that governors do exactly what the legislature wants *without discretion*.

The General Assembly meets only once every two years to approve a budget that covers a period ending thirty months later. As was the case with the effort to control economic development bonds, there is no way the General Assembly can anticipate circumstances which require alteration of the road plan in the interim between legislative sessions. Executive branch discretion in the management of road construction projects just makes common sense.

Legislative Power to Call Itself into Session

The need for either longer or more frequent legislative sessions has been apparent for many years. The General Assembly had been called into special session every year since 1984. However, the Kentucky Constitution limits the General Assembly to one sixty-day legislative session every two years. In Kentucky only a governor can call the legislature into session in the intervening period. The governor also controls the agenda of a special session.

In the debate over the succession amendment, I was offered a compromise which included a short legislative budget session in the even numbered years. I agreed to the short session but rejected the deal because it was coupled with primary election runoffs to which I could not agree. The amendment offered at that time would have limited the session to thirty legislative days (about six weeks) and would have included the organizational activities which now occur at that time anyway. The agenda would be limited to budget adjustments and items on which the governor and legislative leadership could agree in advance.

When the General Assembly convened in 1990, it took a more aggressive approach and passed a constitutional amendment to give the legislature authority to convene itself at any time upon a request from its membership. If this amendment were approved by the voters, the balance of power would have shifted far beyond what the thirty-day interim session would have permitted. The General Assembly could have called itself into session at any time for any reason.

I fought this amendment with a media campaign prior to the November election. The amendment failed along with several others designed to give the legislature greater power. I cannot claim that the amendments failed because of my efforts to defeat them, but clearly they helped. The vote showed the public is not yet ready to greatly expand the power of the General Assembly beyond what it has already granted.

The Budget Memorandum Issue

During the 1982 regular legislative session a whole new section of the Kentucky Revised Code was enacted to spell out in detail how the budget is to be prepared and administered. The new law required the A & R Committees to prepare a budget memorandum after the biennial session ended to explain the legislative intent of the each appropriation. The appropriation act, not the budget, is the document which authorizes the actual expenditure of funds. However, the appropriations act lacks any detail about how the funds appropriated are to be expended. The budget memorandum was created to instruct the governor on the legislative intent for the appropriations which were enacted into law. In effect, it was the legislature's alternative to the executive budget submitted to it by the governor.

Governors Brown, Collins and I regarded the budget memorandum to be advisory only. On the other hand, the General Assembly has contended the budget memorandum has the force of law, since it is a side document which interprets the appropriations act and is incorporated into it by reference. In the 1990 session I used the line item veto authority of the governor to strike from the appropriations bill every reference to the memorandum. In my veto message explaining my action, I said the budget memorandum is an information document prepared by the A & R Committees to more fully inform House and Senate members about the budget. The memorandum is not voted on by the General Assembly and is not in a bill and, therefore, not subject to the governor's veto or signature.

In the 1990 session the General Assembly passed SB319, which by statute gave the budget memorandum the force and effect of law. Enactment of the entire budget memorandum document into law separate from the appropriations act would put it outside of the constitutional line item veto available to the governor. I vetoed SB319, arguing that it was unconstitutional on its face. It went into law anyway when my veto was overridden.

In the case of *Armstrong v. Collins et al* in 1986 the Kentucky Supreme Court reaffirmed its position that the budget cannot be approved by resolution of the General Assembly. In my view, and that of my predecessors, the memorandum must be enacted into law as part of the appropriations act to be legally binding under the Constitution of the Commonwealth. It simply cannot be declared as such by the legislature. For now the legislature prevails on this issue unless some future governor is willing to seek clarification from the Kentucky Supreme Court.

One never knows how the Kentucky Supreme Court might rule on an issue like this since it deals largely with a dispute between the other two branches of government as to what should be the scope of their power. So far the court has limited its opinions to issues of procedure and not ventured into the issue of executive discretion in the administration of the state budget. Neither the legislature nor governor really wants the Supreme Court justices to interpret their respective roles. Far better the parties work out their differences in the political arena than in the courts. However, such a resolution may not be practical.

The Kentucky constitution vests in the legislature the exclusive authority to enact laws, raise taxes, and appropriate money. There is little that stands in the way of a determined legislature committed to expanding its power through the budget process. If there are enough votes to pass the appropriation bill, there are enough votes to override a veto of it since in Kentucky only a simple majority in each house of the legislature is required to override a veto. There is little a governor can do to stop this juggernaut, short of filing a law suit to have the legislation ruled unconstitutional. I will have more to say about this later on.

In a practical sense, much of the budget memorandum is drawn from language found in the governor's executive budget. The problem for a governor is that this document is not open to review until the end of the session. No opportunity is given to lobby for or against changes made by the Appropriations & Revenue Committees. Even with the power to veto some portion of the budget memorandum, at best this would only give a governor the opportunity to eliminate certain items. Nothing left out of it could be restored.

The legislature continues to argue that the budget request of the governor is simply that—a request. The General Assembly will decide on its own, and without interference from the governor, how the public's taxes shall be spent. Every governor will affirm that the budget is the most powerful and political document ever enacted by any legislative body. It is the most tangible expression of public policy. I am gravely concerned about the growing belief among state legislatures that the state budget should be the exclusive province of the legislature.

What offended me most about these attempts to interfere in the workings of the executive branch is the presumption that it is the legislature's role to dictate to the executive how it should conduct its affairs. The legislature on the whole showed a total disrespect for the executive branch. I was plainly reminded on many occasions that a governor isn't supposed to tell the legislature how it should conduct its affairs. It seems to me the reverse ought to be true as well.

VII. EDUCATION:
THE AGENDA FOR CHANGE

An editorial titled "Who will lead Kentucky in drive to upgrade schools?" appeared August 24, 1983, in the Louisville *Courier-Journal*. It began with a reference to a meeting of more than 100 legislators who heard stories about education reform efforts in other Southern states—most notably, Mississippi, Florida, the Carolinas, and Tennessee. The editor then wrote as follows:

> . . . *You'd think Kentucky, which among other dispiriting things has the nation's lowest percentage of high school graduates in the work force, would be among the states trying hardest to pull themselves up by the bootstraps. But it seems depressingly likely, at this point, that Kentucky will have even less to tell at future regional and national meetings.*

> *That's because gains in education, as state Senator David Karem said at the Asheville meeting, hinge on strong gubernatorial leadership. It's inconceivable, as he observed, that a legislature by itself could initiate a strong program of educational improvement.*

> *It's almost equally inconceivable that a majority of Kentuckians would march on Frankfort—at least verbally—and demand that a "play it safe" governor or rudderless General Assembly raise their taxes if necessary, in order to improve the schools. Without strong leadership, the field is likely to be left once more to those citizens who think the educational system costs too much already.*

Apparently, by 1987 the editors had changed their minds about leadership from the governor. It was obvious soon after I started talking about fundamental change in the way we educate children, the *Courier-Journal* only wanted leadership to advance one set of ideas—theirs. The only thing they really wanted from a governor was advocacy for a major tax increase, not new ideas about school reform.

During my tenure as governor I had the opportunity to discuss the need to reform education with other governors across the nation. Each one was trying to lead reform movements in each respective state. They all reported having great difficulty bringing about change. I believe my experience with education reform shows that it takes much more than strong leadership to change a politically powerful, entrenched public institution like public education. Even strong governors encounter enormous difficulty in bringing about change in the priorities and policies of governmental institutions.

The Art and Craft of Policy Development

Public policy is the stated purpose(s) for which action is taken by government in response to a public need. The first task in developing a policy statement is to articulate clearly these four things: (1) the nature of the problem; (2) why immediate action is needed by government; (3) what actions are proposed; and (4) why you believe these actions are an appropriate and effective response to the problem.

The policy debate usually is not about the nature of the problem or of the urgency of governmental action. Politicians would not be considering the issue if there weren't a general consensus on at least these two things. The policy debate usually centers on what constitutes an "appropriate and effective" response to the problem. The need for government action to improve education had already been established in Kentucky. My challenge was to change the focus of Kentucky's approach to improving schools. In effect I had to *re*define the source of the problem and the solutions it required.

Redefining the Solution

The solutions one pursues to solve a problem depend on what one believes is the nature of the problem. Most of the efforts to reform education up to the mid-1980s had presumed that the present system of education was only in disrepair. If we just improved the present system, we would see great improvement in student achievement. Higher standards, better prepared and higher paid teachers, and more money were the remedies.

However, another assessment of the problem appeared in a series of published reports which concluded the basic approach to public education in America was seriously flawed. If we made the present system the best it could become, it still would not enable us to attain the goal of universal education at a level required to remain economically competitive. Nothing short of a complete restructuring of the educational system in America would suffice.

A review of state efforts to improve education since the 1970s revealed they were essentially designed to improve rather than restructure what and how children are taught. The approach taken to improving education focused on its *inputs*—books, facilities, per pupil expenditures, teacher preparation and evaluation, teacher-pupil ratios, accreditation of schools, and the like. Kentucky fell into this category with its much-heralded reforms in 1985.

The arguments for a *restructured* education system seemed more plausible to me than those which sought to reinforce and improve the present system. When I discussed my views with my policy advisers at State Research Associates, I found a well-reasoned argument for restructuring education in a manuscript for a book being written by Jack Foster. The central argument he made was that we needed to focus our attention on what and how children are taught if we want to see real improvement in student achievement. From a public policy standpoint, this meant changing the reform agenda from a focus on the inputs which support the education process to a focus on the education process itself.

Clearly, state policymakers were expressing increased concern about results. They were beginning to look at student test scores as a measure of effectiveness, but the test data were used primarily to measure the effectiveness of the inputs. In fact, this concern about the poor outcomes of a large number of students led some states, including Kentucky, to mandate other kinds of inputs, such as the amount of time which should be spent on certain basic subjects. However, policy makers up to this point had not questioned the assumptions on which teaching and learning were based.

During this time there also was concern about the education and training of teachers. Entrance tests were required as well as more hours devoted to the teaching specialty. Pay scales were tied to advanced degrees teachers held to provide an incentive to get more education. As might have been predicted, these measures did little to change what was going on in the classroom, primarily because there was no change in what teachers were expected to do in the classroom. The teaching-learning model at the college level still was the lecture and textbook. Furthermore, teachers were getting advanced degrees which they often said contributed little to improving their teaching. Essentially, they were rewarded in their paychecks for seat time in the college classroom.

The kind of teaching and learning process we needed could not work within the educational structure as it now existed. First of all, the system didn't focus on helping children learn how to use their knowledge. It was too focused on covering material and learning facts. Second, the lock-step age-graded format didn't allow children of different abilities to move at their own speed. Third, the learning *outcomes* expected were not clearly understood by teachers and were poorly measured. Finally, the adults in the system were not held accountable for the results of their enterprise. In short, assembly line education wasn't working.

As a political leader in an era of school reform, I wanted to change the policy agenda for improving education. I wanted to address the teaching and learning process directly, since I believed our process of schooling was based on outmoded concepts patterned after an industrial model. The American school system was not designed to deal effectively with the vast differences in children, all of whom we must educate. We needed a new kind of institution to educate children for the next century. The policy issue for me was to determine what strategy the government could use to restructure the system so that the desired changes in the teaching and learning process would occur.

A Strategic Policy Approach

It was Dr. Foster's belief that enough was known about how to help *all* children learn that education professionals could get the job done if schools were structured differently. We could achieve our policy objective if the school *system* were designed to focus on achieving specific student outcomes and teachers and parents had the latitude to change the learning *process* (curriculum, materials, use of time, learning strategies, etc.) in ways they thought were necessary to achieve these outcomes. I also felt we needed financially to reward reward success in improving the learning outcomes of children.

The strategy we developed assumed we could achieve the changes we wanted through system design and incentives rather than through direct intervention. The idea was to set the expectations and then provide rewards to those who met these expectations. The results we wanted could be achieved if we designed the system to *enable, reinforce, and reward* the performance we desired. This approach would be indirect and involve much less intrusion of government into decisions which should be made by professionals within the system. It also would move decisions about what is effective from the legislature and state bureaucracy to the teacher in the classroom.

A systemic approach to improving schools was much different than anything attempted before from a policy standpoint. Most politicians offered a series of programs designed to ameliorate certain failures of the present system, but nobody as yet had proposed changing the system itself. While all this made perfect sense to me, I greatly underestimated how difficult it would be to change the reform agenda to focus on *changing the system* rather than creating programs to deal with its inadequacies.

The policy I intended to pursue relied heavily on changing institutional dynamics rather than creating new programs to deal with the things the institutional leaders think will make their organizations more effective. The agenda for change envisioned by most bureaucrats is to have government create and fund more programs for them to administer. Such had been the history of school reform in previous years, but it also could be said of efforts to change almost any institution of government. Even people who proclaim to be the champions of change seem content to work the margins rather than try to force major redesign. They focus on trying to improve what exists, but the underlying policy assumptions are left unchallenged.

The Issue of "Comprehensiveness"

Choosing to pursue a strategic approach to improving education was an option fraught with considerable political difficulties, not the least of which was dealing with the perception that my approach would not have a significant effect on what educators and their supporters thought were the real problems. I was so focused on pushing restructuring of the K-12 education delivery system, I failed to correct the impression that I believed the restructuring proposal was the only thing that had to be done to improve education.

Everyone following school reform knows that in the past "reform" consisted of a collection of special programs or actions designed to deal with a whole array of problems. My critics saw my proposal as just one more program to add to the others. Few people understood the difference between restructuring and improving the education system. The reality was that I had taken *both* a strategic and comprehensive approach. The problem was one of perception due to the way I chose to present my education agenda. How you present what you are doing can affect the perceptions people have of where your priorities are.

The Prichard Committee, for example, said they didn't think my approach to education reform was comprehensive enough. They told me they wanted six areas addressed in any future legislative session on education: (1) early childhood; (2) schools organized for learning; (3) make teaching a true profession; (4) eliminate politics from schools; (5) refocus post-secondary education to meet changing workplace demands; and (6) rectify funding inequities. In reality I addressed all but the last one in the 1988 legislative session, but I was so focused on getting the restructuring plan underway I didn't present my education agenda in a comprehensive way.

I will let my record speak for itself. Even though there was no new money, I found *new or additional* funding for all the education initiatives on the Prichard Committee list and more. Overall I proposed that expenditures for education be *increased* by 12 percent at a time when revenue growth was at it's lowest level in more than a decade. In addition to providing more money, I proposed to base student assessment on demonstrated performance, set high performance standards for all students, remove all unnecessary constraints on professional practice, provide professional development services to aid in restructuring, reward teachers who improve student performance, move vocational education from the Department of Education and place its governance under a new lay board, and move the adult education program to the Literacy Commission for better integration of services.

In addition to these legislative achievements, I announced in Simpson County in September 1988 the creation of ten pilot sites for a program which would bring the social and health services of the Cabinet for Human Resources to the school site to improve services to children and families of school age. Dubbed the Kentucky Integrated Delivery System (KIDS) project, these sites were the forerunners of the acclaimed Family Service and Youth Resource Centers in KERA. The program received national attention through the policy academy of the Council of Governors' Policy Advisors in Washington, D.C., in the months prior to the enactment of KERA. Although not a formal part of my education initiative, they were indeed part of a comprehensive approach to improving services to children who were most at risk of failure in school.

I think this was in fact a comprehensive approach to improving education, but it was not marketed as a comprehensive approach. A major reason for breaking up the agenda was my intention to fund certain early childhood programs with lottery receipts. When the legislature refused to dedicate the funds, these programs were lost in the shuffle from a media standpoint. They were funded in the budget even though not identified as being supported by the lottery. I also backed off my pledge to move vocational education from the Department of Education at the urging of John Brock, Superintendent of Public Instruction. The legislature did appoint a new board over vocational education, and in the 1990 session the vocational education program was moved into the newly created Workforce Development Cabinet.

In retrospect, it is obvious that I didn't present all my education initiatives in a single "education reform package." Taken together, they would have seemed much more impressive, and I might have avoided the impression of being a "Johnny One Note." I don't know that changing the way I packaged my education initiatives would have gained the support of the Prichard Committee or the newspaper editorial boards, but it would have helped to change the perception that the only thing I had to offer was a "little school incentive program."

The lesson here for anyone pushing a major change in policy is to "get it all together" in one place. Even though I regarded the restructuring initiative as the most important set of actions to be taken during in my administration, I left myself open to the criticism that I had a "silver bullet" that would cure all the ills of education. I never felt that way, nor did I conduct my administration as if I did.

Policy is Difficult to Communicate

I found it very difficult to communicate to educators, legislators, and the public what I was trying to accomplish and why I thought my approach was better than what had been tried in the past. First, it was hard to get people to understand how changing the system could result in much improvement in schools. Systemic change was a very difficult concept to explain to the public and news media. It didn't lend itself to slogans and sound bites.

Second, everyone expected a governor to propose special *programs* to deal with specific issues in education such as early childhood education, reading and writing, prevention of drop outs, and attraction and retention of better teachers. What I proposed didn't have a traditional target and seemed off the mark to many people.

Finally, the reasons why the *system rather than the people who run it* was the problem are not easily explained or readily understood. The public believed the problems with schools were mostly due to incompetent or poorly trained teachers, drugs, lack of discipline, and a need to "get back to basics."

There is No Political Forum for Policy Debate

Changing public policy is a political matter. The public interest is at stake. Presumably the political process would allow for an open debate about the issues. Given the General Assembly's desire to be proactive in the policy arena, it is even more important that there be open discussion of various policy options. However, I found debating public policy with legislators to be very difficult for several reasons.

First of all, the medium of communication with the legislature is draft legislation. A governor is expected to put his policy proposals into a bill format which describes very specifically how these policies are to be implemented. Then the legislature will consider them. However, a draft bill doesn't explain why each element of the proposed legislation is important or what it is expected to accomplish. This message must be conveyed through a committee hearing rather than a public discussion.

I often heard people speak of the governor's use of the "bully pulpit" as a way to get his or her ideas before the public. Indeed, one can give many speeches about a policy initiative, but it is legislators who in the end must be persuaded. Yet there is no way to engage them in direct discussions about the proposed policies. They only understand the committee process. I was told time and again that legislative leadership could not just agree on something with a governor and get it done. They said the process could not be circumvented.

Certainly a committee hearing provides the governor an opportunity to set forth the rationale for various parts of the legislation and to clarify any misunderstandings. However, it doesn't provide a forum in which to debate with legislators the merits of the proposal or its underlying policies. The legislative hearing process is essentially a method of getting public reaction to what is under consideration. It does not provide a forum for public debate.

Obviously, a governor can and does lobby individual legislators on behalf of a bill. I frequently had telephone conversations or personal visits with key legislators whose votes were critical, but these were more like negotiation sessions than discussions about why enactment of a bill would be good public policy. It often appeared to me that many legislators either didn't care about or couldn't understand the policy implications of what I was trying to accomplish with public education.

Attempts to Clarify the Policy

Several initiatives were undertaken to make clear the rationale for our approach to improving public education. The initial effort was during the primary election campaign when I released a series of policy statements which later were published as *Kentucky First*. In this policy platform I sketched out the essential ideas and rationale for a different approach to improving education. The policy document got scant attention from the news media.

When we held a news conference in February 1988 to release the details of our legislative proposal, we also distributed to the media and various education constituencies a document titled *The Governor's School Improvement Incentive Program*. The twelve-page report covered all the salient elements of the legislation, including a rationale for each one. However, fixing on the word "incentive" in the title of the booklet, the news media thereafter referred to my reform initiative as the governor's "incentive program," which greatly distorted the message. While financial incentives certainly were a key part of the package, they were not central to our attempt to change what children need to know and how it is learned. At that time, the media never tried to understand what we were trying to accomplish even after hours of discussion with them. They only wanted to talk about money. Thus the focus on "incentives."

Later in 1988 I released another booklet titled *Q.A. — Improving Kentucky Schools.* This thirty-six page document, written in a question and answer format, explained in more detail what we were trying to accomplish and addressed all the questions that had been raised about it. It was here that I first referred to my strategy as "restructuring Kentucky schools." The booklet was widely distributed and seemed to be well received. At least it went further than anything we had previously provided to help people understand the rationale for our approach to improving schools. As we moved toward a planned special session in 1989, I released two more documents titled *A Plan to Restructure Schools in Kentucky* which represented a thorough explanation of our strategy and a plan to implement it. One document was a detailed description of each element of my framework for restructuring. The other document was the proposed legislation.

In addition to the written material, I tried to improve understanding of the issues involved in restructuring through two symposia held during the 1988 legislative session. We brought in high-profile speakers nationally recognized for their understanding of school restructuring. We wanted to open a debate over education reform that would focus the discussion on the need for restructuring rather than just incremental improvement in the existing system. Both meetings were well attended, but they were given very little news media coverage. Always adversarial and skeptical, the media seemed to regard these events as simply a publicity stunt rather than a sincere attempt on our part to begin a policy dialogue with educators, legislators, and the interested public.

The Policy was Plagued by Misunderstanding

No other program or policy during my administration was given so much attention by me and by the media.

Still our initiative suffered from distortions, misrepresentations, and confusion. At one point I was quoted as saying I wanted to deregulate schools—a reporter's errant attempt to understand what I meant when I said I wanted to eliminate system barriers which constrained teachers from doing what they thought was professionally proper to improve the learning of children. My initiative was repeatedly characterized as a very small set of things that might be good to do, but probably were too narrow to have any impact on the "real" needs of education—like tons of new money!

Educators over time had dealt with one program or another until they could not think of reform in any terms other than some kind of "program." Time and again I was asked, "Governor, what is your education program?" Reporters reflected the questions of the education establishment. I was asked from time to time to help them give their readers a proper characterization of what I was trying to do, but I failed ever to get it down to one paragraph. At one point I tried changing the semantics by saying I was not offering a "program" but rather a "framework" within which schools could improve themselves. One political reporter accused me of playing with words while avoiding a straight forward explanation of what I was trying to accomplish.

Perhaps this mutual frustration can best be illustrated by recounting a comment made to Doug Alexander, my press secretary, by John Winn Miller of the *Lexington Herald-Leader* after a rather animated and lengthy discussion between the two about the media's efforts to understand my proposals. Miller told Doug that he couldn't communicate the essence of education reform *a la* Wilkinson unless it could be reduced to two paragraphs!

My education secretary Jack Foster reported a similar experience with Mary Ann Roser, also of the *Herald-Leader*. Responding to a complaint that the newspaper had not fairly reported my views, Roser met with Foster for about an hour after a meeting of educators at the Marriott Hotel in

Lexington in another effort to provide substance to their coverage. In frustration, Roser finally said it just wasn't possible to do. She too related what Miller had said. Everything must be reduced to a sentence or two in a column of newsprint.

As we tried to refine and sharpen our message about education, I focused even more on the theme that we had to redesign a one hundred-year-old system that was broken. In every speech I said, "We must fundamentally change the way we educate our children." While such rhetoric did little to advance the debate or provide a better understanding of my policy on education reform, it did keep the essence of the policy before the public.

Observations About Communicating Policy

In retrospect, I don't believe we ever succeeded in effectively communicating our policy on education reform. Consequently, little credit is given even now to the many months of effort that went into changing the focus of reform. During the campaign my focus group surveys and opinion polls confirmed that the public had little understanding of what I was trying to accomplish. At one point in the election campaign I decided just to say I was for "getting discipline in and drugs out" of our schools. At least this was something the media could capture in one line. All in all, it was a very frustrating experience.

As I look back, I can better understand why political leaders have such difficulty getting public support for major changes in policy. I learned that a *program* initiative designed to deal with a specific problem is much easier to explain than a set of strategic actions which have the potential for much greater impact. The news media simply have too much difficulty distilling into a few paragraphs the essence of what is being proposed, so they tend to use a lot of ink to describe who is for and against it, relying heavily on established power brokers and interest group sources for their information.

At some point it is necessary to challenge the *direction* and *assumptions* of the approach government takes in dealing with problems. I felt major changes were needed in Kentucky's approach to education, the creation and maintenance of a competitive workforce, job creation, economic development in rural areas, rebuilding public infrastructure, and taxation. However, it was in education that I found the greatest resistance to change in policy. I will explore now why I believe it is more difficult to effect structural change in education than to redirect existing programs or just create new ones.

Turning Policy into Legislation

I had always believed that our professional educators had the ability to bring about change if we would allow them to do it, and I said so repeatedly. From my perspective, the role of government in improving education is to set learning outcomes for students, provide a model of the kind of teaching and learning process desired, free teachers from institutional or regulatory constraints on their ability to help all children meet these outcomes, and then reward those who are successful in improving their effectiveness. I proposed that such a policy be implemented in the following manner:

1. establish performance goals for student success which represent the highest expectations for learning in our schools and measure the extent to which students are reaching them.

2. measure how successful schools are in ensuring that all children attain these performance goals;

3. establish "benchmark" schools to demonstrate how to best organize a school and

the instructional process to most effectively meet the different learning needs and abilities of all children; and

4.   financially reward the staff of schools which make progress toward or sustain a high level of student achievement for all their students based on the performance goals for educational attainment.

The legislation to support my policy initiative proved to be more complex to prepare than originally expected. The original bill submitted to the General Assembly in 1988 left many operational details to be worked out by others or through the legislative process. The key elements were to be developed and monitored by a nine-member Council on School Performance Standards. The 1988 bill called for the Council to follow these policies:

... the Council shall recognize that every school is different from every other school in terms of the resources available and the characteristics of their students and community. Taking into account the cooperative effort required to elevate the performance of an entire school, the governor's school improvement incentive program shall encourage people to work together as a school and shall recognize and reward their collective rather than individual efforts. (SB 256)

The Council on School Performance Standards was to be a continuing body with initial responsibility to develop performance goals for students, designate the methodology to be used to assess improvement in student performance, and develop guidelines for the allocation of the incentive bonus. The council would periodically review these elements of the program and make modifications as appropriate and necessary. Vesting much of the responsibility for implementation in the hands of a council appointed by the governor would give us the flexibility to work out some details after the bill became law.

The council was to be independent of the education bureaucracy, but its decisions would have to be ratified (but could not be altered) by the state board of education. The Department of Education would administer the council's policies and procedures once ratified by the state board of education. The council would be staffed cooperatively by the Department of Education and the office of the Secretary of Education and Humanities. The council would be supported by a technical advisory group on matters relating to testing, measurement, and school assessment.

School improvement was to be measured against a baseline established for each school in the commonwealth at the completion of the first year following adoption of the act. Progress would be measured thereafter against the highest previous level of performance for each school. Improvement was to be defined as an increase in the percentage of students at each grade level who made significant progress toward or met the student performance goals set by the council.

The bill required the superintendent of public instruction to conduct workshops to help school personnel identify and explore ways to develop school level plans to improve the academic performance of their students. Each school also would get a grant to secure additional assistance of their own choosing. The bill called for establishment of twenty-one "benchmark schools" to demonstrate ways to restructure school practices and resources to better meet the learning needs of all children. Personnel at every school would be eligible for a salary bonus based on the amount of progress they made toward the goals set by the council. The bonus for certified personnel was to be at least $1,800 per year and could go up to $3,600. Classified staff would receive a lesser amount.

After the original bill failed to pass in the 1988 session, I used the additional time to refine some elements of it. The version of the bill published in my booklet *A Plan to*

Restructure Schools in Kentucky contained some very important features not incorporated in Senate Bill 256. I believe the delay proved to be to my advantage in the end, since many of the refinements later were incorporated in KERA.

Probably the most significant added element was the provision for site-based decision making. The proposed legislation required each school to create an "instructional improvement team" to prepare a plan for attaining the goals for student performance. Unlike the school councils in KERA, these school improvement teams had to secure approval of their plans from the local board of education. There also was more flexibility in the composition of the team membership than was required by KERA. Although parents were not official members of the improvement team, the plan had to document that parents were involved in its preparation. Local boards of education and the state board of education were authorized to waive regulations within their jurisdiction upon request of a school improvement team.

Significant resources were to be available to support the professional development of school personnel and to provide them with more and better instructional materials and equipment. A state-wide Institute for Educational Leadership was to be created to assist schools and school districts in school-based decision making and to promote the adoption of innovative methods of instruction and classroom organization to improve student performance. The institute would provide regional access to its services through three regional professional development centers. The original twenty-one benchmark schools were reduced to six and placed under the management of the institute.

The Council on School Performance Standards was expanded from nine to fifteen members and made advisory to the state board of education. The method of determining progress toward attainment of the performance goals was clarified and made more specific. Authority for setting the performance goals was given to the state board of education. A school improvement index was to be created to measure progress and be the basis for making bonus awards.

Finally, five additional noninstructional days were added to the school year to be used in such manner as the school improvement team determined. These days could be used prior to or during the school term at the discretion of the faculty for planning, collaboration, and professional development.

Policy Change and Political Power

The newspaper editorial boards in Kentucky seem to believe the way to shape public policy is to get consensus among the special interests before you attempt to make major changes. Conventional wisdom says the people affected must first buy into the proposed changes or they will subvert the changes. It is a well-documented fact that well-designed and researched reforms often are thwarted by turf battles and parochial thinking among the groups which must change their way of doing business. On the other hand, it doesn't take a rocket scientist to realize that such thinking means the status quo will always control both the agenda and the outcome of public policy.

When one assumes that a buy in from special interests is the way to shape public policy, then what is important about a policy debate is what the affected special interests think about the ideas under discussion. The resulting public perception is that politicians work to satisfy the *establishment*, not the public in general, when making public policy. That clearly is the case when special interests are the dominant force in shaping public policies which affect their special interest. If this is truly the preferred approach to making public policy, we have little hope of making major changes.

Obviously, all interested and effected parties have a right to participate in a policy debate. However, in this case, educators are like any other interest group which has an economic and personal stake in the outcome, and they often do not act purely in the public interest. The media too often fail to point this out when reporting that certain interest groups support or oppose particular ideas.

I was severely criticized for not spending more time trying to build consensus for my ideas. As I will relate in the next chapter, I made various attempts to get a consensus. What I was proposing did not fit the traditional view of how to improve education. There was very little time in which to change the minds of people who never before had been asked to rethink what they were doing. Because I was unwilling to trade money and old ideas for political support, all these efforts at consensus ultimately failed.

Major changes in policy require much more than good ideas and salesmanship. An enormous amount of personal energy and political capital were expended in the effort to get political support for a major change in how to improve Kentucky's educational system. But it just wasn't enough. As I will show in the next chapter, policymaking is not about how to achieve the public good with innovative ideas. Its about dealing effectively with special interest influence, the exercise of personal political power, and the ability to control the policy agenda.

VIII. EDUCATION:
THE POLITICS OF CHANGE

History shows that major policy shifts seldom originate from the legislature or government bureaucracies. The high public visibility of a governor makes that office a natural locale for the political leadership required to advance a major policy initiative. However, changes in public policy ultimately must be hammered out in the legislative arena. At their best, the processes of government are slow and deliberate.

Getting political action on a major policy agenda at the beginning of a governor's term in office is critical. Without succession, I had only two legislative sessions in which to influence public policy. I realized that it was ambitious to believe you could get a legislature to change its basic approach to school reform in such a short time, but the time required to get all of the elements in place made early passage of the legislation a high priority. It was very important that I quickly seize control of the *political* agenda and maintain that control for an extended period of time.

The political process inherently works against change, as I will illustrate by recounting my own experience with trying to bring about change in education policy. Once legislation is under consideration, a governor has limited ability to control the outcome. In the following pages I recount the ebb and flow of the political currents which ultimately determined the education policy of the commonwealth. While this account focuses on education, the experiences I describe could apply to welfare, health care, environment, tax reform or any other major policy issue.

A Political Strategy for Education Reform

My political strategy for achieving education reform had two simple goals: (1) secure legislative action on my plan to restructure schools before agreeing to raise more money for education; and (2) make achievement of financial equity the first order of business once more money was raised. Timing was a critical element in the political strategy. The tactics to be used to reach these goals were never set in concrete and would have to change with the political process.

The Importance of Getting Legislation First

From a purely political perspective, I could not allow the restructuring agenda to be overridden by the tax issue. I knew that as soon as I agreed publicly to raise more money for education the debate from that point on would focus on (a) how much I would be willing to raise; (b) how I planned to raise it; and (c) how I planned to spend it. These revenue and expenditure issues would significantly change the *political* agenda, and most certainly would take precedence over my proposal to reshape education policy.

Another concern I had about agreeing to raise more money before securing legislative action on my restructuring plan was to avoid getting mired in a political debate over a massive education spending bill to finance programs designed to shore up the *present* system. In my view, we already had spent too much money for too long trying to make the present system work.

I realize that my strategy posed a dilemma for educators and legislators who were wary of my insistence that legislative action be taken on the restructuring initiative before there was agreement to raise more money. No doubt they had trouble believing I would raise more money once I got what I wanted. I would say to them privately that I would raise the money needed if the system were changed, but then publicly continue my strident opposition to any new taxes. The two positions seemed irreconcilable. I had proven that I was willing to take a lot of political heat over the tax issue, so it probably seemed implausible that I would ever change my position.

Equity in Education Finance Was Important to Me

Although I was fighting hard for restructuring the education system, I also felt very keenly that Kentucky had to face the challenge of achieving financial equity in education. Kentucky never could afford to spend on education as much as many other states do, but whatever it does spend should be equitably distributed. I supported the intent of the lawsuit filed by the Council for Better Education and asked to have my name withdrawn as a defendant.

Every state that had been sued over school finance found itself mired for years in delaying tactics, legislative maneuvering, and more legal action. If I were to have the opportunity to influence the course of education in Kentucky, I had to give primacy to equity once I agreed to raise more revenue. The money trough would be crowded with representatives of every special interest under the sun, not just in education. Unless I made equity the first and foremost goal, we would miss the opportunity of a lifetime to rectify the funding inequities that had spanned generations. However, achieving the goal of financial equity would have to wait until the courts rendered a final judgment on the *Council v. Collins* suit.

Controlling the Political Agenda

There are several tactics governors can use to gain and keep control of the political agenda. The visibility of the governor's office can be used to keep a policy issue constantly before the public. Literally hundreds of opportunities were used to keep alive the issue of restructuring our education system. I never eased up in my call for fundamental change in the way we educate our children or on my unwillingness to pay for the same old stuff.

A special session of the General Assembly is another strategy for controlling the political agenda. Since the governor alone sets the agenda for a special session of the General Assembly in Kentucky, it's much easier to keep legislators focused on the issue at hand than in states where the legislature can add to the agenda or is in session all the time. In a special session, legislators can't hold the legislation "hostage" to approval of some other legislation, as commonly is done in a regular session.

As soon as I recognized my education legislation would not pass in the 1988 regular session, I said I would call the legislature into special session to deal with it. I had every intention to call such a session as soon as it was politically feasible to do so. As I said at the close of the 1988 session, calling a special session on education "is a promise, not a threat." I believe my threat of a special session was a key factor in keeping the General Assembly engaged in the debate with me.

A governor has very little leverage on legislators after a regular legislative session adjourns, so a strategy must be employed to keep the political pressure on them in the interim. While my threat to call a special session served in part to keep legislators engaged, I used public speeches and political activism to ratchet up the noise level enough to keep them from ignoring my agenda until a special session could be called. The media, always willing to promote a fight, was more than happy to keep the debate going and thus assisted in my effort to keep the issue alive.

Setting the Stage Early

Realizing that a newly elected governor has little time to build support for a major initiative before it must be presented to the General Assembly for action, I wanted to gain as much support for my ideas as I could before the November election. Even though I kept a heavy campaign schedule throughout the fall of 1987, I approved several efforts to lay the ground work for legislative action. I had only moderate success, certainly not enough to push a major piece of reform legislation through the General Assembly. It is not an easy task to focus on legislation during the heat of an election campaign.

The Support of Educators was Sought

In September 1987 Jack Foster, then with State Research Associates, met with a group of school superintendents assembled by Ken Johnstone, the executive director of the Kentucky Association of School Administrators, to get their reaction to my proposals. Foster thought their early involvement might help us identify any concerns they might have with what was being proposed. At best, we might get the endorsement of some of the KASA leadership for what we wanted to do. At the very least, the groundwork would be laid for later discussions with them.

The meeting was informative and productive. Foster reported cautious support for some of the ideas, particularly the proposal to give schools greater latitude to make instructional decisions. Ken Johnstone became an advocate for our effort to restructure and continued to help during the early months of my administration until he was replaced as director of KASA, at least in part I think because of his strong support for the new ideas I was proposing. However, the other education interest groups in Frankfort distanced themselves from me, primarily over my stand on taxes and the funding of the 1985-86 reforms. Nonetheless, I received strong political support from many teachers and school administrators during the campaign.

In the Fall of 1987, we sought the advice of a small group of superintendents who were generally supportive of what I wanted to do. This small group was later expanded to include teachers and assessment specialists who were leading educators in Kentucky. This informal group met with Foster on different occasions to help with various elements of the proposed legislation as it was being developed. Almost all of their suggestions were included in the legislation that was introduced in the 1988 session of the General Assembly.

I wanted the public support of Dr. John Brock, a personal friend and the Democratic candidate for Superintendent of Public Instruction. He strongly disagreed with what he considered my "top down" approach. I also believe he had trouble with some of the key elements of my proposal. He preferred to let educators determine what needed to be done after he was elected so he neither offered nor provided any help during the campaign. He won the office without a platform for reform.

Early Problems with Legislative Leaders

Coming off the stunning primary victory, I was buoyant about the prospects for doing something meaningful as governor. One can dispute, perhaps, whether I got a mandate from the voters in that election, but conversations with citizens all across the commonwealth convinced me people were ready for a change. I was very critical of the status quo crowd in Frankfort throughout the campaign. On various occasions I had taken potshots at legislative leadership which I felt had been the source of many of Kentucky's problems.

Over the course of the summer months I got embroiled in a debate over conforming the Kentucky tax code with the federal code. Governor Collins was being hard pressed to call a special session, which I opposed. Legislative leaders took umbrage at my getting into the fray before I was even elected governor. The jousting with the leadership of the General Assembly continued into the fall, at which time I turned my full attention to the general election. Needless to say, all of this did little to prepare the way for a smooth beginning with the General Assembly. But it was in education that I stumbled in a way that proved to be more costly later on than anything else I did during the campaign.

After the primary election in 1987, the Prichard Committee for Academic Excellence invited both candidates for governor to present their ideas on school reform at the committee's August meeting at Shakertown. I felt the Prichard Committee was heavily committed to the reforms passed in 1985-86, when they saw much of their agenda become law. It seemed to me their primary interest now was to get these reforms properly funded. I really didn't want to get into that debate during the election campaign.

My initial decision was not to attend. There was little to be gained politically from appearing before them, I thought. Some of my political advisors urged me to reconsider, since the meeting would receive extensive press coverage. It would be a forum where the free media could be used to reach the general public with our message. They also made the point that we should not concede the initiative to my Republican opponent by default. At the last minute I agreed to accept the invitation.

The presentation to the Prichard Committee was the most extensive speech I would make during the entire campaign on the subject of school reform. I gave the rationale for why schools had to be fundamentally restructured and then presented the steps I wanted to take to begin the process. I also spoke of the need to support our university system, particularly in terms of the human resources which make up the university. I promised to address the issue of competitive faculty salaries.

I agreed to take some questions from the floor after I finished my speech. Robert Bell, who was then chair of the Advocates for Higher Education, asked what my position was on funding the reforms of 1985-86. It was a loaded question, the answer to which I probably should have left ambiguous. Instead, I responded in all candor that I had no commitment to anything other than my own proposals. A storm of criticism followed my remarks which completely negated any possible positive gain from my appearance before the group. As usual, the media focused on what it appeared I would *not* do, rather than on what I *would do.*

My political instincts were right. The appearance at this event did nothing to clarify for the public what I was trying to do. My candid answer to a politically charged question stirred up unnecessary concern among those who might have been inclined to help me later and angered key members of the legislature. The political outcome was a widespread perception among legislators and educators that it was my intention to substitute my program for their earlier reforms. The political damage caused by that one highly publicized event proved to be great and long lasting.

Jack Foster had experience working with legislators in other states, so I thought he might be able to explain our approach to school reform in ways Kentucky legislators would understand. Foster held several meetings in late summer and fall of 1987 with Representatives Kenny Rapier, Roger Noe, Harry Moberly, Tom Jones, and Joe Barrows—the people I was told were most responsible for the 1985-86 legislation. One of the meetings included staff from the Speaker's office. The key ideas in my proposal were explained and questions were answered. Foster told me there seemed to be sincere interest in some of my ideas, but these legislators saw no point in discussing them further until I publicly agreed to fully fund their reforms.

There was no compelling reason to make a funding commitment this early. It would have required me to explain in the middle of an election campaign how I planned to pay for the 1985-86 reforms. From a purely political perspective, funding the earlier reforms could be an important bargaining point later on. Making a concession at this stage was premature. As it turned out, I did fund nearly all of the reforms in my first budget, but it earned me nothing in terms of support for my ideas.

There was still another episode involving the legislature prior to the 1988 session. Tom Dorman, who was to become my legislative liaison, suggested that we get Legislative Research Commission staff to draft the legislation. The bill drafting process is supposed to be confidential. I was assured by everyone that details of the proposed legislation would not be released until I had an opportunity to approve the draft bill. We got permission from a friendly legislator to use his name for bill drafting purposes, and work was begun after several conferences between LRC staff and Jack Foster.

During the transition following the election, Carol Marie Cropper of the *Courier-Journal* somehow secured a copy of the draft legislation before I even had an opportunity to review it. The published information, although accurate in many respects, contained several items with which I did not agree and certainly would change before a bill was released to the legislature. Before I was even sworn into office I began to learn how Frankfort worked. I was upset by what appeared to be a the leak to the media, but I was even angrier when I later learned that the draft had been shared with a group of school superintendents and other educators by Rep. Kenny Rapier, House majority whip. Rep. Rapier had little understanding of our proposals and was opposed to almost anything we would have proposed.

As I indicated earlier, communicating my strategy for improving education was difficult enough without having incorrect information out on the street. It's disturbing to get up in the morning and read about your own legislation in the newspaper before you even had an opportunity to review it yourself. Working with the legislature on politically sensitive issues is difficult enough without having to contend with a breach in confidence and premature discussion of proposed legislation in the media.

As can be seen, I approached the first legislative session having made little headway in my effort to gain broad support for the approach I wanted to take in school reform.

Without such support, the road to success certainly would not be an easy one.

The 1988 Legislative Session

My legislative strategy was to have the Senate pass the restructuring bill first, then put political pressure on the House to pass the Senate bill. We did not approach the Senate leadership until the beginning of the 1988 legislative session. Informal discussions with Senator Joe Wright resulted in his agreement to sponsor the legislation in the Senate. While he and Senator David Karem, the leader of the Democratic caucus in the Senate, favored many of the ideas in the proposal, they both said the political problems would be in the House and not the Senate. Their assessment of the situation proved to be accurate. The legislation had no real chance for passage even with the help of the Senate.

Drafting of the bill began prior to the 1988 session, but I wasn't able to give final approval to it until early in February. Once introduced, Senate leadership moved the bill very quickly. Senate Bill 256 was heard by the Senate Education Committee on March 3, was passed by the full Senate by a two-to-one margin several days later, and was sent to the House on Friday March 11. However, this was very late in the session. From a tactical perspective, introducing the bill so late in the session probably gave the opposition an advantage which I could not overcome. House leadership wasn't inclined to approve the bill anyway, but the delay left us little time to lobby House Education Committee members for its passage.

The legislative process gives considerable power to leadership and committee chairs, presumably to prevent consideration of frivolous legislation. However, these rules also can be used to prevent legislation from being considered which the leadership doesn't want passed. Knowing time was running out on us, we worked hard to personally contact each member of the House Education Committee. Rep. Roger

Noe, the committee chair, realized we were about to secure enough votes to call the bill up for consideration and refused to hold any more committee meetings. The Senate bill died in committee without a hearing in the House.

One last personal effort to get the bill released from committee was made in a private meeting with Chairman Noe and members of House leadership. Although the tenor of the meeting was pleasant, nothing changed. Realizing there was no chance now of getting the bill before the House, I then said that I probably would call a special session later in the year to secure passage of the bill.

The Impact of the Legislative Setback

Perhaps passage of the Governor's School Improvement Incentive Act was in trouble from the very beginning and destined for defeat. No doubt the delay in getting the bill introduced, the austere budget I offered, the flap over funding of the 1985-86 reforms, lack of strong support from the education community, and generally poor relations with both House and Senate leadership all contributed to the failure to get it enacted into law in 1988.

In addition to the political problems I had with the House, I didn't have enough time to get a significant number of leading educators to go along with me. Furthermore, the fiscal situation made a reasonable dialog with teachers nearly impossible. My antitax stand angered the editorial boards and tempered the cautious support I had early on from some members of the Prichard Committee.

Perhaps it was unrealistic to think a governor could have enough political clout to get a progressive agenda through a General Assembly determined to demonstrate its independence whenever and wherever possible. Realizing that very few legislators supported my candidacy for governor, I knew I could not count on having a large cadre of legislators waiting to help me through my first legislative session. However, the politics of change reach far beyond the legislature. Public institutions have great resilience to change and are politically powerful.

I was disappointed, but not discouraged, by the outcome and was as determined as ever to get the initiative approved. Although the legislation did not get enacted into law, I was successful in getting public attention focused on the issue of restructuring education. I had learned that when I could get attention focused on education rather than taxes, I fared quite well. The debate still was about the merits of my "incentive plan." Nonetheless, it was politically necessary to keep the debate focused on issues related to restructuring. The threat to call a special session of the General Assembly as soon as possible to approve my plan would serve this purpose.

The Political Fallout from the 1988 Session

By the time the 1988 legislative session was over, I had been raked over the coals in the press, picketed by the teacher's union, and marched on by university students and faculty. I had failed to get a hearing on my ideas in the House of Representatives, and educators and their advocates considered me a great disappointment. Some even thought I was their bitter enemy. It was obvious that I had to quickly improve my political position with these important constituencies if I were to have any hope of getting my legislation passed in a special session. The political liabilities I acquired in this first legislative battle were significant and eventually proved to be very difficult to overcome.

A Quick Overview of the Damage

In order to balance the budget in 1988, I had to do some things educators considered offensive. Among these was a decision not to continue the overmatch for the Kentucky Teachers Retirement Fund. The over match was a special appropriation beyond the normal appropriation to cover what the retirement fund board had been told some years earlier *might* be an unfunded liability in thirty years. In my view and the view of numerous financial consultants, the retirement programs were not in danger, so we could safely divert the over-match money to other purposes. Some interpreted my proposal to drop the overmatch as "borrowing" from these pension funds, which never was the case.

In addition to eliminating the overmatch contribution to the teacher retirement fund, I failed to increase teacher salaries by the amount they expected. The 1986 education reform act promised teachers a 5 percent salary increase each year of the 1988-90 biennium in an effort to raise average salaries for teachers in Kentucky to the average in other southern states. I provided for only a seven percent increase in the 1988-90 budget.

As if that were not enough, a crisis in state health care insurance coverage resulted in creation of a self-insurance program, which slightly increased the premium paid by some state employees. Since teachers participate in the state insurance program, they complained that they would get no real increase in salary the first year because the increased premium wiped out the 2 percent first-year increase for many teachers. The health care insurance program I offered was a "cadillac" model, far better than provided by most states, and certainly better than the private sector average. That didn't seem to matter much to my KEA detractors.

I also did not fund a $300 bonus for teachers who met the requirements of a special evaluation required by the 1986 reforms. Teachers never let me forget this when I talked about *my* bonus program. If I reneged on paying $300, how could I be credible when I promised at least $1,800 per teacher? Of course the General Assembly could have put the bonus back in the budget, but they agreed with my decision to leave it out. In terms of the political cost to me, perhaps I should have paid it, since the amount involved would not have made a great deal of difference in the bottom line of a $19 billion state budget. In any case, it was me and not the General Assembly who took the hit for the bonus not being paid.

I angered the university presidents along with their students, alumni, and supporters when I proposed keeping higher education funding near its current level in the first year of the biennium. I had serious reservations about funding universities on the basis of what other states were willing or able to spend. I objected to the auto- pilot, formula-driven funding policy. The benchmark approach used to determine where Kentucky stood among other states in the level of funding for similar institutions almost guaranteed a continued spiral in higher education spending in all states, not just in Kentucky. I also felt the community colleges gave us the "biggest bang for the buck," but they were way behind the senior institutions in per student funding. I was determined to correct that inequity.

Obviously, I was given no slack by those who are unswerving in their support for giving universities more money year after year without looking at the long-range future of the system. The proper time to deal with inequities among the various institutions would be in the session when inequities in public elementary and secondary school funding were considered. It was my intention to do so at that time, but my refusal to discuss taxes at this point in my administration kept me from promising something better later on.

I had been warned by fellow governors not to "mess with" higher education. They are a powerful political bloc and can be devastating to any politician who gets in their way. But I was tired of bowing to their constant whining that the university system will be hurt if it doesn't get its regular increment in funding each biennium. There seemed to be an unwillingness to contain cost. My offhand comment to a reporter that the presidents "should stop crying and get back to work" gave credibility to the idea that I was anti-intellectual and would not be a strong supporter of higher education.

The Perception that I Abandoned the 1986 Reforms

The most serious political fallout came from the education leadership in the House who continued, even after the session, to characterize the issue between us as one of continuing with *their* agenda set in 1985-86 *or* accepting mine and having their initiatives "unfunded." The idea that I would not fund the earlier reforms came from the position I took during the campaign that I was committed only to my own program. As time passed, my refusal to assure legislators and others that I would at least support what already had been done led to the perception that I had no intention to do so.

In my budget address in January 1988 I said, "I will not abandon or dismantle the successes in education that were enacted in 1985 and 1986. We will continue to fund those priorities." That was more than political rhetoric. When the budget proposal for FY 1989-90 was presented, I had actually increased the level of funding for most of their programs by $16 million and reduced funding for my own from $75 to $10 million. Other than the lower salary increase for teachers, the only major item for which I did not increase funding was a further reduction in class size. The contention that I would not (or did not) fund the earlier reforms was without any foundation in fact. Still the perception remained that I was asking the General Assembly to trade my program for theirs.

Under very austere conditions I did a great deal to financially support the earlier reforms in the 1988 legislative session, but it seemed to be lost in the media's assessment of my role in leading education reform.The editorial boards, the Prichard Committee, and the Advocates for Higher Education all saw higher taxes as the answer to the education problem, and I failed to come through at a critical time from their perspective. What seemed to have escaped everyone's attention was the fact that within the next two years the Kentucky Supreme Court would very likely require the legislature to achieve equity in school funding. A massive increase in taxes in 1988, even if I had agreed to it, would have been a mistake in light of what was ahead.

The Need to Reach Agreement with the Legislature

There was no indication at the end of the 1988 legislative session that House leaders were in a mood to compromise. The residual bitterness from the 1988 skirmishes with leadership in both chambers made meaningful discussion very difficult. By this time it had become a test of wills: who would be forced to give in? It was not an environment conducive to good faith negotiation. I was told that no further consideration of my proposals would be forthcoming unless and until I agreed to support *and fund* the 1986 legislation. This prior constraint was probably the most important reason for the political impasse which continued for the next twelve months.

I was pragmatic enough to know that at some point I would have to concede something to get what I wanted. On the other hand, it was no secret that ideological differences made it difficult for me to support some elements of the 1986 reforms. I wanted to redirect the focus of the education enterprise toward results before agreeing to put more money into it. From my perspective, an agreement with legislative leaders had to involve more than accommodation—just putting together some of their ideas and some of mine. This kind of political "horse trading" was antithetical to the change in *policy perspective* I wanted. But accommodation was exactly what legislative leadership expected. It's their typical approach to resolving political differences.

I don't think this aspect of the dispute between us was ever understood by the legislators I talked with or by the media. Over time my refusal to agree to a "some of this and some of that" kind of legislation got translated into the perception that it had to be "my way or no way." In terms of accommodation, they were right. It did have to be my way or no way. I have never believed in compromising away the integrity of anything in order to get it. As long as the focus of the debate continued to be over which *programs* to fund—mine or theirs —the stalemate would have to continue.

The differences between us were not minor. Take for example the issue of reductions in class size, a very costly but highly valued element in the 1986 legislation. I was told that smaller class sizes were the cornerstone of the 1986 reforms. Research on the impact of smaller class size on improved learning was inconclusive until classes of fewer than fifteen students were attained. Estimates prepared by LRC when the law was enacted put the cost of lowering class size by an average of two students in grades one through six at $59.6 million in 1990. At this rate it would cost the state at least $250 million more to reduce class sizes by ten students each for just these six grades. To reduce class sizes to fifteen in the remaining grades was not estimated, but it would likely have exceeded $450 million more in 1990 dollars for a total cost of at least $780 million for all grades. Based on these estimates, the total cost of pursuing this policy option could reach almost $1 billion by the time it was fully implemented in the year 2000.

My estimate of the cost to equalize the minimum foundation program was about $500 million in the 1990-92 biennium. In other words, we could realistically achieve what the courts were likely to require if we abandoned the class size policy and put that money into equity instead. In light of this information, I simply could not justify the cost of continuing the policy to lower class size in the face of the great need to achieve equity among school districts. While this policy choice was easy for me to make, it required the legislature to abandon one of its major policy objectives in 1986. For this and other reasons, I knew reaching agreement with the General Assembly would be extremely difficult to accomplish.

In retrospect I find the insistence on pursuing class size reduction an interesting one. When the SEEK program was created in 1990, we kept the current cap on class size, but local school districts had the option to lower class size on their own using the new money made available through equalization. Many school districts received as much as a 50 to 100 percent increase in funds, but very few of them used this money to reduce class size. Most of the new money was used to increase teacher salaries instead. Given the policy choice, most teachers chose higher salaries rather than smaller class sizes.

Preparation for the Next Round

Following the 1988 legislative session, I tried to build political support for the legislation before calling a special session of the General Assembly. I decided to mend fences with the education community in the hope that I might find a way to get their endorsement of my legislation. Over the summer months I had a series of meetings with representatives of various education interest groups to see if I could get a breakthrough with them.

I knew money would be central to getting the support of educators, so I was prepared to make a commitment to seek more money for education in exchange for their help in getting my legislation passed in a special session. However, it soon was clear there existed little agreement among the various education interest groups as to what they had to have in exchange. The only thing they seemed to agree upon was that I should raise taxes and appropriate more money for education. Of course I was not about to pledge more money for education until I had some assurance that the structural changes I wanted would be supported by the education community.

Dealing with the Teacher's Union

Improving my relationship with teachers proved to be very difficult. In my travels across the Commonwealth, I had the good pleasure to meet teachers almost everywhere I went. Many of them expressed support for my ideas and offered encouragement. However, their views were offset by a vocal and often boisterous group of Kentucky Education Association (KEA) members who seized every opportunity to cast me as "antiteacher."

My candor before the Prichard Committee regarding the 1986 reforms and some other well-publicized confrontations probably hurt my efforts to generate constructive discussions with KEA on the changes I was proposing. Perhaps a better politician might have been able to bring a more temperate tone to the rhetoric, but I firmly believe it is virtually impossible to achieve significant change in any area of public policy without attacking the sacred cows of special interest. In Kentucky, the education establishment has been the grand champion of sacred cows.

My relationship with KEA was not good from the beginning, and it got no better with time. During the campaign, I refused to meet with the KEA Political Action Committee (KEPAC). To my knowledge, no legitimate contender for the state's highest office had dared to be so brazen as to ignore such a politically powerful organization. For me the decision was simply a matter of how best to use scarce political and financial capital. Meetings between KEA leadership and members of the State Research Associates team during the summer of 1987 made it clear that we had little to agree upon. To me it seemed to be simply a waste of my time to go through a meeting when I knew at the outset it would not result in an endorsement.

Eventually KEA's political arm refused to endorse me in the general election, the first time in its history the teachers' union had not endorsed the Democratic candidate for governor. Perhaps had I at least made an appearance, KEA might not have endorsed anyone. They could not accept my not at least making an appearance. I was openly critical of KEA leadership, and at times I made some uncomplimentary remarks about KEA president David Allen, with whom I had refused to meet. I tried to be careful about criticizing teachers directly. I wanted and needed their political support. However, my public criticism of KEA *as an organization*, especially its leadership, eventually took a political toll among teachers.

As mentioned earlier, KEA sponsored a march on the Capitol during the 1988 legislative session over my reduction of an expected salary increase from 5 percent to 2 percent the first year of the biennium. They also resented my failure to further reduce class sizes and do some other things promised in the 1985-86 reforms and not funded. The situation only got worse after the legislative session when I had to make a major change in the health care insurance program for state employees. The health insurance issue is important in this context, because it was one more monetary issue which KEA used to whip up anti-Wilkinson sentiment.

I got into a war of words with KEA through the media over the insurance issue after KEA held a rally in northern Kentucky to protest the Kentucky KARE program. A *Kentucky Post* article covering the rally quoted Terry Williams, president of the Northern Kentucky Education Association, as saying, "The governor has given us an inadequate raise and has added insult to injury by undercutting our insurance benefits. It isn't fair, and it certainly isn't right." According to the newspaper account, the crowd of "150 teachers, administrators, and politicians" gave Ms. Williams a standing ovation after these remarks.

The rally was scheduled several days before I was to be in northern Kentucky at a "Capitol to the Counties" meeting at Dixie Heights High School in Kenton County. The NKEA planned to picket my appearance. In her remarks at the rally, Ms. Williams went on to say, "Our voice will say, 'Governor Wilkinson, the sale is over. Quality education costs money.'" Of course, quality education in the mind of KEA members is getting paid more and having perhaps the most generous health care program of any Kentucky worker, all at taxpayers' expense. The teachers carried through on their picketing which, of course, was designed to call media attention to their concerns and my "unwillingness to listen."

I agreed to meet with three KEA representatives at Dixie Heights High School during my "Capitol to the County" office hours. The meeting was hostile from the beginning. I wanted to discuss my ideas on improving education, and they wanted to talk money. It was obvious to everyone in the meeting that we had little in common. In a way it was unfortunate, but probably inevitable, that I would come out of this meeting being portrayed as the villain. I did not feel this was a time or place to deal with labor relations issues, and that's what they wanted to talk about.

As promised, there were pickets outside the building, but more like twenty-five rather than the predicted 150. One of the anti-Wilkinson signs even had a misspelled word in it. Nevertheless, here was a small band of vocal teachers demanding that I raise the taxes on every Kentuckian so that teachers could avoid paying an average of $9 a month more for health care insurance while 200,000 Kentuckians had no health insurance at all. And then they wanted me to insult the public's intelligence by saying that this would improve education. Hog wash!

At every Capitol to the Counties meeting I was confronted by a group of KEA teachers, always hostile and carrying placards which described me in unflattering terms. Invariably I met with these groups, but I never found them interested in improving anything other than their own financial position. Of course, there were teachers and school administrators who would stop by to encourage me, but it was clear that the union element of KEA was more interested in confrontation than dialogue.

One incident in particular that really aggravated me was the behavior of a reporter for the *Park City Daily News*. This reporter conspired with the local KEA chapter in Bowling Green to generate a negative story about my position on education. I had come to the city for a Capitol to the Counties meeting. I was confronted by the usual handful of KEA pickets upon my arrival, another made-for-TV "Kodak moment." What ensued at Bowling Green that day is an example of a confrontation organized for the benefit of and in conspiracy with the media.

When it came time for my scheduled meeting with the KEA representatives, they had added a reporter from the *Park City* who had not been part of the group when they originally indicated who would be attending. Although the rule was not universal, we usually did not allow reporters to sit in on meetings during the Capitol to the Counties so as to promote frank discussions and avoid the kind of "made for the media" event this meeting became. Since the reporter already was there, I simply ignored it and continued.

It soon was obvious to me from the way the KEA delegation approached the meeting that the whole episode was being staged as an attack on me for the benefit of the *Park City*. I had come to expect a hostile greeting from the KEA contingents, but I was extremely upset that any reporter would willingly participate in an obvious effort to create news. Needless to say, KEA succeeded in getting the front page story they were looking for the next day.

In spite of the bad political blood between myself and KEA leadership, I was told in private discussions they might be willing to support some of my ideas, but not the accountability or financial incentive provisions. All teachers should be treated the same regardless of their performance. In return for KEA support for other provisions of my proposed legislation, they wanted class size reductions continued, creation of a professional standards board to be controlled by KEA, full restoration of the salary increases not granted in 1988, certain changes in the health care insurance plan, and generally more money spent on education.

Clearly, these were all labor union issues. I fully understand that these are the issues labor unions are supposed to push for on behalf of their members. On the other hand, in my view they have very little to do with quality education; they have much to do with the value of a labor union to teachers. To no one's surprise, I was unwilling to grant what KEA leadership wanted in return for their support of my legislation.

An Appeal to Other Education Interest Groups

Meetings with district superintendents were somewhat more productive, although they never resulted in a public endorsement of my proposals by any of their Associations except for the KASA. In private I told the superintendents I was prepared to ask the legislature to raise more money, but only after I was assured that schools were in a position to improve. In my terms this meant being committed to undertake restructuring along the lines proposed in my policy papers. In almost every case it turned into a "chicken and egg" discussion. Which should come first, a tax increase or passage of my legislation? Everybody wanted to secure someone else's commitment.

I think the problem here was to some extent an issue of trust. I had been so adamant about not raising taxes, I suppose many of these superintendents had private doubts about my commitment to raise the money they wanted once I got my legislation passed. Cynicism is a good defense when history had proven to them that politicians cannot always be trusted when they make statements about what they will do at some later time. These superintendents had experienced a classic example of this kind of political behavior when the legislature met in regular session in 1986 and failed to pass the revenue promised to implement the reforms enacted in the 1985 special session. Would I be any different?

On the other hand, from my perspective it was an issue of political strategy. The moment I publicly promised to raise taxes without being assured of real structural change, I would have lost any opportunity I might have to get the kind of systemic changes I was seeking. Perhaps they were as skeptical of the legislature as they were of me, but clearly there were not enough superintendents willing to publicly support my ideas or work for passage of my legislation to make them an effective political force on my behalf. Consequently, these discussions never produced a political bond between myself and the local school leadership.

I held fewer meetings with David Keller, executive director of the Kentucky School Boards Association, but I received only unofficial personal support from him for most of what I wanted. He was skeptical of the school-based decision-making proposal, but strongly supported the emphasis on performance standards for student achievement and greater accountability for teachers. Once again, I was unable to get a public commitment of support from the KSBA organization.

I came away from these meetings convinced that the political infrastructure of education was too fragmented to be helpful and too scared of the legislature to align themselves with a governor whom the General Assembly considered threatening. I also came to realize that these groups were never going to accept the proposition that schools had to be restructured. They still thought many schools were effective and could not understand why I thought such a radical approach was necessary. At times they seemed tempted to take a chance with me on the hope that I just might be willing to raise the money if I got my legislation passed, but their public support for my restructuring initiative never materialized.

The bottom line here is that I made a serious attempt to reach a reasonable settlement of the issues which had alienated me from the education constituencies. If I could have been successful here, I thought I could push the legislature up against the wall. Money and taxes always came into the picture, but I was prepared to say I would raise the money needed (not necessarily saying I would *raise taxes*) if they would agree to support the changes I wanted. On this point the discussion always seemed to break down. In the end, the education leadership did not have the political grit to stand with me against the legislature. The reason? I would soon be gone, but they would need the legislature long after I was history. As usual, special interests were much more effective in blocking something than in making something happen.

Other Efforts to Gain Support

Efforts to gain understanding and support for my policy initiative went beyond my personal meetings with educators. I asked Jack Foster, then my secretary of the Education and Humanities Cabinet and primary education policy advisor, to meet with various people around the commonwealth to explain and seek support for what we were trying to do. In July 1988 he met with newspaper editors in Paducah, Owensboro, Bowling Green, Ashland, northern Kentucky, and Hopkinsville. We both met with the editorial boards of the *Courier-Journal* and *Herald-Leader* during the campaign, and Foster had a private luncheon meeting with John Carroll, then editor of the *Herald-Leader* in July 1988. Foster also met privately with most members of the state board of education, and at the chairman's request he gave an informal informational briefing to some board members one evening before they met later that summer.

Jack Foster and Sandy Gubser, his deputy, held a number of meetings with John Brock and later on with Betty Steffy in an effort to find a way to get John's support. In mid-September I hosted a dinner meeting in the Governor's Mansion for representatives of all the education interest groups, including higher education, to discuss with them my ideas about how to improve education. The dinner meeting was very helpful, I thought, in clearing up some misunderstandings and misgivings. Although I was not asking at the time for the endorsement of their respective organizations, I did hope to convince them I was not an enemy of education. I recall saying to them at the time I was willing to put more money into education once I was convinced schools were in a position to improve.

Foster had many public and private meetings with school administrators all over the Commonwealth. He

---

continually answered their questions and listened to their concerns about my incentive program and site-based management. At times they felt I was not being responsive because I failed to make any significant changes in these ideas. The bottom line for me was whether or not modifications would lead to political support. In most cases it was clear they simply didn't want to change their roles and relationships, as would occur if my ideas were implemented.

Foster personally sought the help of the leading superintendents on the Council for Better Schools. He carried to them the message that I was prepared to raise the money necessary to bring about the financial equity they sought, but I wanted the restructuring proposal enacted into law before that time. He asked for their strong support of the restructuring initiative. Of course, it never came.

There were influential school administrators like Randy Kimbrough, Jack Rose, and Cliff Wallace who strongly backed my proposal for restructuring. They were successful in getting KASA to endorse the main elements in my proposal, and they also were very helpful in countering resurgence among their peers. They helped counter some of the misinformation that was going around about the program. Undoubtedly there were many others of whose efforts I was unaware. However, there simply were not enough educators like them to make a significant difference.

One Last Effort to Reach Consensus

The media, legislators, and education interest groups persistently maintained that I was the primary stumbling block to further improvement in education. On the one hand, this perception gave me the control over the political agenda I wanted. The political focus would continue to be on how to get me to move. On the other hand, I could not afford to be characterized indefinitely as an obstacle. Somehow I had to turn this political energy into a positive force for change.

In the eight months following the 1988 session, the pressure mounted to do something more in education. Everyone was convinced I would call a special session to deal with my proposals. They also were convinced I would continue to resist raising taxes. In 1985 agreement was reached to hold a special session to deal with the substance of school reform, leaving the issue of funding for the regular session. However, failure to deliver on the promised financial support left everyone bitter and disillusioned. The concern that I would repeat this scenario made it very difficult for me to persuade educators to go along with me on a second round.

During the summer of 1988 John Brock orchestrated the formation of a group called the "Grass Roots Coalition," made up of eight organizations which had a direct interest in education issues. The stated mission of the group was to develop a consensus among the education interest groups on what they considered most important in what some referred to as the "second wave" of reform. The grass roots group was chaired by Robert Sexton, executive director of the Prichard Committee. I was not invited to participate in these discussions. As time passed, it became clear that the *political* objective of the grass roots group was to create a situation where educators could regain control of the reform agenda. Given its organizational makeup, I saw coming a long wish list made up of traditional solutions.

In November of 1988, the Prichard Committee once again tried to get some movement from the General Assembly and me. Wade Mountz, chairman of the committee, in a prepared statement called for a "comprehensive education plan" that incorporates ideas from all parties. Their proposal for getting things moving was to reach an accommodation by taking "some of this and some of that" and making an "education stew." As I discussed earlier, I had serious problems with this approach to achieving the restructuring I envisioned. The committee also had a traditional approach to funding these new initiatives — bring the state tax code into conformity with the federal code and increase various other taxes on property, sales, and unmined minerals.

It so happened I had a meeting scheduled with legislative leaders that same day to discuss a special session on the lottery, which had just been approved by voters. The meeting was congenial, and we all agreed on the need to come up with a plan we could all support. We also agreed that we needed to dispel the idea that we were bickering and unable to come to agreement. However, no specific process was put in place to formulate a political solution.

In January 1989 I met with legislative leaders to discuss among other things my desire to hold a special session on education as soon as possible. We agreed on a tentative target date of March that year. In a move to get agreement before I issued the call, I asked leadership to give me their priorities as soon as possible so I could begin negotiations. I knew reaching an agreement with the legislature would be difficult, but it was politically necessary before calling the session.

Perhaps it was a tactical mistake on my part not to have used the opportunity in November to begin this process. At that time we could have created a working group made up of people from my office and legislative staff to hammer out a political compromise. Creation of such a group then would have gone a long way toward dispelling the notion that I was unwilling to embrace ideas other than my own, and at the same time it would not have diminished the control I wanted to maintain over the political agenda. However, getting the lottery up and running consumed much of my time and attention during the six weeks following the November meeting, and I simply did not follow through. Precious time was lost when progress possibly could have been made toward a compromise.

Having laid down the gauntlet to the legislature, I held one more round of separate meetings with John Brock, Larry Diebold, executive director of KEA; and Wade Mountz and Robert Sexton of the Prichard Committee. I wanted to take a measure of the amount of resistance they still had to my proposals and to see if a compromise could be worked out with them. John Brock said that his grass roots group was close to reaching consensus and wanted me to wait until their report was completed before calling a special session. KEA's position was unchanged, and Mountz and Sexton continued to push their "comprehensive" agenda. As had been the case in earlier meetings, the discussion inevitably turned on whether I would publicly agree to raise taxes in return for their support.

Shortly thereafter, John Brock called to arrange a meeting with members of the grass roots group. On February 7 I met with the group in my office for several hours hours. At that meeting I used every persuasive power in my possession to get a commitment to endorse my proposals publicly. They in turn made it very clear to me that their support for my program would not be considered unless and until I agreed to spend significantly more money on education at all levels. As I had done many times before, I assured them I was willing to spend more money on education, but only after I was assured that schools had been restructured in a way to ensure their improvement.

As the meeting progressed, I sensed we were headed for a standoff. Knowing the political importance of this meeting, I asked for a few minutes alone with my staff. We went into a small room next to my office. After much discussion I decided it was time to take the initiative and tell the group I would publicly state my willingness to raise taxes if necessary to support what was needed in education. This was a politically significant decision on my part, but it was my hope this important concession would lead to an announcement of agreement by all parties at the end of the meeting.

When I returned to the meeting, I tendered my offer to stand by their side in a joint announcement. Jim Wiseman, president of the Kentucky Chamber of Commerce, immediately responded that he could not speak for his organization until he knew how business might be affected by any tax increase. The group caucused for a few minutes and then announced that they appreciated this opportunity to meet, but they were not in a position to publicly commit their organizations to my program at that time. I had finally given them what they wanted in terms of a "raise taxes" statement, and they showed their true colors. The meeting abruptly ended without the endorsement I wanted and expected.

Following the meeting and a brief, informal statement to the media, I was told that some members of the group went directly to a meeting with legislative leaders to discuss the outcome of the meeting with me. Leadership apparently feared the prospect that I might cut a deal with the group and leave the legislature in an awkward position. As it was related to me, the group was told in effect "you have to decide whether you're on his [the governor's] side or ours." I believe we came very close to achieving a political breakthrough that day, but as Jim Wiseman of the Chamber of Commerce explained it, "We can't afford to get caught in a fight between the governor and the legislature. We have to deal with them [the legislature] long after you are gone."

The Decision to Move Ahead

The day after my meeting with the grass roots group I announced that I was creating by executive order a Council on School Performance Standards, a key element in my proposal to restructure schools. The mission of the council was outlined in this statement to the media:

> *Every major education study in this nation has raised questions of whether our schools are focusing on the right things. I believe it is time we finally take a comprehensive look at Kentucky's schools and determine for ourselves if we are addressing that concern. The task is fundamental to our ability to prove to the people of this*

*Commonwealth that we can measure the per-
formance of our schools and account for the
progress of our students.*

*This Council will advise us on the extent to
which the Kentucky Program of Studies satisfies
the learning needs of our young people and
what methods of assessing learning are suitable
for statewide use. The Council also will help us
determine the extent to which the curriculum
can be appropriately adapted to the different
learning styles and speeds of children, and what
we can reasonably expect our children to know
at various stages in the process.*

The decision to create the council by executive order was made in January 1989 when it became apparent a special session to create it by statute would not occur until at least March. The timing for implementing the rest of the re-structuring initiative would be thrown completely off unless this work got under way immediately. I wanted the work to be credible to the public and educators, so the membership consisted of members of the state board of education, business and community leaders, and educators.

I named John Brock and Jack Foster to the council as well. John Brock asked Dr. Betty Steffy, his deputy superintendent, to represent him on the council. Dr. Steffy was very helpful and fully supportive of the report of the council. Of course, it was Jack Foster who knew exactly what I was looking for from the council, and I counted heavily on his ability to keep the work of the group on track.

I asked J. D. Nichols, a Louisville businessman, to chair the council. Knowing the political controversy that surrounded my proposals, J. D. felt the result would have no impact unless the process was open and independent. He agreed to make certain this endeavor did not fall into the hands of the traditionalists in education. Dr. Roger Pankratz, a professor at Western Kentucky University, was hired to be executive director of the council. The council's work had to be completed by August that year, an extremely short timeline within which to accomplish the mission I had given it. Dr. Pankratz had previous experience in guiding statewide projects of this type and did a remarkable job.

From a political standpoint, creation of the council at this time demonstrated my intention to move forward with or without the General Assembly. The mission I gave it needed to be done whether or not I ever was successful in getting the remainder of my program adopted into law. It was the first time in many years the curriculum and testing program was examined in the light of new information about what children needed to know and be able to demonstrate they could do at all ages and ability levels. We were in a new period of our national history. We needed a curriculum which was responsive to the educational needs of the next century. Children who entered first grade that school year were the Class of 2000.

The council did its work in a professional manner under the guiding hand of Jack Foster and Roger Pankratz. As it turned out, the recommendations of the council became the basis for the learning outcomes and accountability system written into the groundbreaking Kentucky Education Reform Act in 1990. The timeliness and relevance of the council's work made extremely fortuitous my decision to proceed with this part of my restructuring plan without legislation. The curriculum committee of the Task Force on School Reform created after the Supreme Court decision could never have completed its work without the work of the council, which by that time had already received national acclaim.

IX. EDUCATION:
GRIDLOCK ENDS

The General Assembly embarked on a series of public hearings around the commonwealth late in the summer of 1988 as a way to maintain a presence in the debate over school reform. From a political perspective, these hearings were intended to build public support for continuing the 1986 reforms and to blunt the impact of my constant call for fundamental change. Unfortunately, while this effort was going on, no meaningful discussions were held between myself and legislative leadership on how to expand the agenda.

It was evident to everyone that no progress was being made. In spite of the rhetoric from both sides, neither of us followed up on working out a compromise, which gave my opponents in the legislature justification for moving forward on their own. After the failed meeting with the grass roots group, I knew there was almost no hope for a successful special session in March. It appeared I was about to lose the political momentum I needed to get action on my proposal any time soon. A political vacuum began to form as the impasse between the legislature and myself continued on into the fall.

Even though it appeared there was no movement on either side, I saw signs that leadership was preparing for a special session. At the legislature's organizational session in January 1989, leadership created a special interim committee to examine site-based management. Hearings on the issue were begun shortly thereafter. I read this to mean that legislative leaders were trying to give the idea a fair hearing before they had to deal with it in a special session. However, I did not think they were prepared yet to embrace the idea. Privately, leadership raised no objection to creation of the Council on School Performance Standards, but I was reminded that the rest of the program could not be implemented without legislation.

The Education Summit

Leadership in the General Assembly finally went on the offensive after being chided by the news media to get something done in education in spite of me. Leadership made a very important tactical move by announcing in December 1988 they would hold an "education summit" in February 1989 in preparation for the special session they still expected me to call sometime in March. Clearly such a forum was intended to move the attention away from my policy agenda and put it back in the hands of the legislature and the education establishment.

The media characterized the event as the opportunity for me to show leadership by offering an olive branch to legislators and educators. I don't know exactly what they expected me to do short of throwing in the towel and "going with the flow." The summit was a political challenge to my leadership, and I fully recognized it as such. Knowing the prospect of a special session in March or even April was now all but lost, I had an important political decision to make. The newspaper editors had determined that it was up to me to make the next move in this political chess game. The political burden of failure to move forward on school reform was placed squarely on my shoulders.

In my prepared remarks at the summit, I gave my response. I said:

> *Our schools need more money. I've never denied that. And I'm willing to spend more money on schools. I'm willing to find more money, but not until we make a commitment to change the system so that we can show the people of Kentucky that they are truly paying for improvement. To put it bluntly, if we are not going to change the system, I'd rather spend less to be last than spend more to be last.*

Martha and I opened the Kentucky
...erback Gallery on Main Street in Lexington
...1962. So many students had lined up to
...rchase textbooks when this picture was taken
...August, 1969, that the fire marshal had to
...ne and help with crowd control.

...ngton Herald-Leader

...pearances by political candidates at the
...ual Fancy Farm Picnic in Graves County is
...olorful tradition. In gubernatorial years
... picnic generally attracts media from all
...oss Kentucky and parts of several sur-
...nding states. ▼

...Alexander
...nson for Governor '87

▲ When I was a boy they dismissed classes so that we
could watch Governor Chandler drive through Liberty. Having
"Happy" endorse my campaign in the rotunda of the state
capitol was one of the great thrills of my life.

Ron Garrison
Lexington Herald-Leader

Glenn, Andrew,
Martha and I share
the thrill of victory!
These are two of my
favorite pictures.

I had promised Daviess County that I would come
Owensboro Election Night if I won. I carried every
ecinct in the county and several hundred people
re there at midnight to greet Martha and me.

en Lake
ensboro Messenger-Inquirer

Among other things Kentucky governors ▶
must swear never to have fought a duel. The
public swearing-in is a formality since it is
preceded by a private midnight ceremony.

Richard Upchurch
Kentucky Department of Libraries and Archives
Public Records Division

idn't get very many endorsements as a candidate.
e Kentucky Firefighters Association really went out
a limb for me. ▼

g Alexander
inson for Governor '87

Everything was congenial when I paid an unannounced visit to Senate chambers on the first day of the 1988 regular General Assembly session. The days ahead were much more difficult.

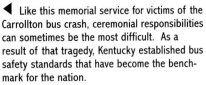

◀ Like this memorial service for victims of the Carrollton bus crash, ceremonial responsibilities can sometimes be the most difficult. As a result of that tragedy, Kentucky established bus safety standards that have become the benchmark for the nation.

Unknown

I bought the first lottery ticket at 6:00 am, April 4, 1989, ▶ in Louisville. In its first year we exceeded the $70 million I predicted the lottery would turn over to the state. The Kentucky lottery is generating almost twice that much now.

Richard Upchurch
Kentucky Department of Libraries and Archives
Public Records Division

When I signed the "samurai" bond agreement in Tokyo, Kentucky became the first state to successfully participate in the Japanese bond market. (Left: L. Rogers Wells; Right: Gene Royalty) ▶

Nomura Securities Co., Ltd.

◀ I spent many productive hours in this conference room. Unfortunately this particular briefing on landfill capacity and long term needs turned out to be a waste of time.

Steve Mitchell
Kentucky Department of Libraries and Archives
Public Records Division

Working with Delta Chairman ▶
Ron Allen was a real pleasure. We
appeared together when he
announced their decision to
expand in Kentucky.

I never saw a community work harder
than Owensboro to land a business
prospect. We got Scott! (Pictured left
to right): County Judge Executive W.
M. "Buzz" Norris, Scott Paper Vice
President Rullie Harris, and Mayor
Dave Adkisson ▼

TOP   I promised during my campaign to make state government more accessible and regularly took the entire cabinet to various locations across the state for Capitol to the Counties. Except when the legislature was in session I spent at least as much time out in the state as I did in Frankfort.

BOTTOM   Besides making state government accessible to more Kentuckians, Capitol to the Counties gave Martha and me a chance to relax a little ourselves.

John Perkins
Kentucky Department of Libraries and Archives
Public Records Division

▲ I don't know who was proudest the day that Martha presented Waylon Jennings with his GED, Waylon, Martha ... or me.

Steve Mitchell
Kentucky Department of Libraries and Archives
Public Records Division

▲ Martha raised thousands of dollars in private donations to defer the testing fee for GED participants.

Dave Crawford
Kentucky Educational Television

◀ I was invited to meet with Prime Minister Kaifu (pictured here) when I visited Japan in 1990. When we closed the "samurai" bond agreement in 1989 I had a similar meeting with then Prime Minister Takeshita.

Office of the Prime Minister
Tokyo, Japan

(Left to right): Deputy Budget Director Ron Carson, Senate Appropriations Committee Chairman Mike Moloney, Budget Director Merl Hackbart, House Appropriations Committee Chairman Joe Clarke, and I had just finished putting the final touches on the measures that would equalize funding of Kentucky schools. ▼

Stephen Castleberry
Lexington Herald-Leader

With the stroke of my pen HB 940 became law
d the road to reform left the statehouse and
ved to the schoolhouse.

ve Mitchell
tucky Department of Libraries and Archives
lic Records Division

You just never know who is going to drop by for a visit.
It might be the President one day and Danny DeVito's
"twin" the next day. Louisville mayor Jerry Abramson and
I greet President Reagan. Arnold Schwarzenegger was
touring the states promoting youth fitness.

DIFFERENCE IN TAX LIABILITY
ENUE REVITALIZATION* vs. 7 CENTS SALES TAX

	SINGLE	COUPLE	FAMILY
500	(169)	(199)	(183)
500	(130)	(166)	(195)
500	(145)	(184)	(219)
4,500	(28)	(76)	(114)
	(16)	(20)	(54)
9,500	(64)	(112)	(148)
9,500	87	(20)	(30)
49,500	140	26	(30)
63,500	559	467	416
88,500			

des Conformity, Deductibility (with low income credit) and Sales
x on Services.

I ultimately lost the fight to broaden Kentucky's tax
se, but the 1990 session was a success for me in just
out every other way.

e Mitchell
tucky Department of Libraries and Archives
lic Records Division

It is impossible to make time for everyone who wants to
see the governor, but who could say no to this group of
school children? ▼

Richard Upchurch
Kentucky Department of Libraries and Archives
Public Records Division

▲ Despite the media's cynicism about these "Whoopee We're Rich" tours, local governments depend on these funds for needed projects. (Pictured: Paducah Mayor Gerry Montgomery and County Judge Executive Gary Hovecamp).

John Perkins
Kentucky Department of Libraries and Archives
Public Records Division

▲ I don't think The Kentucky Press Association was very happy that I chose to give my "off-year" State of the State addresses on statewide television instead of at their annual convention. I am sitting at the desk that Martha and the boys gave me.

John Perkins
Kentucky Department of Libraries and Archives
Public Records Division

▲ Some members of the General Assembly had reservations about my being on the floor of the House when the vote came on the Kentucky Education Reform Act. They were afraid my mere presence would symbolize that they were not suitably independent.

Richard Upchurch
Kentucky Department of Libraries and Archives
Public Records Division

The media gets bored with ribbon cuttings.
When we officially dedicated the AA Highway across
Northern Kentucky I proved there's more than one
way to open a new road.

Kentucky has one of this nation's most unique Vietnam
Memorials. I was honored to be the sitting governor
when it was officially dedicated. ▼

◀ Avon Fogle lobbied so hard for this bridge in Nelson County that everyone simply calls it Avon's Bridge.

Steve Lowery
Bardstown Standard

I sparred with a lot of people in th governor's office but Muhammad A (seated) is the only one who actua ly brought boxing gloves. Governor Chandler (right) is showing why we called him "Happy". ▼

Richard Upchurch
Kentucky Department of Libraries and Archives
Public Records Division

TOP Living in the public eye is hard on everyone in the family. My sons, Glenn and Andrew, handled everything remarkably well.

BOTTOM Skeptical legislators projected that my tax amnesty program would only produce $10,000,000. By the time we finished we had collected over $63,000,000!

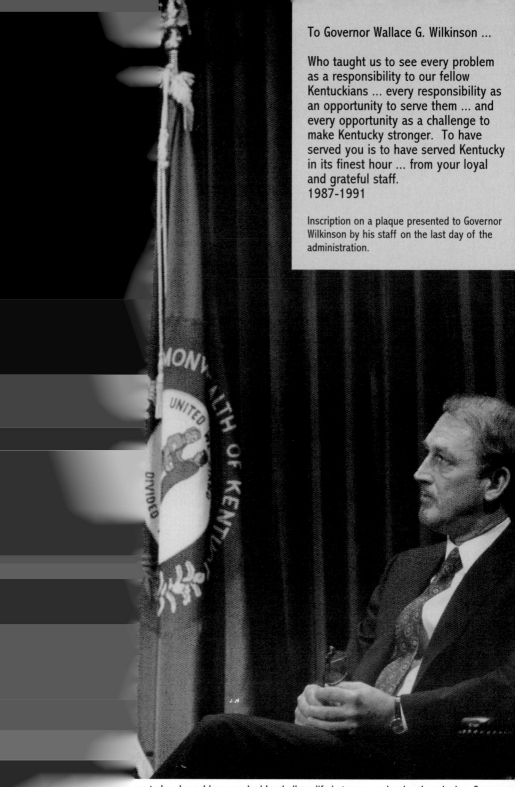

To Governor Wallace G. Wilkinson ...

Who taught us to see every problem
as a responsibility to our fellow
Kentuckians ... every responsibility as
an opportunity to serve them ... and
every opportunity as a challenge to
make Kentucky stronger. To have
served you is to have served Kentucky
in its finest hour ... from your loyal
and grateful staff.
1987-1991

Inscription on a plaque presented to Governor
Wilkinson by his staff on the last day of the
administration.

me to be alone. I have worked hard all my life but never as hard as I worked as Governor.

Although the words "find more money" are not the same as "raise *taxes*," I tried to make it clear to everyone that raising more money for education was not the issue of first importance with me. Time and again I had said that I would do whatever it took to properly fund what we decided to do, including an increase in tax revenues if this were necessary. I repeated that pledge again at the conference. However, from a purely political perspective, I wanted to be able to tell the people of Kentucky that the additional money I was asking them for had a reasonable chance to make a difference. Putting more money into existing programs simply did not meet that test.

The dilemma for everyone was obvious. The basic *strategy* for improving education was not susceptible to the typical form of political compromise. John Brock, while not agreeing with what I wanted to do, astutely saw the political solution when he said he thought the legislature should go ahead and pass everything I wanted except the bonuses and then move on without me from that point. Legislators could not buy into that solution because they knew they could not raise the money for their programs without raising taxes, something they knew they could not do without me.

When asked about my apparent willingness to move on the money issue, leadership complained that I would say one thing in private and something else in public. In reality legislator after legislator came to my office saying one thing in private and something else in public. In every conversation with leadership about the tax issue, I made it very clear I would take the right stand when the time came, but I had no intention of changing my public position on a tax increase. Although they claimed they could not trust me, the reality was they simply were pursuing the path they had taken all along—do nothing with Wilkinson's proposal until he agrees to fund the remainder of their 1986 agenda.

After my speech, the media reported that I had not "budged from my position." But no one else had budged, either! In preparation for the conference, I looked over the list of programs and proposed expenditures which were on the table for consideration at the conference. What struck me most was the absence of anything really new. In an effort to show a spirit of compromise, they had put a few items in the list which dealt with my proposals, but the weight of the agenda was simply to spend more money on what had already been tried. That hardly represented any change in position by educators or legislators. Little wonder people came away thinking nothing had changed. Indeed, it had not.

As I noted earlier, my worst fear politically was that my ideas for changing education policy would get lost in the belly of a huge spending bill designed to reinforce—not change—the present system. That political nightmare was now looming on the horizon. Soon I would be given basically a budget request with a price tag for every program the "educrats" wanted funded. Although framed in terms of goals, the document had no policy for improving education except to invest more money in what was already being done.

Recapturing the Political Initiative

The political strategy of leadership was to keep me on the defensive by continually saying they were ready to meet anytime or anywhere to work out a compromise. No matter what I said or did, leadership always succeeded in getting the media to characterize the situation as though I alone was responsible for not meeting. My door was always open to any legislator who wished to talk with me, and I met with legislators almost daily. It was leadership that did not want to meet with me. It served their purpose better to do nothing and let me take the heat for a lack of progress.

To this day I do not understand how the media could not have seen what was happening. Not once so far as I can remember did the media ever ask me if I had received a call from leadership to set up a meeting. Nonetheless, the reality was I could not find a way to counter the perception that I was refusing to meet with leadership. So I had to take a different tack. At this point I decided to shift the focus of the media from my apparent unwillingness to meet with legislators to the obvious inability of the legislature to get the votes to pass a tax increase. Perhaps I could be successful in shifting the responsibility for inaction from me to the legislature.

After several days of critical press regarding my position on taxes, I held a news conference in Frankfort on the last day of the education conference. It didn't take long for a reporter to raise a question about the tax issue. I took the opportunity to open the new offensive. "I've been thinking about calling their hand on that one," I said, "because a number of members of leadership are hiding behind me on the tax issue. And, quite frankly, I think it would scare them if I came out and said, 'Now produce. How many votes do you have for a tax increase?'" I suggested that reporters should stop talking to leadership about raising taxes and talk to rank-and-file legislators to get their opinion about a tax increase. I summed up the situation by saying "You can't get enough [legislators] on record for a tax increase to do anything!"

Tom Loftus of the Louisville *Courier-Journal* got confirmation from House A & R Committee Chairman Joe Clarke that my assessment of the situation was probably accurate. According to Loftus, Clarke was reported as saying "I agree with the governor. Right now I'd say there are 20 votes (out of 100) for a tax increase." Judging by the irate response my challenge got from leadership, I believe I hit the nail on the head. As long as they could successfully pin the tax issue on me, there would be no need for the legislature to take a hard position on its own.

I also criticized the legislature for coming up with a hodgepodge of ideas that "it would take all the gold in Fort Knox to fund." Leadership retorted that they didn't necessarily support everything in the document which came out of the conference. How could I proceed with negotiations until they set priorities, I asked? Sen. Moloney responded that I needed to show how I intended to pay for my program first, which of course was one more attempt to make me the stumbling block. And so the political bantering continued for several weeks after the conference.

Pressure to give in on the restructuring agenda and move on with other things was growing within my administration as well as from the media and education interests. Some members of my administration felt I had spent too much political capital on the education issue and wanted me to "get this behind us" so the administration could devote more time and energy to other issues. They feared that my "all-or-nothing" position on education would ultimately lead to failure to do anything at all in education and overshadow anything else I might accomplish as governor. They argued for various alternatives which ranged from agreeing to raise more money for education whether or not I got restructuring to abandoning the initiative entirely and letting the court demand that the legislature raise the money. A few simply wanted an end to the contentious wrangling between myself and the legislature over education and money so we could get other important things accomplished.

Kevin Hable, my budget director, was particularly critical of my ongoing confrontation with the legislature over everything in general and education in particular. After my speech was panned in the press, Kevin offered to use his perceived good will with certain key legislators to help make peace with the legislature. I assumed he intended to work through back channels available to him, so I gave him a green light to see what he could do.

Unfortunately, Kevin went public with his concerns the next day in a speech to the Kentucky Chamber of Commerce board of directors. He attributed some of the blame for bad relationships with leadership to the harsh rhetoric of the executive branch. While his remarks were well intentioned, they were in direct contradiction to the strategy I was pursuing with the media. When questioned the next day about this presumed change in attitude, I had to repudiate Kevin's characterization of the situation. It was politically awkward for both of us and certainly doomed to failure whatever Kevin had in mind to do.

The Ball Ends up in My Court

Time was no longer my ally. The March target date for a special session arrived with no action in sight. The Supreme Court was expected to rule on the school finance case sometime that spring. I realized that at best I had one or two months in which to hold a special session on restructuring before the court decision would overtake me. Remember: the case before the court dealt only with school finance. No one was anticipating the kind of ruling that ultimately came down. At this point I knew my political objective of getting the restructuring plan enacted before dealing with anything else could not be achieved. There was virtually no possibility that leadership was going to agree to a special session without their agenda being included.

Legislative leadership said the next move was mine, so about four weeks after the education conference in Lexington I arranged a private meeting with Speaker Blandford and President pro tem Rose to discuss how we might resolve our differences on education reform. The meeting was the first face-to-face discussion between us since January. In the meetings with Blandford and Rose I made it clear that I was willing to consider a reasonable proposal from them as long as my plan for restructuring was part of any final agreement.

The first of several meetings with leadership did not produce any demonstrable progress, but it provided evidence that I was prepared to work something out with the legislature. While we agreed that it would be irresponsible to deal with money issues before the Supreme Court had ruled on the school finance suit, the idea of separating the financing of reforms from the substance was unacceptable to some legisla-tors. We did agree it was necessary to attach a price to each item on the agenda.

Blandford apparently had come to the position that arguing with me any longer over restructuring was futile and said he would help pass "my program" if items of concern to House members were included in the legislation. Senator Rose regarded the inclusion of my restructuring program a very important concession by leadership, but he wanted to see what items in the legislature's agenda I was going to support before he would commit to helping me.

Apparently leadership was sincere about want-ing to get something moving, because within a week they were hard at work preparing a proposal. The next week I met with a select group of House Education Committee members to clar-ify my views on what I wanted from the process. I monitored the process carefully, because I was worried about getting sandbagged with programs or funding levels they knew I would not support. At one point I learned a group of House members were meeting in the Speaker's office, and I asked for and received the opportunity to participate in the discussions. Now, for the first time, I felt some genuine movement toward a political solution.

Work on the legislative proposal continued throughout the month of April. I was hospitalized for a week in Florida during the early part of April, but received the legisla-ture's report shortly after returning to Kentucky. The issue of including revenue measures remained a point of controversy among legislators. The report I received did include some suggested revenue measures, probably to put some pressure on my "no new taxes" position. However, the legislators had pared down the original list to a proposal to spend about $350 million, including the full amount I had requested for the in-centive awards.

Shortly thereafter, I received word that the Supreme Court was getting close to making a ruling. I had to decide whether to hold off on a special session until the justices had issued their opinion. The ball was still in my court, so to speak, so now I had to decide whether or not to continue pursuing a special session in May. Rose and Blanford now were commenting to the media that they thought a special session should not be called until after the Court ruling. It certainly would not be helpful to have the ruling come down while we were in session.

Conceding that there would be no special session, I let up on my public discussion of it. The media continued to put pressure on me to respond to the legislature's proposal, apparently in the belief that I still planned to call the special session. My public response was "I'm still studying it," but privately I was waiting for the Supreme Court decision before making the next move.

Throughout the entire struggle, neither legislators, educators, nor the media ever understood the policy implications of what I proposed. Even in the end, my restructuring proposal was regarded by legislators as another "program" to add to all the others. They failed to see how such ideas as school-based management, a new focus in the curriculum, public expectations for students based on performance rather than memorization, and a powerful accountability system would dramatically change how schools function. All of these elements later were incorporated into KERA and are now seen as representative of some of the most forward thinking in systemic change in education.

One lesson to be gained from this experience is the relatively low position policy actually takes in the legislative process. I hear legislators speak about their policy role in government, but the culture and nature of a legislature makes it truly unsuited as a body to make policy. Likewise, the media seems incapable of advancing the public discussion of policy because it focuses on the programmatic elements of the policy to the exclusion of the rationale for pursuing these programs. Furthermore, the legislative process is captive to special interests, all of whom have something to gain or lose from legislative action.

The legislative process tends to justify every program by its benefits in isolation from the system of which the program is a part. The result is a belief that the public good is served by a proliferation of "good" programs. Never addressed is the question of whether these programs, taken as a whole, give us a good *system* for dealing with the public need the government is trying to meet.

Although in the end I did see most of my ideas become part of the system of education in Kentucky, their adoption came about only after the Supreme Court intervened and allowed a restructuring of the education system to occur. Rather than force me to change my position on raising taxes (a myth that continues to be held by the political pundits), the Supreme Court ruling forced opponents of structural reform to accept the kind of comprehensive, fundamental change I had been advocating throughout the many months of debate.

No one could have been more pleased than I when the long-awaited decision was rendered by the Kentucky Supreme Court. As the months of waiting for the court to rule accumulated, I had a growing sense that it could be more of a turning point than anyone had imagined. I believed that many quarters were recognizing that more than money was at issue.

An Historic Turning Point

The declaration by the state's highest court that the *entire* system of education in Kentucky had to be "re-created, re-established" was a vindication of the position I had taken from the beginning. Obviously, the court went much further than anyone expected, and it certainly went far beyond anything that could have been achieved through the political process alone. In fact, some of the so-called leaders of reform in Kentucky actually thought the court had gone "too far."

The Policy Implications of the Decision

Certain aspects of the court's decision were of critical importance to me from a policy perspective. The rationale the court used to justify declaring the entire system of education unconstitutional was the inequitable opportunities and outcomes for children.

> *The overall effect of appellants' evidence is a virtual concession that Kentucky's system of common schools is underfunded and inadequate; is fraught with inequalities and inequities throughout the 168 [sic] local school districts; is ranked nationally in the lower 20-25% in virtually every category that is used to evaluate educational performance; and is not uniform among the districts in educational opportunities. (Rose v. Council for Better Education, Inc., p. 21)*

The constitutional issue was defined as greater than the equitable distribution of money. It was defined in terms of student equity and the effectiveness of the system overall. While the court clearly expected a "uniform" distribution of funds, it also expected a constitutionally "efficient" system to have more equitable outcomes for all children as measured against various standards other than per student expenditures.

> *The system of common schools must be adequately funded to achieve its goals. The system of common schools must be substantially uniform throughout the state. Each child, every child, in this Commonwealth must be provided with an equal opportunity to have an adequate education. Equality is the key word here. The children of the poor and the children of the rich, the children who live in the poor districts and*

the children who live in the rich districts must
be given the same opportunity and access to an
adequate education. (Rose v. Council for Better
Education, Inc., p 58)

In keeping with the emphasis on the *performance* of the system of common schools, Chief Justice Robert Stephens set forth in the majority opinion what the court considered to be the seven minimum learning outcomes of an efficient system of education:

> *. . . an efficient system of education must have as*
> *its goal to provide each and every child with at*
> *least the seven following capacities:*
> *(i) sufficient oral and written communi-*
> *cation skills to enable students to function in a*
> *complex and rapidly changing civilization;*
> *(ii) sufficient knowledge of economic,*
> *social, and political systems to enable the stu-*
> *dent to make informed choices;*
> *(iii) sufficient understanding of govern-*
> *mental processes to enable the student to*
> *understand the issues that affect his or her*
> *community, state, and nation;*
> *(iv) sufficient self-knowledge and knowl-*
> *edge of his or her mental and physical wellness;*
> *(v) sufficient grounding in the arts to en-*
> *able each student to appreciate his or her*
> *cultural and historical heritage;*
> *(vi) sufficient training or preparation for*
> *advanced training in either academic or voca-*
> *tional fields so as to enable each child to choose*
> *and pursue life work intelligently; and*
> *(vii) sufficient levels of academic or vo-*
> *cational skills to enable public school students*
> *to compete favorably with their counterparts in*
> *surrounding states, in academics or in the job*
> *market. (Rose v. Council for Better Education,*
> *Inc., p 59)*

It is significant that the court defined these capacities in terms of what students not only *know*, but also what they should be *able to do* with a public school education. When the justices concurred with Circuit Judge Ray Corns' opinion that schools should be expected to prepare children with certain capacities, they defined a constitutional standard for Kentucky's education system, i.e. "it must have as its goal to provide each and every child with at least these (seven) capacities." In other words, schools must serve a known public purpose. Efficient management and equitable funding are not sufficient in themselves to meet a test of constitutionality.

The justices may have thought they were leaving public policy to the General Assembly in this opinion, but their affirmation of these goals is clearly a statement of public policy. Publicly funded schools are not the private province of educators. In the view of this court, the constitutional mandate of an efficient system of common schools is to prepare young people to be knowledgeable, productive, and participatory members of society. Furthermore, schools are expected to have as their goal to achieve these outcomes for *each and every child*.

The principles of public policy contained in the court's opinion were the same ones underlying the restructuring policy assumptions I championed. The decision of the court could only advance the policy objectives I pursued whether or not the specifics of my proposal were ever adopted. In that sense I felt we now were in a position to move forward without the necessity of continuing a debate about whether to redesign or to merely improve the present system.

Responsibility for Education

In their opinion, the justices placed full responsibility for restructuring the education system on the General Assembly. In his opinion, Chief Justice Robert Stephens wrote:

*The sole responsibility for providing the system
of common schools is that of our General Assembly. It is a duty—it is a constitutional
mandate placed by the people on the 138 members of that body who represent these selfsame
people. (p 58)*

*Our job is to determine the constitutional valid-
ity of the system of common schools within the
meaning of the Kentucky Constitution, Section
183. We have done so. We have declared the
system of common schools to be unconstitutional. It is now up to the General Assembly to
re-create, and re-establish a system of common
schools within this state which will be in compliance with the Constitution. We have no doubt
they will proceed with their duty. (Rose v.
Council for Better Education, Inc., p 64)*

To further clarify the role of the legislature, the Chief Justice
wrote:

*The General Assembly must not only establish
the system, but it must monitor it on a continuing basis so that it will always be maintained in
a constitutional manner. The state must carefully supervise it, so that there is no waste, no
duplication, no mismanagement, at any level.
(Rose v. Council for Better Education, Inc., p
58)*

Clearly, Section 183 of the constitution required
that a mandate to "re-create and re-establish" a system of
public schools be placed on the branch of government which
can enact the laws required to create and finance a system of
common schools. However, recent history of the General
Assembly gave me little comfort here. The committee responsible for education legislation was also the one which had clung
so desperately to traditional views of the education system.

Could these same people now adopt a new perspective like the one envisioned in the court ruling? I was skeptical.

I was equally concerned about the court assigning the responsibility to "monitor the system" to the legislature, even though historically the General Assembly had delegated that role to the constitutional office of the superintendent of public instruction. But in a period of legislative independence, I anticipated correctly that the General Assembly would interpret this literally as a role which it should retain unto itself in the future. Justice Roy N. Vance dissented in part with the majority opinion and, among other things, shared the same concern:

> *I cannot agree with the majority that the constitution requires the General Assembly to monitor the school system to insure that schools are operated with no waste, mismanagement, or political influence. It is not possible for the General Assembly to oversee the day-to-day operation of the schools. In my view, the General Assembly has discharged its duty when it has provided by law for a school system which, if properly administered, will result in substantially equal educational opportunity throughout the Commonwealth. (Rose v. Council for Better Education, Inc.)*

I fully agreed with Justice Vance's concerns and expected a problem from only this one element of the majority opinion. It materialized when the legislative members of the governance committee of the Task Force on School Reform wanted to establish what eventually became the Office of Educational Accountability. At one point there was discussion of giving the Legislative Research Commission statutory authority to directly intervene in schools and perform other functions which clearly are executive in nature. I threatened to either veto the bill or sue the legislature later unless these onerous ideas were abandoned. Pursuing these ideas would have resulted in disaster. Anyone who understands the LRC staff understands they are not in a position to carry such responsibilities.

A Time for Unity

Justice William M. Gant, in his concurring opinion, wrote what probably was the sentiment of the majority in the court:

> *This decision has provided the Executive and Legislative branches of our government with a rare opportunity to start with a clean slate; to utilize the expertise of its members and others (both inside and outside the state) to study other jurisdictions which have faced a similar problem and successfully solved it; and to stamp a distinguished impression upon the pages of the history of the Commonwealth. Although adequate and additional funding is a necessary part of the contemplated procedure, money alone is not the answer. Efficiency of administration, curriculum, facilities, the ravages of inflation, and many other problems are extant and pleading for cure. (Rose v. Council for Better Education, Inc.)*

The task of totally rewriting a school code was a daunting one under the best of circumstances. No other state had faced a similar task. After months of wrangling over a strategy for improving education, the court gave to both branches a challenge to collectively design a new system of common schools. Given such an historic opportunity, it would have made no sense to have met just to reenact what had already been shown to have failed. It was a time when Kentucky could truly demonstrate to the nation what one state can do to reinvent a major institution of government when given the mandate to do so.

Agreement on a Strategy

The named defendants all received an advance copy of the opinion. Once I sensed its enormous historical significance, I knew the political dynamics would be dramatically changed. Blandford, Rose, and I agreed to have lunch the next day before holding a joint news conference. The discussion was wide-ranging, conciliatory and somber in the face of the enormous challenge before us.

This initial meeting was probably the most important of all the meetings I had with leadership over education. It was essential that I be in a position to exercise influence over the process and that I receive from legislative leadership a commitment not to turn this most important task over to the committee process. If leadership had decided to go it alone and just ask for my help in raising taxes, a political crisis of unprecedented proportions would have been inevitable. But I came away from this critical meeting feeling we had successfully passed the first threshold.

What was significant to me about that meeting was that no compromising or debate was required to reach agreement. There was no mention of "my program" or "their program." We truly did regard this as a historic time when the circumstances required us to lay down our swords and pull together for the common good. We knew no other governor or legislature had ever been given the opportunity to do so much for the people of the commonwealth in education. We still had a long way to go, but this was certainly a good beginning.

We stood together in the capitol rotunda with John Brock as a show of unity. In my public remarks I wanted to assure everyone that I was prepared to be a major player in the process and would not be an obstacle to progress. In my public statement I said:

> *The Supreme Court has given us an opportunity to start with a clean slate. Those of us in the*

executive and legislative branches are in agreement that we need to start from scratch. It is no longer a question of my plan or their plan. As of today, it's our plan. We will begin immediately to take up the issue of what kind of school system we can devise that meets the Supreme Court's guidelines of adequacy and uniformity. We are not looking back. We are moving ahead with our eyes only on the challenge of the future. We are of one heart and mind.

I want to make this final pledge. It is a pledge I have made to the General Assembly and I will make to the people of this Commonwealth. . . . When we can say to the people of this Commonwealth that we've built a better school system; when we can say to the people of this Commonwealth that their money is paying for improvement; when we can say that we have a system that is equitable and adequate for all children in Kentucky; a system, in other words, that provides equal opportunity for an adequate education, I will support the necessary revenue measures to pay for it. (Rose v. Council for Better Education, Inc.)

Notwithstanding my clear pledge to "support the necessary revenue measures to pay for it," some of my critics still thought I would be unwilling to raise the money needed to achieve equity and properly fund the entire system of education. In the next chapter I will discuss in detail my commitment to achieve equity in school funding and at the same time correct many of the fiscal ills which had long plagued the commonwealth.

The Task Force on School Reform

At the historic luncheon mentioned earlier, we agreed on several key matters. The Supreme Court had laid the mandate to create a new system of "common schools" directly on the General Assembly and assigned no specific role for the governor. However, both President pro tem Rose and Speaker Blandford agreed that my involvement was essential. We agreed to create a joint executive-legislative task force to carry out the work. We further agreed that the process had to be under our direct control and involve people in a position to make decisions. In this case that meant at a minimum legislative leadership in both chambers and top-ranking members of my administration.

We also agreed at that meeting that representatives of the various education interest groups and the superintendent of public instruction *should not* be members of this task force since they had a vested interest in keeping the system essentially unchanged except for more money. Finally, at my insistence, we agreed that the Senate and House Education Committees also had to be excluded from task force membership. I felt they were responsible for the system we had and would take this opportunity to reinforce what they had done in 1986 rather than truly restructure the system with fresh ideas. I also believed the education committees were dominated by the KEA, and their membership on the task force would give that organization more influence than I wanted it to have.

The Task Force on School Reform was originally to have fifteen members, five each from the House and Senate and five from the executive branch. This obviously included only legislative leadership. A few days after our meeting I learned that Blandford had unilaterally agreed to include the minority leaders from both chambers. Speaker Blandford then added the chairs of the education committees after pressure was put on him to do so. Finally the A&R Committee chairs were added. We eventually ended up with a task force of twenty-one members which consisted of five people to represent me, five members each from the Senate and House Democratic leadership, four House and Senate committee chairs, and one person selected by minority leadership from each chamber.

We initially were criticized in some quarters for not including John Brock, but he saw the political scenario that was emerging and did not complain publicly. Once the task force process was established I did agree to allow the remaining education committee members to be nonvoting participants in the task force committee meetings. However, most of them by this time were so alienated they did not take advantage of the opportunity when it finally was granted.

My Role in the Process

Left open at that initial meeting was the issue of whether or not I should be a member of the task force. Eck and Don probably took for granted that I would want to be on the Task Force so they didn't even raise the issue. It was a difficult decision touched with irony. After months of lobbying for fundamental change, I finally had moved the education debate from a discussion of how much money to spend to why the structure of the system had to be changed. Whether or not to be on the task force was a decision which would have potentially great impact politically and personally.

Some of my advisors thought my direct involvement on the task force could be a distraction to the important work which had to be done. It was their belief that I would continue to be a lightning rod for the media and everyone who opposed me politically or philosophically. Others were concerned that not being a member on the task force would give my critics an opportunity to say that I "stood on the sideline" and was a nonfactor in education reform in Kentucky.

Although a place in history is something every politician wants, I was more concerned about something else. If I were *not* a member of the task force, how could I be certain the product of the task force would be something I could support? I certainly didn't want to find myself in a position down the road where I would have to disavow the work of the task force. Such a circumstance most certainly would place this historical opportunity in jeopardy.

In the end, I decided not to place myself on the task force, a decision which no doubt came as a surprise to most people. I must admit it was not an easy one. However, after fully evaluating the situation, I agreed with those who thought my presence on the task force could be disruptive and distract from the important work it had to do. The issue was not whether I could make a meaningful contribution. I certainly thought I could. But the climate between the legislature and myself had grown so acrimonious, it didn't seem reasonable to believe that I could sit at the table with them and not find decisions being made based almost entirely on whether I was for or against something.

At this point, I felt there was an informal understanding between myself and leadership that my proposals would be included in some fashion in the final product. At this moment in history, it was far more important to do whatever had to be done to improve Kentucky schools than thrust myself into the process simply to get a share of the public credit for the end result. As for my concern about the end product, I would have to find less direct ways to influence the work of the task force than by being a working member of it. On this point, several key issues had to be resolved with legislative leadership before I could agree to not being a member. One issue dealt with how task force decisions would be made and the other dealt with the selection of consultants.

Before I publicly announced that I would not be an official member of the task force, I insisted that decisions of the task force *not* be made by formal vote. Clearly, the numbers were such that the legislative members would control every vote. Although we never made a public issue of it, we finally agreed that "straw votes" could be taken when necessary to get the sentiment of committee or task force members, but final positions on the legislation itself had to be acceptable to legislative leadership and myself. In effect this gave both sides a private veto that either of us could use if necessary to avoid a public rift over task force decisions which either of us could not support.

I recognized the important influence outside consultants would have on the legislative members of the task force. Given that I would not be a member, it was critical that the consultants guiding the task force deliberations be people who understood and would be supportive of the policy objectives for which we had worked so hard. Rose and Blandford agreed that any consultants hired by the task force would have to be acceptable to me, but waiting until a list was brought to me was too risky. I asked Jack Foster to get involved in the selection of the consultants to ensure they would be acceptable to us before there was closure on their selection.

Jack learned that L.R.C. staff had arranged a meeting in Chicago in mid-July with education experts from the National Governor's Association, National Conference on State Legislatures, and the Education Commission of the States to discuss candidates for the consultant positions. Since Jack was a personal friend and former colleague of all of the participants, he went to Chicago to be part of the discussion. The representatives of the three organizations were asked to prepare a prioritized list of consultants they would recommend. Jack was either personally acquainted with or knew something about most of the people on the list. It appeared that John Augenblick was the favored candidate in school finance and David Hornbeck was highly touted as the person to help with curriculum and related matters.

Mike Cohen, then director of NGA's education policy program, was very familiar with my ideas for restructuring and was a strong advocate for this approach. He also had been a speaker at the first education forum I held in Lawrenceburg in 1988. Mike and Jack discussed at the Chicago meeting the importance of getting the right person in all positions, but particularly in the curriculum committee position. Mike knew that David Hornbeck was probably the only one on the curriculum consultant list who shared our views and suggested that Jack meet with Hornbeck while they both were still in Chicago. Hornbeck was in Chicago at the time attending an ECS meeting. Mike helped get the two together later that afternoon.

Jack shared with Dr. Hornbeck my views on various education policy issues. Jack gave Hornbeck some of the documents I had prepared and discussed with him the need for assurance that the key ideas of restructuring I had advocated would be part of any legislation he proposed. Dr. Hornbeck agreed in principle with my views as described by Jack, but he wanted an opportunity to read the documents before committing himself. In a telephone call to Jack several days later, Hornbeck confirmed that we were all on the same wavelength. Jack was reasonably certain that Hornbeck was sincere and that we could count on him to support the key ideas in our restructuring plan.

At this point I felt a level of comfort in knowing that the key consultants were supportive of the approach I wanted taken. However, there remained a concern that certain legislative members of the Task Force might oppose even their own consultant if they thought he was acting directly on my behalf. As it turned out, ideas like site-based decision making and a performance-based curriculum and assessment program were adopted by the Governance and Curriculum Committees with only modest resistance. The Curriculum Committee recommended that the Council on School Performance be reconvened by statute to continue its work on the learner outcomes and to recommend a new assessment system to support them.

The financial incentive for improved student learning was perhaps the most controversial element of my restructuring proposal. To his credit, Dr. Hornbeck took enormous heat from some members of the committee over his insistence that the new system include strong "rewards and sanctions." He personally believed this was an essential element and stuck to his guns on it. In the end, the approach which was implemented in KERA had all the key elements of the reward system proposed in my restructuring plan.

As the work of the task force moved forward, I monitored everything that happened. I was especially pleased that at no time was it necessary to get publicly involved in order to assure that Kentucky came up with a truly restructured system of education. For the most part, the process went smoothly. There were several instances when I had to have my representatives on the Governance Committee take strong positions against certain proposals which I could not support. In particular, I had concerns about the role given to any legislative body created to have oversight of schools. I also had a problem with a proposal by certain legislators that the new state board of education be appointed directly by the General Assembly.

At several points the rift within the committee got so deep that I was concerned we might end up with something I would have to openly oppose. Unlike the situation in other committees, the consultants to this committee didn't seem able to control the process, or they simply failed to recognize the problems these ideas would create. Fortunately, these issues were resolved without my having to go public with my concerns. The process went smoothly from my standpoint largely because we made certain at the outset that the consultants would be advocates of what I wanted to see happen.

In retrospect I must admit that the politics of special interest was rougher than even I had anticipated. Special interests have become entrenched in the legislative process and make it very difficult to achieve real change in public policy. No matter how hard you work to explain and justify your position, it comes down in the end to hard-ball politics. I sincerely believe that Dr. Hornbeck, who often is cited as the "author" of KERA, would have had little chance of selling the legislature on ideas like rewards and sanctions, site-based decision making, a performance-based curriculum and testing program, and family and youth resource centers if I had not made these ideas a matter of public debate for many months before he ever set foot in Kentucky.

Change is extremely difficult. No doubt many will look back on this period and give the Supreme Court credit for setting the stage for school reform in Kentucky. Certainly the Supreme Court played an historic role in breaking the political gridlock over education reform, but the politics of change would have worked against the kind of reform law we finally adopted had I not made the need to totally restructure the education system a major political issue. Certainly the belief that I would not support the end product with increased revenue unless most (if not all) of my concerns were addressed in the legislation provided the political leverage needed to ensure that many of the ideas education experts now acclaim as so progressive would be present. I am very proud of Kentucky. Other states have had court mandates which produced little or no change in the system. In the end we produced the real model for restructuring the nation's schools.

X. EDUCATION:
EQUITY IN FUNDING

From the time public schools were first created in Kentucky, the issue of how to finance them adequately has been a matter of continuous debate in the legislature. A review of the history of education in Kentucky reveals there never has been a time when financial resources were thought to be adequate. I knew the struggle with the legislature and education establishment would not be over a need to make funding more adequate and equitable. Rather, the debate would center on whether it was necessary to revamp totally the existing approach to school finance to reach that goal.

In my view, there were sound policy reasons for fundamentally changing the present method of financing schools. On the other hand, we had to make changes in the way education was financed within the context of an overall fiscal and tax policy for state government. Education makes up almost two-thirds of the general fund budget, so major changes in the funding of education have a direct and profound affect on every other public service. The decisions we made about school finance had to fit into a larger framework for state fiscal and tax policy and other revenue needs of the state.

A draft document containing my ideas for school finance reform had been on my desk for almost a year. Due to the prolonged, contentious debate over school restructuring, it was never published, so my position on many of the issues was not generally known. About all that people thought they knew about my position was that I would refuse to raise taxes no matter what the consequences. In one sense this might have been to my advantage. Opponents were unable to subject my ideas to long debate or hold them hostage to the reforms of 1985-86.

Why the Present School Finance System Had to Change

The Minimum Foundation Program was the basic vehicle for funding public schools in Kentucky. The foundation program was created in the 1950s to guarantee a "minimum" amount of money per pupil. A school district received a salary grant based upon the number of classroom "units" taught by teachers with various levels of education and years of experience in the system. The classroom units varied somewhat from the lower to upper grades, but the unit funded was teachers and not students. Additional money for administration, operating expenses, and instructional materials also were allocated using the same classroom units.

My analysis of the foundation program showed that it was responsible for most of the disparity in funding among Kentucky schools. The structure of the program was such that it fostered the great disparity in the money available per child from one school district to another. Here were my concerns about the foundation program as it was implemented in Kentucky.

First, the foundation program was essentially a teacher salary subsidy program. Teacher salary funds made up about 70 percent of the total amount of money distributed through the program. The level of funding for the program was determined primarily by the state minimum salary schedule rather than by student instructional needs. The salary scale was determined by demographic and educational characteristics of the teaching staff, so some school districts received more money than others only because their teaching staff had longer tenure in the system or held more advanced degrees, which in turn entitled these districts to a larger salary subsidy.

Second, the foundation formula did not take into account the local district's contribution. Foundation money was distributed as though it was an entitlement program. Neither a demonstration of need nor the ability to raise local money were factored into the foundation formula. Rich and poor districts were treated alike even though they were not similarly situated in terms of their ability to raise funds locally with a comparable level of effort.

Third, there were great differences in the value of the available tax base and a wide range in tax rates levied by local school boards. A tax rate of $0.26 per $100 assessed property value in Fayette County, one of the most property-rich counties in Kentucky, raised $771 per student in 1988, whereas the same tax rate in Elliott County, one of Kentucky's poorest counties, yielded $117 per student, a ratio of about 7 to 1. Every time Fayette county increased its tax *rate* by a penny, Elliott County fell behind Fayette County at a rate of $7 to $1 even if it increased its millage by the same penny.

In summary, nearly all of the variance in the amount of money available for the "typical" student could be attributed to three factors: (a) the number of teachers at each salary rank and longevity level; (b) the amount of money raised per mil of property tax levied by the school district; and (c) differences in the millage of property tax levied by the school district. The foundation program made no adjustment for distortions in the amount of money available per student that were created by any of these factors.

An Earlier Attempt to Remediate Inequity

A special program was created by the General Assembly in the 1970s to offset the disparity the foundation program created. The Power Equalization Program, as it was named, attempted to "equalize" the local revenue derived from the same tax *rate* when applied to a different tax *base*. The equalization program was easy to administer compared to the foundation program. The assessed value of property in a school district was divided by the number of students in the district. The state then allocated the money appropriated to the program according to the ratio of each district's revenue capacity to that of the state's two wealthiest school districts, Fayette County and Anchorage.

At the time I reviewed the program, we were "equalizing" a tax rate of about $0.13 in Fayette County. Since the state required a $0.25 mil local school tax rate to participate in the program, less than half of what was required in local effort was being equalized by the state. Furthermore, the $0.25 mil rate was well below the $0.55 mil (excluding millage for construction) in Fayette County at the time. Given the rapid growth in property values in Fayette County, the state equalization program fell further behind each year. More money had to be appropriated each legislative session just to keep equalization from falling below the level of the previous biennium. Trying to keep up with Fayette County's ability or willingness to raise money for schools was clearly the wrong benchmark for an equity policy. There had to be a better way to equalize funding.

The approach to equity taken by the legislature when the power equalization program was created probably represented the wisdom of the time, but it had the practical effect of creating two school finance programs in Kentucky. Political considerations probably made it much easier for the legislature to create a new program rather than reform the foundation program. The amount of money invested in the equalization program was a fraction of the amount appropriated through the foundation program, so the ratio of equalization money to the money spent creating the disparity almost guaranteed that the goal of equity could never be met.

Power Equalization Was Not the Solution

There were several reasons why I did not want to continue the bifurcated financing system. First of all, the equalization program did not adequately redress the inequities created by the much larger foundation program. Second, there would forever be two ways to fund schools since there was no provision for the historically disadvantaged schools to ever escape the dual funding scheme. The latter situation was compounded by the fact that the state imposed different rules on the use of equalized funds than applied to foundation program funds. All school districts were allowed to use local funds in any manner they chose, but the state equalization money was strictly controlled by the state.

It was clear to me the state was using the equalization mechanism for other policy objectives beyond achieving equity. The finances of school districts which happened to be located in economically impoverished areas were being subjected to greater external control than those with a wealthier tax base. These poorer school districts were treated as if they were receiving something they didn't deserve and warranted more supervision as a result. Being poor was equated with being inept.

In my view, the policy objective of an equitable school finance program should be to *eliminate* the "financially disadvantaged" distinction rather than to perpetuate it indefinitely. Continuing to maintain two methods of funding schools, one of which is based solely on economic disadvantage, would never achieve that objective. Eventually a "fiscal schizophrenia" would evolve as these districts tried to cope with administration of two major sources of funds, each with different regulations governing their use. Continuation of the power equalization program would make permanent welfare subjects out of the poorer school districts.

A Proposal for Reform

A system of school finance must be equitable among schools, taxpayers, and students. Court cases in other states and experts on school finance generally agree that "equity" must be viewed from three perspectives:

    a) equity in the level of resources available to educate each "typical" child;

    b) equity among communities in the level of local effort put forth to support their schools; and

c) a recognition that some children have unique learning needs which require resources beyond those needed for the "typical" child.

The Kentucky approach to financing schools failed to satisfy these criteria for more reasons than underfunding.

The approach I wanted to pursue would abolish the existing minimum foundation and power equalization programs and create a "power equalized" finance program which established a minimum funding level for every student without regard to the salary levels of the teaching staff. The state would take into account how much the local school district could contribute toward that minimum funding level at a specific, uniform property tax rate set by the state. State funds would then make up the difference between the local contribution and the guaranteed minimum. This approach would ensure a uniform financial base for every *student*, regardless of their residence.

I realized that equity in educational opportunity did not mean treating every child the same. More resources are required to support the unique educational services for children with special needs. The federal government for many years has provided money to states to support special educational services to children with handicapping conditions or who come from impoverished social and economic conditions. These programs all require a state contribution which is allocated in tandem with the federal funds. In the new foundation program, these state and federal funds would be distributed based on the identification of specific children deserving of the extra support rather than through the foundation formula.

Equity for Taxpayers

Several other issues had to be addressed if the new school finance program was to be equitable to *taxpayers*. Property is the most stable indicator of community wealth and is widely used as an index for determining the level of local effort to support public schools. It would continue to be the best index to use to establish the level of local support desired. However, a school finance program which uses local property taxes for school purposes has to assume the tax system itself is equitable.

In spite of several rulings by the Kentucky Supreme Court, real property still was not assessed uniformly throughout the state. The state was gradually gaining greater control over administration of the assessment process, but certainly more needed to be done in this area. The property assessment issue could appropriately be dealt with as part of school finance reform, but the problems associated with inequitable property tax administration also needed to be part of a larger package of tax reforms.

Linking Compensation to Performance

One other issue of importance to me was my proposal to provide a financial reward to the faculty and staff of schools which demonstrated continuing improvement in the educational success of their students. Various ways to create a compensation system more closely associated with personal performance had been debated nationally for at least a decade.

I had no objection to the state setting a minimum salary level for teachers, but I could not support a compensation system which financially rewarded people for just hanging around or for putting in "seat time" taking graduate courses at some university. In my opinion, the policy governing teacher compensation had to be changed. My approach was to provide a cash "bonus" to those teachers who *collectively* met certain performance goals. I thought this was a much sounder approach than programs like a career ladder or a personal merit system.

Other Views of School Finance

School finance equity was not addressed in the special legislative session on school reform in 1985, or in the regular session in 1986, except to increase the amount of money appropriated to the power equalization program. The General Assembly did create by resolution a Task Force on School Finance. The task force consisted of House and Senate Education Committee members, representatives of the major education interest groups, the Department of Education, and Sandy Gubser of Governor Collins' office. Sandy was a deputy secretary in the Education and Humanities Cabinet in my administration, and I later appointed her as the first secretary of the new Workforce Development Cabinet created in 1990.

The Task Force on School Finance, Chaired by Rep. Joe Barrows, completed its work in December 1987, but its report was not published by LRC until just before a so-called "education summit" was convened in February, 1989. The consultant for the task force was Dr. James Melton, a school finance expert formerly with the Kentucky Department of Education. It was interesting to note that most of the task force recommendations dealt with technical elements of the school finance program such as teacher salaries, building needs, district organization, textbooks, and the like. It appeared that the mindset of the task force members was only to tinker with the present system. There was an admission that a foundation program based on classroom units had serious deficiencies, but the members were split on what to do about these deficiencies. The basic conclusion coming from this group was that the present approach was only in need of refinement and a higher level of funding.

Between the time the Task Force on School Finance completed its deliberations and before publication of its report, another report on school finance was prepared. After announcing his preliminary findings on the school finance suit on May 31, 1988, Judge Ray Corns of the Franklin Circuit Court ordered formation of a select committee to advise him on the issues that should be addressed in his final order. The committee, made up of John Brock, Larry Forgy, James Melton, Sylvia Watson, and Kern Alexander, submitted its report to Judge Corns on September 15, 1988. Corns' formal ruling on October 14, 1988, incorporated some elements of the select committee report.

I was not surprised that Dr. Kern Alexander was appointed to chair the select committee. Kern was president of Western Kentucky University at the time and a highly regarded expert on school finance. He had been involved in school finance issues in other states prior to coming to Kentucky and had a reputation of being open to new ideas. Along with Bert Combs, Kern was an advisor to the Council for Better Education which filed the law suit seeking to have the way schools are funded in Kentucky declared unconstitutional..

The report of the select committee was helpful, but the committee was constrained in the recommendations it could offer. The report Kern prepared for Judge Corns did not get into specific details of how the finance system should be changed, since that would be beyond the prerogative of the judicial branch. But Kern had ideas of his own which called for much more change than the other members of the select committee would have supported.

As part of a visit to Western Kentucky University during my first year in office, I had the opportunity to have dinner with Kern. We talked at some length about what he personally thought Kentucky should do to correct the disparity in funding of schools. I indicated my desire to see a major change in approach and asked for his views on some of my ideas. It was clear to me then that I was on the right track. As we concluded our discussion, I suggested that he and Jack Foster get together to develop a set of proposals for me to consider. The two men met in Frankfort shortly thereafter and came away from the meeting realizing they held similar views about what needed to be done.

It is interesting to note in retrospect that upon learning of the Supreme Court decision, some members of the select committee thought the court had gone too far. All they thought was needed was an order requiring the governor and legislature to raise taxes and put more money into education. They were not interested in major changes in the way the funds were allocated and certainly didn't expect to have the entire statutory basis for education eliminated. Even Judge Combs told me that he thought we had done more than was needed to satisfy the court and that the Supreme Court justices had gone too far.

Without a doubt the Council for Better Schools got more than it expected from its legal action seeking equity in funding. But one thing was clear to me. While many ideas were being offered on school finance, none of them required a fundamental change in the way public education was financed in Kentucky.

Support from the Task Force Consultant

I was obviously pleased with the selection of John Augenblick as the consultant to the Finance Committee of the Task Force on School Reform. I knew Augenblick's ideas on school finance were consistent with my own and that he would be open to my suggestions. His credentials in school finance were excellent, and he clearly was not satisfied with the structure Kentucky had been using. Early in the process Jack met privately with Augenblick to share ideas. Jack was satisfied that Augenblick would recommend a finance proposal very similar to the one I had envisioned. Quite frankly, I would have found any consultant unacceptable who was not in agreement with our basic policy approach.

Nevertheless, the first steps toward reforming school finance were not promising. It appeared in the early going that the Finance Committee of the Task Force on School Reform was not using Augenblick to work out a proposal, but simply to send up "trial balloons" instead. Meanwhile, Merl

Hackbart, my budget director at the time and member of the Finance Committee with Jack Foster, was preoccupied with the budget process and the legislative session. It was obvious as we moved toward consensus on curriculum issues that I would have to take a more active role in finance deliberations to keep them headed in the direction I wanted them to go.

Agreement is Reached with Legislators

Jack Foster had prepared a computer model of the finance structure being considered by the committee. We had a good handle on the projected cost of the program by mid-February, so I sent word to Mike Moloney and Joe Clarke, the two legislative budget chairs, that we needed to meet to set the final budget figures. By the end of February 1990, I had reached agreement with Sen. Moloney and Rep. Clarke on the basic elements of the Support Education Excellence in Kentucky (SEEK) program, which replaced the minimum foundation and power equalization programs.

The SEEK program had all the key elements I wanted in a school finance program: (a) a guaranteed amount for every child set by the General Assembly; (b) a uniform minimum local tax effort; (c) the revenue produced by the uniform local effort is credited toward the guaranteed amount and then the state makes up the difference; and (d) additional money is provided for children with special needs on a qualifying basis.

The connection between the foundation program and teacher salaries was severed, although we agreed to retain a minimum salary schedule to prevent an unreasonable lowering of a teacher's salary for political reasons. There also was a requirement that a performance-based salary schedule be developed by the Kentucky Department of Education before the next legislative session, something which I do not believe was ever done. The SEEK program had other refinements which I could readily support. A struggle never developed

---

between myself and the legislature over whether it should be "my way or their way" on school finance. All that remained now was to agree on the level of funding.

Agreement on Funding

When the executive budget for fiscal years 1990-92 was prepared, I had to estimate what would be needed to properly fund the new programs envisioned by the task force. I used projections we had developed to determine the amount of money needed to close the equity gap and to fund other things as well. I set aside $263 million in new money for equity in addition to planned increases in the foundation program. I then added about $100 million for new programs to support the reforms envisioned by the task force. At the time the budget was made, many KERA initiatives had not been finalized. Even so, given other commitments in the budget, the ultimate bottom line would not be very negotiable, regardless of what the task force finally decided.

I invited Mike Moloney, Joe Clarke, John Augenblick (the finance committee consultant), and Tom Willis of the LRC staff to meet with me and my staff at the Governor's Mansion to work out the final numbers. It was my goal to fund as much of the equity as practical in the first biennium of the program. There had been too much disappointment in the past when such decisions were delayed. Any future increase in the level of funding would have to come from growth in revenues rather than another increase in taxes.

In the first meeting we set the initial guaranteed amount per student for the first two years of the new SEEK program. We set it high enough to cover roughly 80 percent or more of the inequity, with the rest to be achieved in the following biennium. As it turned out, we could not have wisely spent more than the amount I had budgeted for the first two years of the SEEK program. The numbers indicated that the amount of state money some districts would receive if the SEEK were fully funded would more than double.

We readily agreed that no district should get an increase in funds so large it would likely be wasted, a distinct possibility. We decided, therefore, that no district should receive more than a 25 percent increase in state funds in any single year of the program, even though this would mean that some of the poorest school districts would get less than the guaranteed amount per student in the initial years of the program.

We also quickly agreed to increase the uniform local equivalent tax rate from $0.25 to $.30 per $100 assessed property value *exclusive* of taxes dedicated to debt service. We found many districts had met the original $0.25 minimum millage, but most of the money went to retire building debt rather than for instruction. In some communities, this meant local tax rates had to be increased more than the $0.05 to meet the minimum local effort we expected. But the provision to exclude debt service ensured that each school district put forth the same level of effort to support instruction. A uniform rate for instructional purposes assures equity among taxpayers, since the level of effort is determined by the amount of the tax *rate*, not the amount of *money* it produces.

As an incentive for communities voluntarily to increase the local effort beyond the mandated minimum, we agreed to equalize money raised locally from millage above the mandated amount up to 15 percent of the state-guaranteed amount for every child. This became known as "Tier I" funding above the SEEK guarantee. We had a lot of discussion about how much money to appropriate for this part of the SEEK, since we had no idea how many districts would use this option. As it turned out, we grossly underestimated the willingness of local school boards to raise taxes even more than the required $0.05 mil and unfortunately did not appropriate enough money to fully fund this provision of the finance program.

We had extensive discussions on two crucial issues: whether to cap the amount of money local schools should be permitted to raise, and whether to apply a "hold harmless" policy toward districts which would get less state money under SEEK than they received from the old foundation and equalization programs. I did not favor putting a cap on local effort for several reasons. You have to cap either a tax rate or the amount of money that can be raised. Clearly, it would be difficult to regulate either one. Furthermore, I felt it sent the wrong message to the public.

Augenblick contended that not having a cap on maximum local spending could lead to imbalance once again and future litigation. A review of the impact a cap might have on various school districts showed that it was unlikely any district would reach the proposed cap in the near future, so I agreed to cap the dollar amount at 15 percent above the combined state guaranteed level and the 15 percent Tier I incentive amount.

The "hold harmless" proposal was more contentious. I had a problem with continuing to increase state funding *above the SEEK formula* to the wealthiest districts beyond a brief transition period. I took the position that the state should not commit itself to forever subsidizing the wealthier school districts above what they were entitled to under the SEEK formula. A better policy would be to use extra funds to steadily increase the guaranteed amount for all schools until the disparity was eliminated.

Legislative leaders were concerned that it would be difficult to pass a large tax package in the name of education if the two most populous counties were not guaranteed to get something significant out of it. The argument was made that no schools in Kentucky were adequately funded, so we needed to do something for even the best-funded schools. Such were the political realities of reaching "equity."

The initial understanding was that we would freeze the state amount at the 1989-90 funding level for the first four years, when the new school finance program would be phased in. At the end of the four years, no district should receive hold harmless funds from the state. It was estimated that the primary impact would be a reduction in the *rate* of income growth for these districts, most of which was coming from the increase in state funds anyway. Furthermore, these districts also had the greatest opportunity to experience a natural growth in revenues due to local economic activity to help offset any possible reduction in state funds. We decided to limit hold harmless funding to the four years.

A Last-Minute Glitch

Just how precarious negotiations on school finance were became obvious when legislative committee hearings began on the education appropriation. Action was taken in committee to require local districts to provide at least a 10 percent salary increase in FY 1990-91 for teachers *in all districts* regardless of the amount the district received under the SEEK program or under the hold harmless provision. Such an idea had never been discussed in my earlier meetings with legislative finance committee members.

The legislative committee's action was obviously an attempt by legislators beholden to KEA to get a larger salary increase for teachers in the wealthier school districts than might have been provided through the SEEK or the additional 5 percent hold harmless money. After some negotiation, the increase was reduced to 8 percent, the hold harmless provision in HB 940 was ignored, and the SEEK appropriation was increased by an amount sufficient to cover the additional cost. The salary issue was a sobering reminder that special interest politics was still alive and well in Frankfort. Far too many educators saw "reform" only in terms of more money. Furthermore, the more populous urban regions of the state had to make certain they got something in return for their agreement to let the others try to catch up.

I considered the creation of the Kentucky Successful Schools Trust Fund to pay for rewards to schools an important policy victory, so I wanted it funded in 1990 even though the rewards would not be granted until sometime in the next biennium. I wanted to make sure money would be there when the time came, and putting the money into a trust fund did that. We appropriated $30 million in the first biennium as a show of good faith to teachers. A formula for distribution of the rewards would be worked out later, but wording in HB 940 gave guidance to that process.

Crossing the Horizon on School Reform

It was gratifying to me, after so many months of contentious debate over education reform, that I now was in a position to do something very concrete to improve the educational opportunity of all Kentucky's citizens. The breadth and innovativeness of the ideas emerging from the Task Force on School Reform gave me hope that we would come up with something I could support without reservation. That hope was fulfilled on March 8, 1990, when the task force approved the draft HB 940, later known as KERA, and sent it to the House and Senate for action.

My critics have suggested that I had to be dragged kicking and screaming to the decision to raise new revenue, and my only role in education reform was to "get out of the way" of a tax increase. I would never have raised taxes, so their reasoning goes, if it had not been for the Supreme Court decision on education. In reality, we probably could have raised far less money and satisfied the court. Furthermore, in my mind it is entirely possible that the court would not have ruled the way it did if it were not for the emphasis I had placed on the need to change the *entire* system of education, not just how it is financed. That was the issue which had dominated the political debate over how to improve education for almost two years.

As I will discuss further in a moment, the revenue package to support the reform had to accomplish more than simply yield more money. It had to bring with it reform of the entire revenue structure of state government as well. I was determined to make that one of the hallmarks of my administration. But the struggle over school reform was only the first battle leading up to the next one to overcome resistance to my proposed revenue package.

Equity Expanded to Higher Education

The budget recommendations for higher education in the 1988-90 biennium were interpreted by some in the colleges and universities as a bias on my part against them. I will admit that I had then, and still have, reservations about how many of our universities spend their money. Nonetheless, I was fully aware of the serious financial inequities which existed among the institutions in the higher education system. With all the focus on reforming the elementary and secondary school system, there had been little public debate about the inequities in higher education funding. Even though the Supreme Court did not address that situation, I wanted the funding disparity in higher education remedied at the same time we dealt with inequities among public schools.

I took this opportunity to redress these inequities to an extent not done by any previous governor. Unlike the finance approach in the K-12 system, the Council on Higher Education approves the budget for the system and recommends it to both the governor and legislature. The council then becomes an advocate for the budget request when it comes before the legislature. The governor can ignore these requests and submit a different budget, just as I did in 1988, but governors have no authority over the university budgets or how they are administered at the institutional level. These decisions are reserved for the university boards and their presidents.

Some years earlier, the Council on Higher Education developed a formula for funding the various universities in the system after the legislature decided it was politically difficult to deal with the university presidents directly. The amount of money requested by the individual universities in Kentucky was justified primarily in terms of what their benchmark counterparts received in other states. I never liked a formula-driven, automatic-pilot funding program. I believe our spending decisions should be judged against our own priorities, not by what other states might be able or willing to spend on higher education.

The reasons given for retaining the funding formula were basically political ones. The regional universities had a better chance in the legislature if their requests were buffered by a neutral body, in this case the Council on Higher Education. I realized early on that trying to restructure finance in higher education was not a fight I wanted at this time. On the other hand, I did want to eliminate the interinstitutional funding inequities. Universities were funded at different levels in reference to their own benchmarks. I was told the formula was supposed to remedy this inequity over time, but I saw no way the fast-growing community college system would be funded at or near its benchmark level any time soon under the formula.

In my opinion the community colleges were dollar for dollar the best higher education buy in the commonwealth. They had done more per student with less than any other higher education entity. I insisted that the community colleges get their "fair share" as I worked to break the formula approach which had distorted funding decisions. I threatened to fund the community colleges outside the formula, which none of the university presidents wanted to happen. They were so scared that I would "break" the formula they conceded on this point, even though they detested it. The University of Kentucky was less interested in funding the community colleges than they were the main campus. I was able to get the community colleges funded on a parity with the other higher education entities for the first time in their history. They were no longer funded as stepchildren.

Higher education represents a significant part of the budget, so I wanted to get the higher education appropriation request settled as early as possible. Late in December 1989 I met with the university presidents to determine how much of an increase in funding they thought they needed for operating expenses and capital projects in the next biennium. We agreed on an increase of about 18.5 percent in operating funds for the 1990-92 biennium, the largest increase they had received in many years. This would bring all the universities and the community colleges up to at least 90 percent of their benchmark level, with some up to as much as 97 percent, and would virtually eliminate the disparity in funding among the universities and community colleges. In addition to the large increase in operating funds, I also developed a capital projects budget for the universities and community colleges which totaled more than $100 million.

Increasing Access to Higher Education

In the Summer of 1988, I was invited to a meeting of the Education Commission of the States in New Orleans to talk about my ideas on school reform. In one of the sessions, I listened to Louisiana businessman Patrick Taylor tell about his effort to get disadvantaged students to complete high school by offering to pay for their college education. He called them "Taylor's Kids" and gave them T-shirts and other items which publicly identified them as aspirants for college.

At first Mr. Taylor did this with his own money, but he then tried unsuccessfully to get the Louisiana legislature to adopt the program by paying for at least the first two years of college for disadvantaged students. I commented at the time that every state should be willing to guarantee access to at least 14 years of education. I had a hard time understanding why we should not do this for all students.

When I got back to Frankfort, I inquired about what Kentucky was doing in this regard. We had a grant-in-aid and loan program which was grossly underfunded and was based primarily on the financial need of students who wanted to go on to college or a university. The program was intended to supplement other student aid programs, and it was not a *carte blanche* guarantee that any student who wanted to go on to higher education would not be prohibited from doing so for financial reasons. I thought we could do better than this.

Later that year I proposed a new effort called the "College Access Program" to assure that every student who wanted to enroll in a college or university in Kentucky could afford to do so. We had a community college system which brought higher education within easy driving distance of everyone in the state, but some families still could not afford to send their children to college. It was inequitable that many of these families were paying taxes so other children could attend college while they could not afford to send their own.

The College Access Program was a tuition and book subsidy for freshmen and sophomores enrolling in any public or private college or university in Kentucky based on the Pell Grant income formula. I was determined to guarantee access to 14 years of education to every citizen of the Commonwealth. In the 1990-92 budget I proposed that $12 million new dollars be added to the grant-in-aid program for this specific purpose. I was as proud of that as anything. I wish it had been available when I was trying to attend the university the first time.

XI. A BETTER
FISCAL FUTURE

One of my goals as governor was to correct the persistent fiscal problems of state government. Revenue estimation errors, overly ambitious budgets, economic malaise, and an eroded tax base all had contributed over the years to chronic revenue problems in state government. The seriousness of the revenue problem was demonstrated in stark terms in 1988 when I was forced to prepare the most austere state budget in nearly a decade.

Kentucky had suffered for many decades from an irrational tax structure. The long-term solution to Kentucky's fiscal problems required more than to simply raise tax *rates* on the same tax base, a policy previous administrations and legislatures had pursued for years. A change in the basic approach to taxation at all levels had to be made, and I had a unique opportunity to do it. Raising more revenue is never politically easy, but when it is necessary it should be done in a responsible manner. As in education, I saw the opportunity to do more than just raise more money. I saw the opportunity to revitalize the revenue base and restore the capacity of the commonwealth to meet its growing economic, educational, and social needs.

Increased Tax Productivity vs. Increased Rates

The "productivity" of a given tax is measured in terms of the amount of revenue actually produced compared to what the base is capable of producing if it is fully taxed. The productivity of general revenue taxes in Kentucky has steadily declined over the years due primarily to the practice of granting tax exemptions to various taxpayer groups. From a revenue

...dpoint, this means that whatever is being taxed yields less than the full amount of revenue it is capable of producing.

The consequence of these tax exemptions is that the state must find other sources of revenue to make up for the lower tax productivity. The general tax burden remains the same; it is only shifted from one taxpayer or tax base to another. Before raising *rates* for a particular tax, it is incumbent that policy makers examine the *productivity* of that tax. In other words, determine if it is producing all the revenue of which it is capable.

The most popular thing a politician can ever do is *reduce* taxes, and the easiest way to do that is to grant an exemption to an existing tax. Many tax credits or exemptions were created for purely political reasons and served no identifiable public policy objective. Individually, a tax credit or exemption appears to have only a marginal effect on state revenues, but collectively they represent a major loss of revenue with no economic or policy benefit to the state.

In light of the enormous need for more revenue to support basic programs like education, the first step in a search for increased revenue had to begin with an examination of the public benefit gained from tax expenditures associated with each tax base before considering a general increase in the tax *rate* assessed against that tax base.

Tax Exemptions and Credits as Public Expenditures

From a budget standpoint, all tax exemptions or credits are considered "tax expenditures," meaning they are equivalent to budgeted program expenditures except there is no exchange of money between the recipient and the government. Government decides to forego a certain amount of income to achieve some public purpose. In some instances the exemptions are justified in the name of equity. In other instances the tax system rather than a government appropriation is used to advance a public policy. The key point here is that tax expenditures should be made to further a public purpose, not just to give tax relief to certain special interests of political importance to public officials.

Tax credits and exemptions can be effective tools to advance a public policy. IRAs, tax free bonds, tax credits for training low skilled workers or for locating businesses in certain areas are well known examples of tax incentives. Most states provide tax incentives of some kind to attract and hold business and industry. Although I was critical of the cost of the Toyota deal, I fully recognized the role tax concessions play in attracting and retaining business and industry. Generally, it is preferable to provide such incentives through tax expenditures than direct grants. Taxpayers may look at tax incentives as "tax breaks," but from a policy perspective they are considered public investments just like those made through budgeted appropriations.

A *Tax Expenditure Analysis* report, prepared in January 1989 for me by Secretary of Finance L. Rogers Wells, identified almost $2.4 billion in exemptions and tax credits in FY 1988-89. This amount of revenue was spent before it was ever received. Unlike direct appropriations, which must be continually reviewed and approved by the General Assembly to remain in effect, tax expenditures are rarely examined once the tax code is amended. Tax expenditures are made "off the top" before any consideration is given to other government programs.

It was my opinion that many of these tax expenditures would not receive the same priority if they had to compete with programs more directly funded in the appropriation process. That is to say, if one had to choose between continuing a tax exemption or increasing the direct funding of a program, the decision might yield a different result. As I examined the various exemptions and credits on the law books, it was obvious that politically powerful constituencies had been successful in gaining tax advantages for themselves with no clear public purpose in mind.

I firmly believed Kentucky could satisfy most of its revenue needs through a broader application of existing taxes at *present* rates rather than by increasing the rates for people already paying these taxes. In most instances, a tax *increase* means an increase in the tax *rate*. In the education debate, I was confronted repeatedly with proposals to raise tax *rates*. I would respond that I would raise the needed revenue, but it was not my intention to "raise taxes" which I knew always meant in their terms *raise tax rates*. I chose this rhetoric carefully to deflect the common perception that the only way to increase revenue was to raise tax *rates*.

Everyone had a difficult time understanding the difference between increasing revenue by extending an existing tax to taxpayers presently exempted and raising rates on those already paying the tax. Of course, a tax increase is in the eye of the beholder. If you're asked to pay a tax from which you were previously exempted, you no doubt regard that as an increase in your taxes. Eliminating a tax credit or exemption can be just as politically difficult as raising tax rates, and in certain instances it has proven to be even more difficult. Undoubtedly that is why it always seemed easier to just pass a rate increase rather than take away a tax advantage from an influential political constituency.

In the past, tax policy in Kentucky always seemed to focus on increasing the *rate* of an existing tax rather than improving the *productivity* of the tax. Ironically, tax *rate* increases often were accompanied by rate adjustments and the granting of new exemptions which in turn reduced the amount of revenue the increased tax rate could have produced. I wanted to change that practice in favor of a tax policy which improved the productivity of the tax structure at present rates before looking at the need to raise the rate for those already paying the tax.

A Revenue Revitalization Program

I began early in my administration to prepare for the revenue revitalization program I proposed to the General Assembly in the 1990 session. The three major tax bases— property, income, and goods and services—would be the target for increased tax productivity. Each tax base required a different approach, but the overall policy that guided the development of my revenue revitalization proposal was to expand the productivity of existing taxes before giving consideration to raising tax rates.

The revenue proposal I finally came up with had the following key elements. First, it adjusted the personal income tax to conform to the federal tax code; eliminated the deductibility of federal income taxes; and granted a low income tax credit to offset any increase in tax burden due to the first two actions. Second, it broadened the sales tax to include selected services currently exempted. Third, it increased the tax rate on cigarettes and corporate income. Only the last action actually changed tax *rates*. The program was designed to raise over $1 billion in new revenue for the 1990-92 biennium. From a fiscal policy perspective, it put an emphasis on those taxes which are most likely to keep pace with economic growth in future years. Of equal importance, it was designed to improve the fairness of the tax structure overall.

Among other things, the program implemented the "no tax *rate* increase" element of my political rhetoric. It also was designed to demonstrate the wisdom of taking aggressive action to improve the productivity of the existing tax structure, especially the business transaction (sales) tax. However, it also ended up as a demonstration of how difficult it is to go against powerful special interests, even in the name of a fairer and more productive tax structure.

I will begin with the property tax reform initiative which was necessitated in large part by changes I wanted in the school finance program. Then I will explain how I adjusted the personal income tax to make it more progressive and provide tax relief for an estimated 110,000 low income taxpayers. Finally, I will explain why I fought so hard to broaden the applicability of the sales tax to include selected services which directly affected businesses more than consumers, and fought *against* raising the rate of the sales tax.

Property Tax Reform

Maximum productivity from the property tax can be secured through a uniform application of the property tax law throughout the state. Section 172 of the Kentucky constitution requires that all property not specifically exempted by the constitution be assessed for taxation purposes at its fair cash value and taxed accordingly. The Kentucky legislature cannot grant exemptions from the property tax, so this was not a place to look for exemptions to expand the tax base.

The major problems with real property tax productivity were these: (a) lack of uniformity in property valuation; (b) failure to apply the tax to 100 percent of that valuation; and (c) lax collection of taxes which are assessed. Real property taxes in 1988 constituted something less than 9 percent of all general fund revenues for state government. However, property taxes were the primary source of revenue available to support government services and education at the local level. Local governments were not getting the revenues they badly needed from their real property tax base, largely because of inequities, inefficiencies, and abuses in the property tax system. This meant they had to turn to the state for subsidies to support basic public services.

In 1965 the Kentucky Court of Appeals ruled in the *Russman v. Luckett* decision that all real property had to be assessed at 100 percent of full market value. Assessments were running as low as 12.5 percent of fair market value at the time, so this meant that property taxes would dramatically increase unless the *rates* were rolled back. The legislature responded immediately to the ruling and passed a roll back law which reduced real property tax rates sufficiently to keep the amount of taxes paid by the property owner the same as before the reassessment. In spite of the court ruling some twenty years earlier, uniform valuation and assessments based on the full fair market value of real property still were not a reality in 1990.

The lack of uniformity of property valuation and its assessment was due primarily to the state's failure to enforce the Kentucky constitution. Responsibility for making proper assessments is vested in a Property Valuation Administrator (PVA), a local elected official. The political nature of the PVA office almost assured that assessments would be subject to uneven administration or outright corruption. Some properties are taxed on a valuation far below their fair market value. The impact on local tax revenue is obvious. The actual value of a particular property could be as much as ten times the value being taxed. Revenues, then, are only 10 percent of what they would be if the tax were levied against the full fair market cash value of that property.

We were asking for a significant increase in local school taxes as part of the new school finance program, so it was very important that the property tax be administered fairly and uniformly across the commonwealth. Legislative leadership and I agreed that, as part of the implementation of the new school finance law, a reassessment of *all* real property statewide should be completed by 1994, something Revenue Secretary Calvert had already been working on. I also requested a special appropriation to beef up the Revenue Cabinet's ability to audit the work of the PVAs and to take over any office where there appeared to be gross abuse or neglect of duty.

The school finance program was indexed to tax rates on real property, so it was most important to local school boards to have real property fairly assessed and taxed. However, the impact these reforms would have on state revenues was minimal. The state actually raises almost four times as much money from twenty-one other ad valorem taxes than it raises from the tax on real property. On the other hand, state expenditures to support education would be affected, since the SEEK program reduced the size of the state subsidy by the amount of money raised through local taxes .

Unlike the real property tax, the assessment and collection of ad valorem taxes on tangible and intangible property is difficult to administer since declaration of the property is the burden of the taxpayer. The Revenue Cabinet has worked for years to improve the effective and fair application of these taxes. However, nine of the twenty-one ad valorem taxes yield very little or no revenue. I did not see them as good candidates for increased productivity.

Income Taxes

The Kentucky tax code in 1989 allowed forty-one exemptions to the individual income tax, reducing the overall productivity of this tax base by an estimated $893.5 million in FY 1989. The Revenue Revitalization Program I proposed was designed to improve the productivity of the individual income tax by roughly 37 percent through conformity to the federal code which eliminated some of these exemptions and elimination of the deductibility of federal income taxes paid. Since the individual income tax represents about one-third of the total general fund revenue stream, an increase of this magnitude could have a significant impact on Kentucky's fiscal problems.

Prior to 1986 Kentucky had conformed its individual income tax law to the federal tax code, which means that exemptions allowed at the federal level are accepted by the state. Among other things, conformity greatly simplifies administration of the state income tax law. The adjusted gross income declared for federal tax purposes is accepted as the taxable income base for Kentucky personal income taxes. President Ronald Reagan and the Congress made extensive changes in federal tax laws in 1986, but Kentucky had not yet taken any action to conform.

Editors of the two major state newspapers and certain legislators urged Governor Collins to conform the Kentucky tax code in the Fall of 1987. As was noted earlier, there was considerable objection raised to my public opposition to conforming to the tax code at that time. "Why not benefit from the revenue and let Martha Layne take the political hit?" was a frequently asked question. Although I agreed with the policy of conformity, I disliked the idea of using it at that time to simply shore up the budget. I also knew that early passage of conformity would make it all the more difficult to address revenue needs in the context of a more comprehensive reform of fiscal and tax policy which I wanted to pursue later.

My revenue revitalization program did include conforming to changes in the 1986 federal tax code. The federal tax code changes impacted these major income and expense items: dividends, unemployment compensation, employee business expenses, non-business interest expenses, medical expense deductions, sales tax deduction, and capital gains. The exemptions eliminated by conformity to the federal tax code were projected to increase state revenues by an estimated $252 million over the biennium.

In addition to conformity to the federal income tax code, I proposed elimination of the deductibility of federal income taxes from the Kentucky income tax, an exemption which primarily benefited the wealthy. The federal tax deduction was the largest source of revenue loss, estimated at $220 million a year in 1989. We determined that elimination of the deductibility of federal income taxes paid would produce an additional $554 million in general fund revenue over the 1990-92 biennium.

Elimination of the federal tax deduction improved the productivity of the individual income tax, and it also made the state income tax law fairer by progressively increasing the tax liability of those who could better afford to pay higher taxes. To further improve the fairness of the state income tax, I proposed a low income tax credit for people with less than $20,000 adjusted gross income which eliminated a tax liability for about 110,000 additional taxpayers.

Taxes on Goods and Services

It was in the sales and use tax that I saw the greatest opportunity to increase tax productivity. Kentucky's first sales tax was enacted in 1934, but was repealed in the next legislative session. It was enacted again in 1960, some twenty-six years later, at a rate of 3 percent. The rate was raised to 5 percent in 1968 and became known as "Nunn's Nickel" named after then Governor Louie Nunn. Sales and use taxes now produce slightly more than one-third of the state's general fund revenues. It represents a major source of income for state government.

The sales tax actually is assessed against a retailer's gross sales and not the consumer's purchase. However, since most retailers pass the tax on to the consumer and visibly add it to the sale price, consumers believe *they* are the ones being taxed. In addition to the retail sales tax, Kentucky has what is called a "use" tax which is assessed against materials in storage or consumed in Kentucky but purchased outside the state. Among these items are such things as mail-order and automobile purchases which would be considered taxable retail sales if purchased within the state.

The Kentucky Tax Code contained forty-nine specific exemptions from sales and use taxes for a total of $939.5 million in lost revenue in FY 1989. Many of these exemptions were granted in the original law in 1960, particularly those which had a direct impact on business, industry, and farming. Services were specifically exempted from the sales and use tax at that time. Undoubtedly, these concessions were politically necessary to get enough support in the legislature to pass the sales and use tax bill.

Although sales and use tax exemptions are numerous, 56 percent of the almost $1 billion in exempted revenue came from the exemption of services, medicine, and food items. An additional 11 percent came from the exemption of sales to nonprofit educational, charitable, and religious institutions, schools, and units of government. All the remaining exemptions accounted for less than one-third of the total exempted revenue.

The exemption of food, medicines, and certain purchasers were not likely candidates for change. Imposing a sales tax on food and medicine in particular would have a particularly unfair impact on the poor and people on fixed incomes. It also would add to the cost of health care, some of which is born by government through Medicaid and other programs. On the other hand, given the enormous growth in the service sector of our economy, the continued exemption of other services from the sales and use tax had to be examined. My policy preference was to extend the sales tax to previously exempted services rather than to increase the basic tax rate on nonexempt sales.

In the interest of fairness and ease of administration, I wanted to choose carefully the exemptions to be eliminated. Personal services like car and home repairs, hair care, dry cleaning, and medical care would continue to be exempted. Services used primarily by businesses or less consumer-driven, such as advertising, air charters, lobbying, janitorial, security, legal, and accounting services would be taxed. Implementation of these changes would reduce the cost of exemptions by about one-third. We estimated elimination of exemptions on fourteen services would raise about $200 million in new revenue in the 1990-92 budget.

The "No New Taxes" Pledge

I maintained strong opposition to increasing *tax rates* throughout my campaign and during the first half of my administration, a position criticized by nearly everyone who challenged me to increase revenue. Foremost among the proponents of raising tax rates were the two largest newspapers in the state. I wanted to pursue a different course, one which would restore integrity and fairness to the existing tax structure, but not at the expense of the ordinary taxpayer. Clearly I was marching to the beat of a different political drummer.

In the first several months of my administration, Wilson Wyatt Sr., Al Smith, Bert Combs, and some others met with me to discuss several matters, among them education. They made a plea for me to relent on my position against new taxes and raise the money needed to meet the real needs of Kentucky. I told them privately that I thought that was a reasonable goal if we could achieve systemic change in education, and we took the time needed to prepare the public for what needed to be done. I said I thought it would take $1 billion to meet the most important needs of the state. Combs didn't think so and didn't believe I could or would raise it. None of them ever helped me do what they wanted me to do, and I never got their public support.

I don't know if they left my office believing I was sincere in my pledge, but I was convinced at the time that I had to be unwavering in my public opposition to raising new revenue until a new policy agenda was firmly in place. That experience was repeated time and again as I maneuvered my way through the tax minefield. Each effort I made to assure people that I was prepared to meet the fiscal needs of the commonwealth was met with skepticism.

I believe what I initially proposed fulfilled my promise not to "raise taxes." Of the $1.03 billion in new revenue I proposed, all but $150 million of it was achieved by increasing the productivity of existing taxes *at existing rates*. This was exactly what I had promised I would do. A one percentage point increase in the corporate income tax rate and an increase in cigarette taxes were the only actual increases in tax *rates* proposed by me.

As in many other things during my administration, I would not have the last word on the tax issue. Legislators had other ideas about how to raise revenue, and a battle ensued which proved to be just as intense and even more acrimonious than the one over how to improve education in Kentucky. Once again, the role of special interest in blocking progressive actions in government was demonstrated. At times the fight seemed to be about everything *except* tax policy. How and why we mounted a campaign to pass my revenue proposal, and the sometimes bizarre events related to it, deserve more attention later.

Building Public Support

As the policy issues fell into place, the time arrived to deliver in public what I had promised in private. Key decisions on the budget were made in late December with the final numbers to be worked out by mid-January. The day before Thanksgiving I had an all-day meeting at the Mansion with Budget Director Merl Hackbart and Deputy Directors Ron Carson and Bill Hintze. These three men were real professionals in public finance and budgeting. I was fortunate to have them as part of the administration, particularly at this critical time. They were a joy to work with and offered helpful guidance on this and many other occasions as well.

Hackbart, Carson, and Hintze presented various options for raising revenue, ranging from a minimalist approach which would raise only enough new money to satisfy the school court case to what came to be known as the "whole enchilada," an increase in revenue large enough to have a major impact on all areas of state government and a tax reform measure that would have a lasting and positive impact on state fiscal policy.

We thoroughly discussed the pros and cons of each option in terms of practicality, policy, political legacy and leverage. After we considered all the options, there was little question in my mind that we had to go for the "whole enchilada." Three strategic decisions were made at that meeting. The first was to present the budget in pieces before releasing details of how it would be paid for. The second decision was to make the revenue measure part of the education bill. The third decision was to enact the education and revenue bills in the regular 1990 session of the General Assembly.

The decision to combine the education bill with the revenue measure was critical to passage of the tax bill. Education reform was the political linchpin needed to ensure passage of the revenue measure. History had demonstrated that the legislature would probably pass the education bill in a flurry of excitement, but then would not pass the revenues needed to support it. I was not about to repeat the fiasco of the 1986 legislative session when the General Assembly balked at raising the revenue needed to implement the education program it enacted the previous year in special session.

The decision to enact the education reform bill during the regular session was a change in plans. I had earlier agreed with legislative leaders that we would take whatever time was required for the Task Force on School Reform to come up with its recommendations. The leadership was pushing for a special session on education in June because of concerns about having to take action on taxes just before the primary election in May. However, it was impossible for me to put together a budget in January with nearly half of it off the table. Action on the financing of education had to occur in the regular 1990 session.

The budget meeting was followed a week later by one with Finance Cabinet Secretary Wells to discuss the results of the tax expenditure analysis report. The revenue study identified various tax exemptions, exclusions, deductions, credits, deferrals, and preferential rates that currently existed in the tax statutes. It was prepared under the direction of James Ramsey, Chief State Economist and executive director of the Office of Financial Management and Economic

Analysis in the Finance and Administration Cabinet. I found Dr. Ramsey to be another real professional with outstanding expertise in making budget projections. The study he prepared on tax expenditures gave me the information I needed to finalize the revenue proposal.

Setting the Stage

Budgets are very complex documents and difficult for the general public to comprehend, given the limited information they receive through the media. Since I was about to ask the public to support the largest increase in revenue in Kentucky history, it was important to make clear where I wanted the money to go. The first of seven press conferences on various elements of the budget was held in the state room of the Capitol on January 4, 1990, with the last one occurring ten days later. My budget proposal for education was saved to the last since that was the item of greatest public interest.

Many people commented that this approach was probably the smartest public relations effort any governor had ever attempted as a way to sell a tax increase. Not surprisingly, the two most experienced veterans of many budget wars—Ron Carson and Bill Hintze—proposed the plan and implemented it with great expertise. I personally felt good about it at the time.

The Strategy Worked

After haranguing me for months over my apparent unwillingness to deal with the fiscal needs of the commonwealth, it was interesting to watch the media's response to my budget proposals. After the first few announcements, the political pundits and capitol reporters started raising their eyebrows as the numbers kept getting bigger. Bill Bishop, a *Lexington Herald-Leader* columnist, quipped that "the budget looks great, but so did Fantasia." The figure which had been bantered about for months was somewhere around $700 million in new revenue, $170 million of which was expected to come from growth in the economy. We reached that number before education was addressed, the largest single item in the budget.

For the most part, newspaper editors across the state were supportive of the initiatives outlined in the press conferences. However, the cynical editorial types muted their enthusiasm. I suppose it would be the height of *naivete* to expect words of praise from them, but I did expect a somewhat less skeptical view of the historic political action I was prepared to take. Somehow they thought I was not sincere in proposing to support so many things without showing how each one would be funded.

Comments by legislative leaders reported in the media indicated they thought I was just building a political trap for them by proposing all of these good things and then dropping an unacceptable tax package on them in order to make them out to be the bad guys. I know they were scared to death over my building public expectations in such a visible way. After all the months of talk about taxes by legislative leaders, it was now time for them to put up or shut up.

In reality the majority of legislators dreaded being faced with *any* tax measure, no matter what it was for. Many of them had expressed to me privately their hope that I would keep the expected tax increase small, and perhaps limit it to the least amount required to satisfy the court's demand for equitable funding of education. Perhaps the hardest work of my administration now lay ahead of me. Getting the legislature to support my approach to fiscal policy would be a tough sell under the best of circumstances.

Confrontation Over Tax Policy

As was the case in education policy, it was politically necessary to control the debate on the tax issue. Legislative rhetoric constantly focused on the need to raise tax rates. My job was to change the focus from raising tax rates to addressing the inequity and poor productivity of the tax system, and to bring it more in line with economic reality. Most of all, I wanted the debate to be over my proposal, not theirs.

In mid-December, the legislative budget chairs released their version of the budget for FY 1990-92, an unprecedented move on their part. In the absence of a proposal from me, I knew their proposal would become the starting point for the debate by default. Over the next four weeks I could expect news reporters to repeatedly ask me what I planned to do about their proposal unless I launched a pre-emptive strike now. I could ill afford to lose the initiative on the most important political issue of my career in public life. Thus, the same day the legislative budget proposal was released I held a press conference to trash it publicly. My rhetoric was strident and calculated.

"Let me tell you what this is all about," I said. "This [debate] is not about good times. It's not about parties. It's not about receptions. It's not about the good old boys over at Flynn's. It's not about schmoozing around in friendly relationships. This fight is about and between the daddies and mammas who take their children fishing on Saturday morning and the lobbyists who take legislators golfing on Wednesday afternoon. The fight is about whether you are going to be on the side of special interests or going to be on the side of working men and women in this commonwealth."

Once again the stuck pig squealed, and the editors jumped on me for picking a fight with key legislators just when their support was needed to pass education reform and higher taxes. From my vantage point, there was little likelihood of ever negotiating a settlement of our differences, so there was little to lose. What I wanted was too contrary to the legislative mind-set and traditional legislative politics. I saw little hope of ever getting the support I needed from a recalcitrant and heady legislature which was not inclined to give me anything I wanted, no matter what merit my proposal might have. What I needed most at this time was support from ordinary taxpayers, so my rhetoric was primarily for their consumption.

The media gave extensive coverage that day to the legislature's proposal, but the headline was "Wilkinson blasts legislative leaders." My immediate objective was achieved. The media focused on the fight rather than the substance of the legislative proposal, giving me the opportunity to paint legislative leaders as the ones who wanted to increase rather than reform taxes. The public exchange between myself and the legislature continued over the next few weeks as they tried to keep control of their destiny. However, characterizing my opponents in the legislature as being in the pocket of special interests was a theme I would hammer on time and again throughout the debate.

What the Fight Was All About

I knew from the outset that the struggle would be over my proposal to expand application of the sales and use tax to include services. During the campaign in 1987 Mike Moloney and Joe Clarke had proposed raising the sales and use tax by a penny, a 20 percent increase in the most regressive tax we levied. Conventional wisdom among legislators was that the public viewed this tax as fair because "everyone paid it." Legislators believed it was politically easier to raise a tax which the public thought was fair than to take an exemption away from politically powerful groups like lawyers and newspapers.

I had good reasons for wanting to tax services before raising the sales tax rate. Growth in the economy is not reflected in a corresponding growth in tax revenues. The reason is clear. When the sales tax was enacted in 1960, the General Assembly specifically defined the tax as a retail tax which applied only to goods sold and not services. In the intervening thirty years, services became the fastest growing sector of the economy. I wanted to be in a position such that the revenue stream would grow as the economy grew. Then perhaps in future years, Kentucky would not always be behind the "eight ball" and always raising rates. At least half the money needed to meet the current fiscal needs of the state was potentially available if the exemption on services was lifted.

Tax experts generally agree that a sales tax is the most regressive of all taxes. Property taxes vary according to the actual cash value of the property. Incomes taxes are graduated and indexed to the income level of the taxpayer. The sales tax, however, applies the same to everyone regardless of ability to pay. I contended that to impose a 20 percent increase in a flat tax like the sales and use tax is insensitive fiscal policy when other options are available. It seemed unjust to want to raise taxes on the blue jeans and winter coats our families work so hard to buy, while corporations and special interest buy millions of dollars in advertising and legal advice on which no tax is paid.

The Battle Begins

When the revenue bill was delivered to the House in mid-February, I personally appeared before the House A& R Committee to make the case for my revenue proposal. Curiously, I was asked if I was prepared to work for passage of this bill. The question surprised me. Did they really think I would lay out such a proposal and then just walk away from it? Perhaps they thought I was just trying to corner them with a proposal I knew they could not support. Of course I was willing to fight for it.

In the weeks that followed, I aggressively lobbied individual legislators to support the tax on services and not to consider raising the sales and use tax a penny. Many of them confessed they found it hard to determine how their constituents would be affected. But some of the problems I faced surfaced immediately with most of the opposition coming from predictable sources. Farmers complained about the tobacco tax. Lawyers, who make up about a third of the General Assembly, didn't want their services taxed. Cable TV opposed the tax on their product. Lobbyist for various other professional and service providers flooded Frankfort with literature.

I was waiting to see what reaction the newspaper editors would have to the proposal to tax intrastate advertising. Almost all of them had favored a large tax increase to fund education. Even though most were generally in favor of the tax proposal, they all were opposed to taxing advertising services. Particularly hypocritical in their reaction was the *Courier-Journal*, which repeatedly used its editorial page to level harsh attacks on me for not having the fortitude to "suck it up" and raise taxes. After months of demanding that taxes be raised, they were the first to oppose a tax on themselves. It should be noted they found little problem with the taxes proposed for everyone else.

The cable television industry also used their medium to attack the proposed tax on cable services. Advertising "crawlers," which move across the bottom of the television screen, were used to attack the proposed tax on cable services. They were unscrupulous in their open use of a virtual monopoly to lobby their viewers to oppose the tax. At one point I threatened to demand equal time to combat their campaign against the proposed tax on their services. There are pages of law addressing the rights and responsibilities of the media to present all sides of an issue, all of which were ignored in the cable television industry's determined effort to defeat the part of the revenue package which affected them.

The tobacco lobby was out in force contending that the proposed increase in the cigarette tax would "destroy the industry." I knew the increase probably would not fly, but I wanted to flush out as many special interests as I could. As a smoker myself, I could not be accused of picking on that constituency. Reaction was typical of special interest politics. For years Philip Morris had sponsored a Derby Party for the Commonwealth in Washington. They canceled the event that year long before there was even a vote taken on the proposed tax.

These and others like them were the special interests I railed against when the details of my revenue revitalization program were released. I knew they would be out in full force. Noticeably absent from the legislative hallways and offices were representatives of ordinary, hard-working taxpayers who had no organization through which to express their voice or to lobby on their behalf. I tried my best to take their view, but unfortunately legislators continued to get the impression that they preferred an increase in the sales tax, even though few of them would have felt any impact from the services tax. Unfortunately, a lack of understanding of the importance of the issues being debated left many citizens ill prepared to argue the fine points of state fiscal policy.

As time was running out for debate, I made one last effort to get support for the services tax, the only part of the revenue bill which had organized opposition of any significance except for the tobacco lobby. I met personally with almost every member of the House of Representatives and presented my case. We talked about other changes they might want, but I urged them not to take the route of an increase in the sales tax rate.

Although I gained support from some legislators, clearly I didn't get enough to assure passage of the tax proposal in its present form. Speaker Blandford leaned heavily on House members not to yield to my pressure and undoubtedly kept some of them from publicly supporting me. At the last minute I picked up public support from KEA and the League of Women Voters, but it came too late to swing any votes.

The "Great Compromise"

I had been to Washington, DC, early that fateful week. On the return trip I reviewed my situation. I knew the tobacco tax was gone and the services tax was in deep trouble, even with the thirty-seven votes I thought I had lined up. The finance measure had to have fifty-one votes in the House, regardless of the number voting. I knew some members might abstain or conveniently be "out of the chamber" when the vote was taken. I have never been one to give up a fight when I thought I was right, but the very thought of having to veto the education bill because of a sales tax provision was abhorrent. To give in to the legislature on this issue was unthinkable. So I was faced with a real dilemma.

In a last-ditch effort to keep my revenue measure intact, I hastily called a press conference and again threatened to veto the entire bill if it contained an increase in the tax *rate* on property, income, or sales. Perhaps it was in part a bluff and in part an act of political desperation. Legislative leadership, sensing a lack of support for the bill with the services tax in it, met after my press conference to decide what to do. In the mind of leadership, it was decision time.

House Speaker Blandford was under severe pressure to resolve the issue before legislators had to go home to face the voters. He was convinced that I would rather see everything go down the tube than relent on my stand against the proposed penny increase in the sales tax. There was good reason for him to think so, for I had just concluded a press conference at which I emphatically said, "I think any further talk about a sales tax is a waste of time and energy that would be better devoted to something else."

House leaders met late Thursday to examine the list of votes I said were lined up in favor of my proposal. I claimed we had thirty-seven of the House members, but their own count was much lower. The Senate had basically backed the proposal and was waiting for the House to decide what it was going to do. Thinking they probably would have to go it alone, House leaders agreed to abandon both the cigarette tax increase and the tax on services, and replace them with a penny increase in the sales tax, which they wanted all along to do. Apparently they were considering an announcement to this effect the next morning, which would have laid the gauntlet down with no further discussion.

Perhaps fearful of my reaction or just out of courtesy, Greg Stumbo suggested that they approach me one more time to see if I could be persuaded to change my position. He proposed that an offer be made to support my $600 million road bond issue in return for agreement not to fight the effort to pass an increase in the sales tax. Don Blandford thought I was a lost cause, but agreed to have Greg contact me that Thursday evening to extend the offer and to seek my agreement to what they were going to do without me anyway.

The rage I felt inside is indescribable. Over and again I tried to make my point with Greg, only to have him say that the game was really over already. This was the only opportunity I would have to salvage something from the fight. We both agreed that open warfare with the legislature on this issue would guarantee that nothing would get done in this session and everyone would lose. History would condemn us all. The issue was not about what makes good sense or good policy; it was about what the legislature could pass into law—with or without my help. After several hours of intense discussion, I agreed to think about the offer. I simply was not prepared to just walk away from something I felt was so important to the future of the commonwealth. I knew the deadlock had to be broken, but at what cost to myself and to everyone who had put faith in me?

I met with House leadership in my office the next morning to discuss the terms under which I would agree not to fight the sales tax increase and give up the idea of taxing services and increasing the cigarette tax. In addition to the $600 million road bonds they had offered, I wanted my community development bonds and assurance from leadership that the education bill and my budget would be passed "essentially intact" with the education money in it.

The discussion was tense, and several times the meeting almost fell apart. At one point Speaker Blandford got up and started for the door. All would certainly have been lost if I hadn't convinced him to sit back down. It was a real give and take session, primarily their "giving" me the facts of life on the general sales tax increase and my "taking" it. At last a compromise was reached, but Senate leadership at this point had not been consulted.

A call went out to Senate leadership for an urgent meeting in the governor's office. When they arrived and learned about the agreement we had reached, they were very upset at being expected to sign on to an agreement when they had no part in its making. There was a heated exchange between Joe Wright and Don Blandford over the decision by House leadership to proceed on its own to negotiate a deal with me without consulting the Senate. The Senators felt they had been ambushed by the House, but they were in an untenable position. After a private caucus, the Senators agreed to the compromise, but warned they could not promise delivery on the items I wanted until they could meet with the Senate Democratic caucus.

The tentativeness of Senate leadership left me uneasy. I suggested that perhaps we should put the agreement in writing. The idea was accepted and I prepared a handwritten list of the items that leadership had agreed to in return for withdrawing my opposition to the penny increase in the sales tax rate. However, after it was written, Joe Wright said he thought their word should be good enough and wanted the document torn up. After further discussion, I finally tore the paper up, and we proceeded on a good faith basis.

The impasse was broken and the pathway cleared for education reform, but I had given up an important part of the revenue reform agenda for which I had fought so hard. Obviously, I was disappointed at having to give up on a cardinal element in my political platform. Just as disappointing was the opportunity we missed to address the long-term revenue problems of the state. I thought at the time, "How long would it be before another governor will have the courage to advocate a tax on services?"

Some of the old pork barrel practices common to the legislature surfaced near the end of the session. Senator Mike Moloney proposed that the changes in the personal income tax be made retroactive to January 1990, which would yield about $200 million more in "one time" revenue. The legislature eventually included this provision in the revenue measure. Unfortunately much of this additional one time money was used by House leadership in a last minute "projects for votes" trading frenzy.

Even though I was able to show how every element of the revenue revitalization program would impact the taxpayer, the nuances of "regressive taxes and deductibility" were beyond the understanding of ordinary taxpayers. I was unable to mobilize general public support for what I was trying to do, which left the politics to those with ample resources to lobby the legislature. To this day I believe the decision to increase the sales tax rate rather than extend it to certain services was a tragic mistake and a missed opportunity. The state ran out of money within two years after I left office. How could the state be broke right after the biggest tax increase in twenty-two years? It makes me sick to my stomach.

In the end I achieved most of what I wanted from the effort to put Kentucky on a sounder fiscal basis. The achievement of a major restructuring of education finance, passage of a revenue bill large enough to have a major impact on many of our most pressing needs, addressing problems in the administration of the property tax, and a significant restructuring of the personal income tax were in themselves historic. This is a legacy of which I am proud.

But the opposition was formidable. I must admit that special interests are alive and well when it comes to influencing public policy. The issue with them never was what might be in the public interest. The issue was plain and simple—don't put a tax on *me*! And in the end, they won. Once again the legislature showed its inability to develop or implement a rational public policy. Pursue the path of least resistance and don't offend your supporters is the legislator's "bottom line." The public cannot help but be cynical about government and politicians when they so obviously and blatantly subordinate sound public policy to special interest politics.

XII. GROWING THE ECONOMY

It is a widely held assumption that business people don't make very good politicians. On the other hand, no one would do business the way politicians do government. For my part, I readily admit to being a better businessman than politician. I do not have the patience for the indecisive, go slow, consensus-building approach that pervades politics at every level. Nor have I ever been particularly adept at another of the common attributes of many successful politicians— subtlety. Like it or not, the critics are right. The characteristics which make one successful in business are not necessarily the best attributes when applied to politics.

That's not to say that they shouldn't be. Just because few people are willing to challenge the conventional wisdom doesn't mean it shouldn't happen more often. One of the reasons that education in Kentucky was so badly in need of fundamental reform was that the existing system was the product of years of compromise with and appeasement of special interest groups. In other words, it was a product of the political process.

Economic development is another thing altogether. If there is one area of state government that ought to respond to a business approach and is less encumbered by the pressures of special interests, it's economic development. Where my tenacity and determination were perceived as threats to the status quo when applied to the politically charged area of education reform, those same characteristics were essential to success in economic development.

I have no quarrel with those who say I am tenacious. I also am competitive, and I like to win. When I laid out my goals for education and said I would settle for nothing less than a complete restructuring of education in Kentucky, I was called a tyrant and heard a chorus of "You can't do that, Governor." When I laid out my goals for economic development and said I would settle for nothing less than making Kentucky number one in jobs, I was called a dreamer and told again, "You can't do that, Governor."

The fact of the matter is that the roots of my approach to economic development were nurtured in the same rural, up-from-the bootstraps background that prompted my passion for education reform. Indeed, building Kentucky's infrastructure is as much about education and workforce development as is about roads and bridges and water lines. As usual, the nay-sayers said I would fail. I enjoyed proving them wrong in both cases.

One of the weaknesses in Kentucky's economic framework has always been our neglect of rural Kentucky and the resultant clash between rural and urban interests over priorities. Most politicians have avoided the rural/urban crossfire by simply taking a *laissez faire* approach. It is easy to say all the right things about creating jobs and stimulating the economy while avoiding the hard decisions that have to be made. Benign neglect, however, is still neglect.

Fundamental economic needs in Kentucky have gone unmet in part because there hasn't been a political downside to doing nothing. Except for the historic strength of agriculture and coal, rural interests have never had the expertise or clout to challenge the status quo. It is just too easy for politicians to pledge support for a new bridge in Owensboro, for example, "when Indiana promises to build a road to it," knowing Indiana never would. Or to profess support for a road project (Paris Pike comes to mind), knowing they could always blame inaction on others.

My style is to say what I mean and mean what I say. I meant it when I told people I was for something and did everything I could to get it done. Likewise, if I could not support a project I generally said so. I was unequivocal in my support for rural Kentucky and my belief that there needn't be two Kentuckies. "Fifteen counties can't continue to support the other 105" was as much apart of my campaign message as was "we need more Casey County thinking in Frankfort and less Frankfort thinking in Casey County."

Kentucky is Open for Business

Success in economic development is as much style and attitude as it is policy. Attitude is one of the things that had always held Kentucky back. To be successful in any competition, you have to believe you can win before you will win. Kentuckians have been told for so many years what we can't do. Sometimes it's hard to find anybody who thinks there is something we can do. I was appalled during the education debate when one of the more innovative features of the reform was questioned by a legislator because he didn't think Kentucky ought to be the first to try it. With thinking like that, no one should wonder why Kentucky kept finding itself somewhere back in the pack.

We must think like winners before we can be winners. That means making every county and every region in Kentucky feel like it has a chance to succeed. We had to take affirmative action to attract attention. Declaring Kentucky "Open for Business," and adopting that as our economic development slogan, was one of the first steps I took. The slogan itself had no real significance, but the marketing effort we put behind it and the simple message it sent to existing companies and prospects helped generate interest and enthusiasm. As it turned out, the slogan even received international exposure.

Excerpts from a speech I gave to top CEOs and politicians in Tokyo during one of my visits to Japan were later included in a public television documentary about competing with the Japanese. The focus of the speech which was shown all over the world was our "Open for Business" attitude. That speech and our success with the yen bond agreement also led to an audience with the Japanese Prime Minister.

As described in a previous chapter, my legislative goals in the 1988 budget were hampered by the more pressing and immediate need to right the fiscal ship of state. However, important legislation was implemented which contributed greatly to our effort to direct more resources to previously neglected areas of the state. Among these was the Rural Kentucky Jobs Act. First dubbed the Depressed Counties Act, the idea was brought to me by then Pike County Judge Executive Paul Patton as a way to specifically help eastern Kentucky.

The legislation provided special incentives to companies that would locate in counties with the highest rates of unemployment. Additionally, the Infrastructure Act provided funds for water, sewage treatment, and other basic needs required for economic growth. Expanding the scope of the Kentucky Development Finance Authority to include non-manufacturing related companies opened the door to a whole new range of companies previously outside the purview of KDFA.

Given the General Assembly's reticence to support gubernatorial discretion in economic development, funding my efforts to create jobs proved to be a somewhat daunting task. In the 1988 session, we had to put up a major fight to protect a rather meager $30 to $35 million in state funds available for job creation programs. Only my veto and the legislature's failure to override protected it.

Few areas of state government are more responsive to the personal involvement of a governor than economic development. The active, visible participation of the governor signals a state's aggressiveness. Over the years, the General Assembly has gradually reduced the ability of a governor to personally direct the state's economic development efforts. In 1992 they finally succeeded in subordinating economic development to a committee, effectively eliminating the governor from any meaningful role. There probably are many reasons why the General Assembly wanted to strip the executive branch of any real opportunity to develop and implement an economic development policy. Our success with the "samurai" bond probably was the last straw.

First Steps and the Yen Bond

Throughout the 1980s, states competed against each other for Japanese investment through location of new plants, routinely selling bonds to finance various projects. No one, however, had ever participated in the Japanese bond market. The regulatory and public relations gauntlet that one faces in the Japanese financial market effectively kept foreign governments out of it. Many states, including Kentucky, welcomed the expansion of Japan's manufacturing base to the United States, but no one had yet succeeded in attracting a significant amount of Japanese capital for other projects. The yen bond offered a way to generate funds for state projects and at the same time elevate Kentucky's visibility in corporate board rooms around the world.

I quickly pushed our interest in the Japanese financial markets to the forefront of our economic development plans. We could we use the additional capital to reinvest in new projects, but I also felt like the exposure in business circles would give a positive spin to our new aggressiveness. Secretary of Finance L. Rogers Wells, himself a successful businessman, worked diligently for many months to forge a working relationship with Japanese banks and investment companies.

There was no one in my administration I relied upon and trusted more than Rogers Wells. We had been friends and business associates for many years before I entered politics. One of my first jobs was working for Rog's father in Glasgow. Besides sharing a common philosophy and enthusiasm for business, I knew Rog shared my determination to get Kentucky on track economically.

By the time I went to Japan for the March 10, 1989, signing of the yen bond agreement, we had put together a strong consortium of Japanese financial interests headed by the International Bank of Japan (IBJ) and Nomura Securities. An economic development seminar we held in Tokyo prior to signing the agreement attracted virtually every major financial and industrial interest in Japan.

With the signing of the bond agreements, Kentucky became the first state ever to successfully complete an issue on the Japanese financial market. Within hours of signing the bond agreements, Kentucky's yen bond issue was sold out and we had $80 million in new capital to invest. Prime Minister Noboru Takeshita in particular had high praise for Kentucky. In a private meeting before we returned home, he told me that when he was Finance Minister of Japan he advocated more outside participation in their financial markets. Our success, he said, proved him right.

The benefits of the yen bond went beyond the capital it gave us to invest in new economic development projects. Through a series of "swaps" with IBJ, Kentucky was able to provide incentives in most major world currencies, thus eliminating the concern over effects international currency fluctuations might have on borrowing and repayment. It sent a clear message throughout the world that Kentucky was a serious player in the competition for new investment and economic growth. It meant Kentucky was "open for business" world wide.

An unexpected benefit came from *Institutional Investor* magazine when it named the yen bond one of its "Deals of the Year" for 1989. The next year, as a result of our overall efforts in education and economic development, the National Alliance of Business named Kentucky its "State of the Year."

The usual nay-sayers questioned the effort we put into the yen bond, most notably Senator Moloney and others in the General Assembly who had been endeavoring to hamstring the executive branch's prerogatives for a number of years. That a governor could single-handedly initiate an innovative and cost-efficient approach to generating capital was contrary to their efforts to micromanage state government.

Changing the Way We Do Business

In the context of a campaign, the media presumes everything a candidate says has only political significance. My criticism of Kentucky's negotiating posture with Toyota, however, was not mere campaign rhetoric. For long-range success and stability of the state's economy, Kentucky needed to be viewed as a partner in economic development, not simply a sugar daddy.

Success in economic development ultimately comes in the trenches in the head-to-head competition for new and expanded industry. The competition has stiffened over the years as states have increasingly sought to gain an advantage through the use of various kinds of incentives which generally involve some kind of preferential tax treatment. No one likes to compete strictly on the basis of who can offer the largest financial package for a prospective company, but every state feels like it has to in order to be competitive.

States have received criticism, some of it justified, for the various incentive programs used to attract new jobs. However, states which want to be competitive have no choice but to play by whatever rules govern the game. That doesn't mean that incentives alone drive every corporate decision. Success generally goes to the best negotiator, not necessarily the highest bidder. This is where a governor who understands business can make a difference.

The focus in most economic development projects which involve incentives is generally on how much the state is willing to invest. One of the things I made clear to all prospects from the outset was that we would expect commitments in return for our investment. While most people would assume as much, I was surprised at how firmly entrenched the practices of the past were and at how many people in and out of government assumed that state participation in a project would come with no strings attached.

Just how different our approach was going to be was apparent at a meeting I had in west Kentucky with a local economic development group soon after Gene Royalty came on board as my Secretary of Economic Development. The group specifically wanted to ask us about a letter they had received from the cabinet outlining the expectations the state would have should we agree to provide an incentive package for the particular company in which they had an interest. The fact that the state would require anything for its participation seemed to surprise them, and they truly felt like they would be out of the running if we did. "But the state's never required anything of companies before," said one of the locals. Spontaneously and in unison, Gene and I said, "We just started."

I must say that Secretary Gene Royalty and his staff have to be considered among the many unsung heroes that made things work during my administration. There are a lot of reasons for Gene's effectiveness, but among them was his success in convincing Jeff Noel to return to state government as deputy secretary despite Jeff's other interests and general reluctance to become a part of the bureaucracy. Jeff's handiwork and skills are evident throughout all of the major projects we completed during my term in office.

You Just Can't Make Some People Happy

As population and resources concentrated in central Kentucky, the gap between the haves and have-nots widened over the years, creating the "two Kentuckys" I talked about during my campaign. Prior to my taking office, all of the attention in economic development had been focused on locating Toyota Motor Manufacturing in Georgetown, further exacerbating the disparities between rural and urban Kentucky. Rarely a day went by in the months before my election that some mention was not made of Kentucky's Golden Triangle formed by Louisville, Lexington and northern Kentucky.

Despite my belief that being prorural Kentucky didn't make me anticity, I think some people were quick to draw conclusions about my potential interest in and support for their priorities. In Louisville, especially, nothing I did seemed to satisfy them. Perhaps it was because I had campaigned as a rural Kentuckian and had made it clear that I intended to help rural Kentucky address some long-standing needs that many in Louisville were so predisposed to believe that I couldn't be prorural Kentucky without being anti-Louisville. My assurance that no area of the state would be neglected fell on deaf ears. They never seemed to understand that by "raising the river all boats would rise."

I think another reason some people in Louisville developed such a negative attitude toward me stems from a conversation I had early in my administration involving the Greater Louisville Downtown Economic Development Foundation. Several representatives of the foundation came to my office to discuss their needs and priorities. Among them was George Gill, then publisher of the *Courier-Journal.* Speaking for the group, George made a plea for an additional one million dollars in state funds for the foundation. Since I was aware that the foundation already had $11 million in the bank, I was reluctant to take another million out of what I knew was going to be a tight budget in 1988 and give it to a project that was flush by most people's standards.

My response to George was something like "I am not going to give the Greater Louisville Foundation a million dollars when you already have $11 million and there are areas of the state that don't even have clean water." George's response was that I didn't care anything about Louisville. He talked about the symbolism of the state's participation and the positive effect it would have on potential corporate donors. In effect he was saying, if the state wouldn't participate, why should corporations? Finally, he simply concluded that I didn't care about Louisville and said so. Once tagged as anti-Louisville, especially by someone in a position to influence editorial opinion, I don't think from that point on that it really made any difference what I did. I wasn't going to satisfy my Louisville critics.

It probably didn't help either that I later insisted that Louisville repay a loan made during the Ford administration. The state had loaned Louisville $12 million to cover the city's share of the cost of renovations to the University of Louisville Hospital prior to its being taken over by Humana. Louisville signed a note establishing the loan so they could delay selling bonds to cover their share of the cost until a more favorable time.

The problem was that Louisville never sold the bonds, never paid the debt back, and had never given any indication that they had any intention of paying it back. It seemed perfectly reasonable to me to expect repayment on a good faith loan. The Louisville fathers thought otherwise and objected. Apparently my insistence that they meet their obligation was seen as another example of a negative attitude toward Louisville. Ironically, after having been criticized for demanding repayment and having reservations about accepting the property in the first place, I was asked by Pat Malloy, state secretary of finance in the Jones administration, to help negotiate a land swap with CSX Corporation which probably will make possible the construction of a new football stadium for the University of Louisville.

I'm sure the early departure of Bill Lomicka as secretary of the Economic Development Cabinet probably contributed to my problems in Louisville. Bill came highly recommended. I was excited about the prospect of having someone from Louisville in that position, hoping it might ease concerns about my administration's relationship with the state's largest city. Despite speculation in the media, there wasn't any great mystery about Bill's departure. I don't think either of us ever was completely comfortable with our relationship and the relationship of the governor's office to the cabinet. From the beginning of my campaign, I made no secret of my intention to play an active role in economic development. Bill and I just didn't seem to click. For my part, the separation was amicable but necessary. However, it did nothing to soothe the feelings of the "River Road boys."

For my part, I tried to look at every project or request based on its merits regardless of where it was. The irony of all this is that, other than George's million dollars, I don't think there was a major request made by Louisville that my administration didn't try to address. The airport expansion was certainly the largest in terms of cost at $50 million. I also funded major expansion projects at the Kentucky Fairgrounds, most sewer and road projects requested, and a much-needed but hotly debated expansion of Hazelwood Hospital.

Toyota and the Kitchen Sink

John Y. Brown Jr. made "running the state like a business" the centerpiece of his gubernatorial campaign. It was a very successful campaign theme, but it really had nothing to do with the state's ability to stimulate economic development. Realizing that successfully landing Toyota would be her legacy as governor, Martha Layne Collins negotiated herself into a "must win" situation which, to their credit and benefit, Toyota exploited. Both John and Martha Layne elevated Kentucky's stature in economic development, John with the UPS success and the aura of celebrity he brought to the state house and Martha Layne with her Toyota success. However, long-term economic success would take more than personality and an occasional home run.

My criticism of the Toyota deal during the campaign was directed toward Kentucky's negotiating posture. There seemed to be no end to what we were willing to offer Toyota, and that's never a good position from which to negotiate. One of the first things I did as governor was change our thinking from "how much can we give you" to "what do you need to make your project work?"

Justification for my concerns about Kentucky's approach to Toyota became apparent later on during the campaign. Familiarity with one aspect of our relationship with Toyota illustrated my problem with the Economic Development Cabinet's "how much can you give" approach to economic development deals. State bureaucrats from the cabinet contacted one of my companies to inquire about the availability of suites on the top floors of the Capital Plaza Hotel in Frankfort. A request for one suite led to a request for others until it looked like they would need at least one entire floor if not more.

It wasn't long after inquiring about the cost of leasing the suites that we received another call asking how much it would cost to decorate and furnish them. Every few days we would get another call regarding another upgrade to the suites until it didn't seem like money was an object at all. If we were this generous in this case, how much were we giving away in other areas? And why were we still offering to pay items which couldn't have been talked about in the original deal?

I was preparing to schedule a news conference to discuss what I considered to be this very liberal approach to economic development when I was preempted by a news article with an entirely different spin on the issue of the Capital Plaza Hotel suites. Mark Chellgren of the Associated Press published an article suggesting that my ownership of the suites and their possible use by Toyota could represent a conflict of interest. Had I already been governor, I would have seen the point, not necessarily that there actually was a conflict but that it warranted a story. But how I had a conflict when I had been the one criticizing the Toyota deal has never been clear to me. Chellgren's story didn't amount to a whole lot in terms of the campaign, but it effectively killed my chance to illustrate one of the reasons I had been critical of the state's negotiations with Toyota.

The media was a lot more concerned about my relationship with Toyota than either myself or the Japanese. Besides understanding American politics extremely well, I think the Japanese realized the precarious public relations position they were in throughout the negotiations. I have long felt that Toyota finally made its decision to locate in Kentucky at just about the point that the public relations curve was going to turn against them.

It is hard to measure how much Kentucky benefited from having been chosen as the site for the first Toyota plant when the time came for Toyota to consider a second plant, but I'm sure it didn't hurt. From the beginning, however, Toyota made it clear that they viewed the second plant as distinct from the first in every possible way. At least ten states were considered by Toyota before they decided once again on Kentucky. No incentives were asked for or offered in this case. But I did relate to Toyota that, given all the incentives granted on the first round, it was only fair that they give us the second plant. I really think in that sense they agreed.

We're Winning in Kentucky . . .

. . .with General Tire.

Rather than approach prospective companies with an open checkbook, I tried to analyze their position and devise ways the state could provide incentives that met specific needs. One of the first major projects that needed attention was not an effort to generate new jobs for Kentucky, but to save existing ones. It also turned out to be one of the most unique financing agreements we would make.

General Tire's parent company had recently been acquired by Continental Tire of Hanover, Germany. Observers were speculating that Continental would move immediately to close at least two of its seven United States manufacturing plants. The Mayfield plant seemed an obvious target since it was not currently equipped to manufacture radial tires.

After meeting with Continental officials in Hanover in September of 1988, it was obvious that the odds of Continental keeping its plant in Mayfield were slim. It was also obvious that General Tire didn't need tax abatement, the customary approach to most state incentives, as much as it needed up-front capital to finance renovation of the plant in order to manufacture radial tires. Had we approached them with a traditional incentive plan, it is very unlikely that General Tire would have been operating in Kentucky by the end of my administration.

What we devised was a unique plan which met Continental's need for capital, but did so at a minimal cost to the commonwealth. The idea behind the state's participation was really quite simple. Continental needed to invest more than $100 million in the Mayfield plant in order to convert to the manufacture of radial tires. To make this bottom line work, Continental needed $50 million in capital from Kentucky.

Businesses don't fear cost as much as they do risk. In this case, Continental was reluctant to borrow the money needed to convert the plant, fearing a rise in interest rates. We were able to show Continental how they could save at least $50 million over the life of the loan if they allowed Kentucky to participate in the financing. Continental would borrow funds based on a "floater" rate, a much riskier approach than a "fixed" rate. Kentucky would agree to reimburse Continental the difference whenever the lower floater rate went above a fixed rate set to the London Interbank Borrowing Rate (LIBOR). Conversely, when the floater rate fell below that fixed rate, the state earned credits applied against future payments. The state's participation was capped at $18 million.

General Tire got what it needed the most, risk-free debt and a substantial cost saving below what their corporate credit rating would have allowed at a fixed rate, and the state was able to retain the largest employer in west Kentucky. Our plant not only didn't close, we got an expansion. Theoretically at least, if interest rates stayed below LIBOR for the duration of the deal, it could cost the state nothing and we might even have made money!

. . .with Scott Paper.

The Scott Paper project was unique for the way the community presented itself. I have never seen people work as hard as those in Owensboro did to convince a company to locate there. Owensboro was a community that deserved to have something good happen to it.

During one of many campaign trips to Owensboro, the *Messenger-Inquirer* carried a front page story about the local economy. It cited a national study listing Owensboro as one of ten communities of similar size with the highest unemployment rates. To make matters worse, the story noted that Owensboro was the only community among the ten that wasn't either in Texas or Louisiana, where employment problems could be directly attributed to recessions in the oil and gas industries. I promised that day to move the Capitol to Owensboro if we couldn't get the unemployment rate down. As it turned out, I didn't have to move the Capitol, but I was in Owensboro enough to be considered a resident.

Scott Paper took a long time to decide where to locate, and not a day went by that Owensboro didn't do something to let the company know it was welcome. I would like to think my trips to Philadelphia to meet with company officials made a difference. Certainly every time a problem arose in this deal we worked out a solution one-on-one. But the credit belongs to the people of Owensboro who showed the spirit and hospitality of the community and simply out-hustled the competition.

. . . with South Central Bell

One of our more interesting efforts that deserves attention was in fiber optics. Obviously, no business or industry was going to locate in an area of the country which lacked the capability to provide high speed data and facsimile transmission and related communication services. At the time, most of Kentucky could not provide these basic communication services. In October of 1989 I announced a joint effort with South Central Bell to take fiber optics throughout their service area, a major investment in Kentucky which would help build the communication infrastructure of the future. I believe it may have been the first such agreement in any state.

Few projects were as satisfying as Delta Air Line's expansion in northern Kentucky. Besides being the largest expansion Delta had ever undertaken, it was the most coveted prize on the economic development scene in 1990. I was certain that a Delta expansion would ensure the economic future of northern Kentucky for decades to come. The Delta project was one where I thought the rapport we were able to establish with top management was a determining factor in the decision to locate in Kentucky. We made it clear from the beginning in both deeds and words that Delta was foremost in our minds.

Most of Delta's top executives had risen in the company ranks under the leadership of Chairman Ron Allen, a hands-on, no-nonsense executive. I knew Chairman Allen would never approve a deal without at some point being personally involved in the negotiations. Sure enough, when it came time to "fish or cut bait," the negotiations teetered between success and failure for several days. Just how tenuous our position was became evident at the very moment we thought we were close to a deal.

As the delegation I had dispatched to pick up Chairman Allen in Richmond, Virginia, prepared to leave, Delta Vice President Harold Bevis advised them that there was no sense in going to get him because the terms we were preparing to discuss were unacceptable. When John Cubine, deputy to Finance Secretary Rogers Wells, told Wells what Bevis had said, he was advised in rather colorful but forceful words that they were to get on that plane and not return without Chairman Allen. It is still a mystery to me how Cubine, Ray Kring, and Denis Fleming kept us on track.

Cubine had been the lead negotiator on the deal and proved to be a persuasive salesman. In due time he returned with Chairman Allen. Wells pulled John aside when they arrived and asked him if they were coming to make a deal. Only people who know John personally can really appreciate his response. John is one of the most talented, decent, and humble people I know. He also possesses a dry wit. "Are they staying?" Wells asked. "Yes, sir" John replied. John calls everybody "sir." "How do you know that?" asked Wells. John quickly responded, "We have their luggage, sir."

Chairman Allen proved to be every bit as tough and gracious as you would want a chief executive to be. After almost a year of back and forth discussions between various people on both sides, the two of us finalized the deal on a yellow legal pad while sitting alone on the back patio of the Governor's executive mansion. This deal was a winner for both of us, and dealing with Ron Allen was a pleasure.

. . . but, not with United Airlines

Ironically, the project which probably generated the most media attention for Kentucky was the one we didn't get. Our discussions with United Airlines just never seemed right. In contrast to Delta's focus and decisiveness, it was very hard to get answers to even the most basic questions from United. Whenever we did get an answer to our questions, a different management group would often change or overrule it. Still, United was talking about the biggest project on the horizon, and we were as anxious as any state to be a part of the negotiations. After all, when they started their search for a location, they were talking about 7,000 jobs and a project worth a billion dollars.

Kentucky's offer was a combination of state, city and county funds totaling $341 million. Again, we tailored our proposal to meet what we guessed was United's greatest need. Like most airlines at the time, they needed cash, and we were offering $300 million of our package up front if they wanted it. Twenty-two months of intense negotiation ended in a late-evening telephone call from United headquarters inviting us to Chicago for final consideration the next morning. United made two requests of us. Come prepared to stay until the process is complete, and bring only the people absolutely necessary in order to avoid news leaks. We kept our side of the bargain, but by the time we got to Chicago it seemed like everyone in America knew we were there and why.

It was evident very quickly why the long negotiation process had been so frustrating. Instead of a final session to close a deal, United had invited four states to make final presentations. Each state was ensconced in a meeting area separate from the others to await a meeting. As the day wore on United officials would periodically drop in to update us on the course of their deliberations. I was immediately uncomfortable with the way United was conducting the process. We had been led to believe we were coming to Chicago to complete a deal. Instead we were involved in an bidding war.

When the time came for Kentucky to make its presentation, things deteriorated even more. At least twenty people were in the room representing various divisions of United. When United's Chairman Stephen Wolf was not among them, it was obvious to me that a final decision would not be made by the group in the room. The meeting was pretty much a three-ring circus. As soon as one division seemed satisfied that we had answered their questions, another division would raise the same questions, and we would go back over the whole process again. The fact that we had spent almost two years preparing detailed responses to all of the same questions seemed to have no bearing on the discussion. To make matters worse, I considered some of United's questions insulting and told them so, such as a request for a performance guarantee on certain aspects of the deal.

Throughout the many months of discussion, we had based our proposal on United's commitment of 7,000 jobs and a billion dollar investment. As we were going through a point-by-point review of our proposal, United suggested that the number of jobs might only be 6,300 and the level of investment substantially lower than a billion dollars. Furthermore, the salary levels that we had been told were projected in current (1991) dollars were in fact estimates for 2004. Actual salaries for the first thirteen years of the project would be substantially less.

As we did in every other project in which the state participated, we expected United to commit formally to meeting these projections or be required to refund a proportionate amount of the original incentive package. I was astonished that a company would reach this point in negotiations and think it could change the terms of a deal we had been talking about for two years. It didn't seem to occur to United that substantial changes in their investment would affect the level of our commitment.

Finally, at about 5:00 that afternoon, we were told that a decision would not be made that day, or possibly even the next day. We were told a new proposal had been presented and had yet to be evaluated. We were shown a news release to that effect and were advised to plan to stay over while the process continued. This was the last straw. If we had the best deal on the table, and I believe we did, and we were supposed to be in Chicago to make a final decision as we had been told, then it was obvious that United had no intention of coming to Kentucky. We were simply being used to help United squeeze more out of whatever state they had finally selected.

As we discussed what might be going on in United's mind, Joe Corradino, a consultant for the Regional Airport Authority of Louisville and Jefferson County who had been working with us throughout negotiations, interrupted and simply said, "We could walk." The room fell silent as every head turned to see how I would react. Even though Joe had expressed what we all felt about the whole process, we continued for a time to deliberate among ourselves what options we had and whether or not it was in Kentucky's best interest to stay. When our decision to withdraw Kentucky's proposal became public, there was some speculation that it might have been made in anger and haste. But it was nothing like that. I always said there is a point at which I would just as soon let someone else own something. The time to put that belief into practice had come in the United deal.

Our hosts were in yet another meeting, but no sooner had we sent word that our offer was withdrawn and we were leaving than Louis Valeria, senior vice president for finance and treasurer and Richard Street, vice president of airport affairs, literally raced down the hall after us. They pleaded with me as we walked outside to our cars, at one point even suggesting the Kentucky was leading. "You have conducted a public auction," I told them, "and no corporation is bigger than the Commonwealth of Kentucky." Even into the next day, United continued to insist that Kentucky was still under consideration despite our denials.

Indianapolis, Indiana, was eventually named the site selected for the expansion. It was Indiana's last minute proposal which caused United to renege on their commitment to finalize the process. Had we not done what we did, it's highly likely they would still be trying to make a decision. Even so, to no one's surprise in Kentucky, United has yet to begin the project as of this writing.

I don't know if it was possible for United to be embarrassed over their behavior, but I hope they were because they deserved to be. They were unprofessional, disorganized, and worst of all, disrespectful of their potential business partners. Even if Kentucky had stayed in the race, I don't think United would have ever located here. There was no way they would ever have agreed to our demand for specific levels of employment and investment.

Response to my decision to withdraw Kentucky's offer was universally positive. A member of the Colorado legislature even suggested that I be invited to run for governor there. Even the editors of the *Courier-Journal* and *Herald-Leader* agreed that we had done the right thing. Ironically, one of the few things on which the editors and I ever agreed was something that *didn't* happen.

Because I put so much emphasis on the needs of rural Kentucky, I tend to think of our major economic development deals more in terms of location than size. Seaboard Farms in Mayfield and Avian Farms near Somerset helped open new doors of opportunity and diversity for farmers throughout the commonwealth. Tibbals Flooring in Somerset was a first step in establishing a secondary wood products industry in Kentucky. North American Stainless located in Carroll County because it was uniquely suited for river access.

Two factors stand out among our many successes in economic development. First, I kept my promise to be a governor for all of Kentucky. By the end of my term we estimated that almost three-fourths of the jobs created had located in rural Kentucky counties. Furthermore, we had success attracting industries that showed long-term promise for helping diversify Kentucky's economy, particularly in areas where it was sorely needed, such as food processing and secondary wood products in eastern and southeastern Kentucky and poultry farming in west Kentucky. I could write an entire book about the negotiations with all the smaller deals to locate plants in Kentucky, but let it suffice to say I enjoyed them all.

"Whoopee, We're Rich!"

In addition to Economic Development, the two agencies on the front lines attacking infrastructure problems are the Departments of Transportation and Local Government headed by Milo Bryant and Lee Troutwine, respectively. The foundation for economic growth is public infrastructure. Kentucky's infrastructure is woefully inadequate in some areas even to this day.

A University of Kentucky study I cited in our *Kentucky First* platform estimated that some five billion dollars of work was required just to meet basic infrastructure needs. When I took office, there were still areas which did not have adequate clean water or sewage treatment facilities. Only a fraction of the state, virtually none of rural Kentucky, was served by fiber optics. Major road projects needed attention. Many areas of Kentucky could not accommodate new industry even if a company had wanted to locate there.

For a governor, the department of local government is like a warm blanket on a cold night. It provides one of the ways government can make someone happy. However, balancing need against available funds is a major challenge under the best of circumstances. I was particularly interested in making sure that counties and communities with more resources and sophistication in dealing with the system didn't have an advantage over those less well positioned.

Block grants and other funding tools administered by the governor's office are awarded on the basis of a scoring system calculated by local government staff. Nevertheless, I still expected Lee Troutwine, his assistant Sally Hamilton, director of community programs, and the rest of his staff to explain why each application was scored as it was. Every application was presented by the supervising staff member. I frequently challenged them to justify their scores. I was always impressed with the level of expertise and professionalism in the department. For their part I think they enjoyed the challenge of making a good presentation and having to justify their decisions.

I started every day with a bowl of fresh fruit on a table in the office. After a few of these sessions, the staff began to characterize our meetings based on the amount of fruit eaten. The better the presentation and explanation of scores, the shorter and smoother were our meetings. A "one banana" meeting was short and uneventful. Apparently I was more contentious in "two banana" meetings and downright difficult in "three banana" meetings. Eventually no one had to go into detail to describe our sessions. Everyone understood perfectly how things went based on the number of bananas eaten.

Over time I noticed a change in the way presentations were made. Word apparently got around that there were certain things you simply didn't say during our meetings. Gradually such tried and true bureaucratic cliches as "but, that's the way it's always been done," "use it or lose it," "it's never been done that way," and one which inspired the title for this book—"you can't do that, Governor"—disappeared from the presentations. It was a naive and uninformed presenter who tried to justify a project using one of these bureaucratic crutches.

The best part of the process is going on the road to announce the award of the grants. Local governments eagerly await the results of their applications. The reception is always positive when the governor shows up with a check. The fact that these grants rarely warrant much media attention except in the community specifically affected is one reason why so many areas have been neglected. Lack of political clout and indifference by the statewide media are enough to put any project on Frankfort's back burner.

Just how indifferent the statewide media are to the awarding of local grants is revealed in the attitude of Mark Chellgren, Frankfort bureau chief for Associated Press and an otherwise sensible reporter. Mark calls them the "Whoopee, we're rich" tours. True, grants of this nature represent a minuscule part of the overall state budget, but for the communities that receive them the money often is the difference between having clean water or not; remodeling a senior citizen's center, or being able to provide any number of other important local services. Come to think of it, I didn't hear a whole lot of hooting from Mark or anyone else on press row when I decided to include $50 million in the Community Bond Program for Louisville's airport project. Whoopee, *they're* rich too!

Most areas of Kentucky rarely see a governor. Early in this book I talked about the impact Governor Chandler's visit to Casey County had on me as a boy. Although television has changed how people are able to view public figures, I think the majority of people still appreciate it when their elected leaders think enough of them to visit now and then. I tried to use every mechanism available to me to bridge the gulf between what most people consider important and want to *hear* about, and what the media consider important and want to *talk* about.

Paving Our Way to Prosperity

Roads and road construction have been inextricably woven into the economic and political fortunes of state governments since colonial days. Anyone who has traveled Kentucky either as a candidate or elected official will tell you that at times it seems like road construction is thought by many to be the only function of state government.

Unquestionably roads, or a lack of them, are a critical part of Kentucky's infrastructure. Over the years, far more effort has gone in to fulfilling political promises than meeting the real economic needs of the state. Huge gaps, literally and figuratively, can be found on Kentucky's road map. Much of the cynicism directed toward Frankfort comes from those who have watched candidate after candidate pledge action only to be disappointed as their pet project got buried in budget negotiations or mired in the bureaucracy.

Getting a project funded is not nearly as hard as actually getting it built. That was the area I was particularly concerned about as I entered my tenure as governor. Allowed to work at its own pace, the bureaucracy in general—and transportation in particular—will operate at a snail's pace unless someone or something forces it to act. Without someone to keep cracking the whip over it, government and its various parts will bog down within itself in endless studies and committee meetings.

There never was any doubt about my priorities in transportation. I had been very specific during the campaign about the major projects I intended to pursue. We started with an ambitious agenda and added to it as we went along. Responsibility to move projects along and implement administration priorities is in the hands of the secretary of transportation, and I think Milo Bryant was one of the best ever.

Milo successfully negotiated both the bureau-cratic and political pitfalls in transportation and deserves far more credit than he received or will ever get for his contributions to Kentucky. I set what some people would consider unreasonable goals for the department of transportation, but the majority of them were met. Although he had every reason to say so on many occasions, never once did Milo tell me "you can't do that, Governor." His standard response was "we'll do the best we can," and he always did.

The William Natcher Bridge in Owensboro is a good example of Milo's determination and intensity. Owens-boro has needed a new bridge for a long time. As I noted earlier, every candidate for governor for years has promised the bridge "if and when Indiana decides to build a road to it on their side." I also promised the bridge, but I was committed to getting it built. Getting Indiana to agree to build the road was only one obstacle among many which had to be negotiated, however. Alternative designs had to be considered and envi-ronmental impact studies conducted on each option. Right of way had to be acquired and many other details worked out. It can take years to complete all of the preparations needed to build a major project before the first shovel can actually be put in the ground.

Month after month I asked Milo for an update on the bridge. He always assured me that we would be able to pour pilings before I left office. The closer we got to December 1991, the more I doubted that we could make the deadline. Milo gave me the best surprise of my administration when we poured concrete for the first footers on the Kentucky side on December 5, 1991, just four days before I left office.

The bridge is a fitting tribute to Congressman William H. Natcher. There is no way anyone will ever be able to calculate the contributions Chairman Natcher made to Kentucky over the years of service in the Congress. I can't speak for other governors, but I can honestly say he was always there when I needed him. A man of few words but eloquent deeds, the Chairman would listen to my explanation of what was needed and invariably respond, "Governor, the President will have an appropriations request on his desk." And he always did. The Owensboro bridge was just one great example of his ability to deliver.

Another success story I enjoy telling involves a bridge proposed in Nelson County and newspaper columnist Steve Lowery at the *Kentucky Standard* in Bardstown. The bridge itself came to be known as the Fogle Bridge because Avon Fogle made such a persistent and impassioned plea for its construction. When I told Avon that I would build the bridge, Steve portrayed my pledge as just another politician's promise. Periodically during the administration Steve would remind his readers of my promise in his column and invariably question its sincerity. In one column he made a promise of his own to put a photograph of Avon and me on the front page of the *Standard* if the bridge ever got started. I am happy to say that I kept my promise, and so did Steve.

Because transportation issues are among the more politically charged in state government, transportation secretaries generally take an inordinate amount of abuse from all sides. Naturally when something goes well, everyone thanks the governor while the secretary is busy explaining to others why their projects can't get done. The things nobody ever sees, and the media certainly doesn't care about, are the hours of time and effort that go on behind the scenes keeping a project on track.

While Milo was busy making sure that every road with a Kentucky state highway number was paved, many for the first time in the history of the commonwealth, the press was busy exposing his effort to brighten working conditions at the department offices by changing the light bulbs or criticizing him for trying to keep Kentucky's interstate highway system presentable. The *Lexington Herald-Leader* had a particular problem with our mowing program, apparently preferring to see wildflowers adorn the highways than mown grass.

While the newspaper's position might have merit from someone's perspective, I never fully appreciated the major policy standing they afforded the issue. All I know is that while Milo was secretary of transportation, Kentucky's roads never looked better. While they didn't mean it as a compliment, and Milo didn't particularly like it, not a spring will ever pass that I won't think of Milo and the *Herald's* description of his philosophy: "When it stops snowing, start mowing."

By the time the administration ended, we had either completed or substantially begun all of the major projects I talked about in my campaign: the two legs of the AA Highway, U.S. 23, 25E, U.S. 119, U.S 68 from Bowling Green to Cadiz, and U.S. 27. We had paved every mile of previously unpaved state road. We had begun a bridge replacement program to rebuild every state bridge that would not bear the weight of a loaded school bus. In addition to the Natcher Bridge, we had made substantial progress on four other Ohio River bridges in Maysville, Louisville, and northern Kentucky. We even had equipment on sight and contracts let to begin the · construction of Paris Pike, one of the most controversial and most delayed road projects over the past twenty years.

One thing I learned quickly about state government is that the bureaucracy will rarely present an option that is not already acceptable to it. Wading through the history and research on a project in order to break their "envelope of acceptability" can take months or even years. That is one of the reasons why governors have such a hard time getting anything done. Should a governor dare to propose something outside the "envelope," the bureaucrats simply "hunker down" and wait out the rest of the administration. Limited to four years in office, many governors never saw the beginning of a major project, much less the completion of one. The construction of a major road or bridge can take years, but far too many projects are needlessly delayed simply because of the legislative and bureaucratic obstacle course they must traverse.

Subsequent vacillation or inaction on a number of projects has denied Kentuckians the benefits of the projects themselves and potentially cost millions of additional dollars should the projects ever be done. For example, I had a commitment from Congressman William Natcher to fund the new bridge in Louisville until bickering over its location delayed it. After we left office and before his death, Chairman Natcher told Secretary Bryant that he could have made sure funding was in the budget for a new bridge in Louisville if only someone from the Jones administration had come to Washington and asked for it. They had not. Furthermore, we had a written agreement with Governor Evan Bayh that has been ignored that Indiana would pay for half of the bridge even though they would normally be responsible for only twenty percent of it.

These projects have either died or been delayed because of neglect. In a couple of other cases, deliberate action by Governor Jones killed the project. He canceled what remained of the county bridge replacement program that wasn't already under construction and, in an act of incredible selfishness, stopped construction of the Paris Pike.

Paris Pike is one of those issues that comes along now and then to which there is no easy answer. There are powerful and appealing arguments on both sides, either to widen it or preserve it as a scenic and historic thoroughfare. Despite opposition from preservationists, every study conducted over a twenty year period concluded that the Paris Pike needed to be widened, and there was no reasonable alternate route. The federal court was about to lift the final barrier to construction when Governor-elect Jones announced his opposition to it. Either Jones didn't understand the consequences of what he was saying, or he deliberately torpedoed the project because of opposition from his fellow horsemen in the area. Whatever his reason, all he did was delay the inevitable even longer.

While much has been made in the media about the reconvening of the various groups for and against the Paris Pike for additional study, the end result was simply to delay the project further while those groups came up with the same design that was on the table and ready to begin in 1991. As of this writing construction still had not started on Paris Pike. The only way it is ever going to get done is for some governor to once again put his foot down and simply say, "We've addressed every objection; we've answered every question; we're going to build it."

Creating Jobs

It is generally recognized that a state economy is influenced greatly by the condition of the national economy, but I felt we made considerable progress in job growth at a time when job growth nationally was in decline. By the end of my administration, we were able to elevate Kentucky in virtually every statistical category. However, creating the conditions for *sustainable* economic growth is a goal pursued by every governor. The work begins with a clear policy for building the human infrastructure of the domestic economy.

A Policy for Workforce Development

Three historic developments brought about significant changes in the American economy in recent years: (1) the emergence of global competition for the markets of American goods; (2) a dramatic growth in the information and service sector of the economy; and (3) increased automation of the workplace.

The erosion of the American share of the world market caused serious structural dysfunctions in the manufacturing sector of our economy. Over the last decade many companies either closed their American plants or substantially reduced their workforce, as production of manufactured goods slowed or moved offshore. As these market changes were occurring, important changes also were taking place in manufacturing technology and business processes. Scientific advances in microelectronics led to the automation of many aspects of business and commerce. In less than two decades, we evolved into a technology and information-driven economy.

One very important outcome of these economic events was a significant change in the nature of work and job security. Many jobs have been lost in recent years as highly automated machines now perform the work previously done by people. Perhaps of even greater importance, the introduction of automation created a much more sophisticated work environment. Clearly different skills are required of today's workers than were expected of them even two decades ago. Rapidly changing technology also has affected job security, requiring workers to undergo retraining every few years to keep their jobs. In a paper I delivered at the International Roundtable on Educational Reform at St. Peters College, Oxford, England in August 1989, I said that:

> *a properly educated and trained workforce is just as essential to a healthy economy as superior technology, plentiful energy, good public services, and transportation. Any strategy for improving one's competitive position through technology must take into account the need to prepare and sustain a workforce that can match the sophistication of the workplace.*

> *It seems quite clear that the transition to an information and technology-based economy is going to require us to develop and sustain over time an educated, flexible, and trainable workforce that can be productive in this kind of work environment. The public and private investment we make to develop and continually upgrade the workforce as technology changes will largely determine the ability of American business and industry to remain competitive in a global marketplace.*

In my view, workforce development had to have the same standing and importance in government as the more traditional "economic" development, since the two are now inseparable. We must change the way we do our business not only in the recruitment and retention of business and industry, but in the development and maintenance of a highly skilled workforce. As I told the Oxford participants:

Economic growth in the past was fueled primarily by significant investment in capital goods. Industrialization required heavy investment in manufacturing plants, energy production and distribution facilities, necessary public services, and an extensive transportation system, but required little investment in the workforce. Workers for these industries were generally in sufficient supply, and the cost to make them productive was small and relatively insignificant compared to the investment in capital goods.

However, as we moved toward an information and technology-driven economy, the nature of work significantly changed. Automated machines now are the "workers," and employees are supervisors of machines that do the work they formerly did. Clearly, different skills are required in this new work environment.

And herein lies the strategic role that our education systems must play in the future economic well-being of the state and nation. It is my view that, for at least the next quarter century, the economic competitive edge will belong to those nations that succeed in developing a cost-effective system for educating and training its population to be productive workers in a technology and information driven economy. Education and economic advantage are now interdependent variables.

As a governor leading a state into this new era, I wanted Kentucky's business and industry to be competitive in both the domestic and international marketplace. Toyota's success in Kentucky clearly demonstrated that we could provide as good a workforce as could be found anywhere in the world. Their experience also told us that many Kentucky workers could not qualify to work in this new environment. Of the thousands of employees they interviewed, far too many did not possess the qualifications needed to work in the new technological workplace. It was obvious we still had a long way to go to develop and maintain a highly competitive workforce in the years to come.

A strategic approach to developing and maintaining a competent workforce begins with our youth. As the high school diploma becomes the entry level education requirement, workers without a high school diploma will find it increasingly difficult to find new employment once they lose their present jobs. Clearly we must get every Kentucky youngster to complete high school so they do not add to this pool of ill-prepared workers. Hopefully, the changes we have made in our public education system will make us more successful at this in the future. However, even the dramatic changes being made in our K-12 school system will have relatively little impact on the workforce until well into the next century.

Helping the Poorly Educated Worker

Kentucky has a substantial number of workers and prospective workers whose educational skills are so poor they make job training difficult and costly to the employer and the state. Most of these workers do not have a high school diploma and some are not literate enough to undertake the kind of training required of today's workers. Erasing such a long-standing educational deficit is a daunting task. At least one-third of the adult population in Kentucky has less than a secondary school education. It was obvious that we had to engage in a serious effort to raise the educational level of the existing workforce to at least the equivalent of a high school education.

My wife Martha led the charge in our fight against illiteracy and undereducation. In the early months of the administration she traveled across Kentucky giving graduation speeches to recipients of the General Educational Development (GED) diploma, a national high school equivalency education program. She was struck by the courage of these people. She also was beseeched by relatives and friends of these graduates to encourage others to do the same. She felt a deep compassion for these people who were struggling so hard to succeed without the benefit of a high school diploma. She honestly felt she should do something to help.

At that time she was working primarily with the GED program offered by the Kentucky Department of Education through its thirty-eight adult learning centers scattered around the commonwealth. After visiting some of these centers, it was obvious that this approach was not getting the job done. Martha met with the officials heading up the program and was basically given a tale of woe about a lack of funding and not enough staff to do the job. Martha wasn't very satisfied with what she heard.

KET, the Kentucky educational television agency, offered a very successful GED program on television which also was available on videotape. She met with O. Leonard Press, then director of KET, to discuss how she could help get the people of Kentucky to take advantage of this program. It seemed to her that this would be a much quicker and possibly more effective approach than the one used by the Adult Education Division of the Department of Education.

On a summer day in 1988, Martha was meeting with "Len" Press to discuss plans for a campaign to inform the public of the opportunity to earn their GED diploma through the KET program. Martha mentioned that there was a whole "army" of people across the commonwealth just waiting for this opportunity if they could only be reached with the challenge. Len right then proposed that the campaign be called "Martha's Army." She was immediately named the "General" of the newly organized "GED Army." Thus was born perhaps the most intensive effort ever undertaken in any state to enlist people in a campaign to earn a high school equivalency diploma.

The KET promotional program was launched that August at the state fair in Louisville with posters of Martha in army fatigues asking people to join her GED Army. One of the first volunteers Martha recruited was her own mother Lucille Stafford who helped organize a hotline for GED information at the Capitol Annex. The response was phenomenal.

As Martha traveled across the commonwealth pushing her campaign, she learned that the ten dollar test fee was an obstacle for many people. She approached the staff at the Department of Education for help, but they said their funds were committed to the adult education program they operated and could not be used for the KET program. Disgusted with this attitude, Martha appealed to private industry and our supporters for private donations.

Just before Christmas that first year, $10,000 was donated by Columbia Gas of Kentucky, Inc., to pay the testing fee for 1,000 Kentucky adults who wanted to earn the GED diploma and could not afford the testing fee. At a press conference announcing the gift, Columbia chairman and chief executive officer C. Ronald Tilley said the company also would sponsor workshops on resume preparation, job application completion, and job interview skills for those who passed the test.

Appearing before a legislative panel in March 1989, Martha urged the state to open its GED incentive program to more state employees. She spoke in favor of a proposed regulation which would make all state workers eligible for a one-time 10 percent bonus for earning their GEDs. At the time only permanent, fulltime state employees were eligible. She thought state government, one of the largest employers in the commonwealth, should set an example for business and industry.

Perhaps one of our most memorable moments was when Waylon Jennings told Martha he was going to get his GED because of her influence. In September 1989 Bill Farley, chief executive of Fruit of the Loom Corporation, sponsored a benefit concert on behalf of the GED Army. Jennings was the featured attraction. During the concert he commented that one of his great disappointments in life was his failure to complete high school. When the program was over, Martha went backstage and promised Waylon she would get him copies of the KET videotapes so he could get his GED. Waylon laughed at the time and said he probably should do it.

The next night Waylon was giving a benefit concert for Muscular Dystrophy in Louisville. True to her promise, and probably to his surprise, Martha showed up in Louisville with a set of the KET videotapes in her hand. She encouraged him to get his GED now. She kept in touch with Waylon, reminding him of the impact this could have on others in Kentucky and elsewhere. In October we visited Waylon and his lovely wife Jessie Colter at their home in Brentwood, Tennessee. He promised Martha he would have his GED by Christmas. Well, he kept his promise. He studied the KET videotapes, often with the help of his young son Shooter, as they traveled around the country in his tour bus. In December he took the GED test at the Hyatt Regency Hotel in Lexington.

When Martha called Waylon to tell him he had passed, he told her to keep the certificate until he could come to Kentucky in January for a special two hour television show on KET during which people could call in and register for the "GED on TV" program. Waylon had helped her in September 1989 with the first one which was a great success. But this time there would be a difference. This time he too would have earned his GED. He came to Frankfort early the day of the telecast so Martha could personally award the diploma to him.

During the first telecast in 1989, Martha offered to give away 500 free GED enrollments if people would call in to register for them during the program. She awarded 686 that night because, as she put it, "the phones just kept ringing, and I couldn't say no." The second telecast with Waylon was successful beyond anyone's wildest dreams. This time Martha offered 1,000 free enrollments to people who called in during the show. KET had received 2,520 calls from 112 counties by the time the two-hour program ended! She funded every one of them from money raised by her GED Army volunteers.

The local telephone company said that over 107,000 calls had been placed to the KET telethon number during the two hours of the telecast. Only a fraction of them were able to get through. Martha could barely contain her excitement when she came home from the telethon. "We could enroll 50,000 people if we had the money," she told me. At about $20 per enrollee for materials and the testing fee, she estimated that $1 million would do it.

In a March 1 letter to the chairs of the House and Senate Appropriations Committees, I requested $1.5 million to KET to fund a modest marketing program and the cost of materials and fees for additional GED enrollees. Had anyone but Martha been responsible for the surge in GED enrollments, this amendment would have sailed through the budget process. However, in as vengeful and selfish an act as any I witnessed as governor, House Education Committee Chairman Roger Noe and others killed the request.

There is no telling how many people would have achieved their GED by now had the momentum generated by Martha's Army not been snuffed out by Governor Jones and the few bureaucrats who resented her success. As soon as possible the new administration acted to bury any aspect of the literacy program with which Martha had been involved. The Literacy Commission was absorbed by the Department for Adult Education and ceased to exist. Not wanting to irritate Jones, and lacking Martha's enthusiasm and private fundraising support, KET stopped sponsoring the telethons.

Although Martha's GED Army received a lot of great publicity, including a national story in *Parade Magazine*, she also dedicated much of her time to the literacy program of the state. I appointed her to the Literacy Commission, where she was an active member. She worked to get a local literacy program active in every county of the commonwealth. She also promoted reading in a variety of settings and encouraged people of all ages to learn to read and write. She even established some job-site literacy programs for workers at industries throughout Kentucky.

Martha promoted the importance of literacy skills by joining with the Jesse Stuart Foundation, the Kentucky Jaycees, and the United Parcel Service in the distribution of a copy of Stuart's book *The Beatinest Boy* to every sixth grade student in Kentucky. She also sponsored a statewide essay contest in which students were asked to write up to one page about what they learned from the book. Awards were given for the best essay in every class, county, and congressional district.

Martha's success with her "army" and adult literacy efforts is one of the many assets she brought to my administration. She never was one to just be seen and not heard. She is a great motivator and found her own way to contribute to the governorship. What she accomplished was something of which I am extremely proud. I know she will be remembered by literally hundreds of Kentuckians as the one who inspired them to pursue a lifelong dream—the completion of their formal education.

Sustaining a Highly Qualified Workforce

The most glaring gap in the workforce education and training structure in Kentucky was a strategic approach to upgrading and retraining the existing workforce. We are told that at least four of every five persons who will be working in the year 2000 are already in the workforce. Thus, the most serious challenge facing Kentucky was the need to develop *in the existing workforce* the skills and knowledge required to be productive in a rapidly changing workplace.

Kentucky has not had a coherent approach to workforce development, in part because policy decisions and management of the delivery system have been highly fragmented. Furthermore, we lacked a clear policy for job *retraining* which could guide the public investment in the job training system. Until the last decade or so, publicly funded job-related education and training focused almost exclusively on *new entrants to the workforce*. Training of workers already in the workforce was left primarily to business and industry.

Various estimates of the investment in training made by American business and industry indicate that private expenditures for job training now surpass what all the states together spend on higher education. Clearly the private sector was already investing in training, so the policy issue here is how government and the private sector can equitably share responsibility for creating and sustaining a flexible, responsive training system which meets the unique needs of business and industry. Given the rapid and continuous changes occurring in the workplace, retraining certainly will continue to require intensive capital investment well into the next century.

A number of states, including Kentucky, offer to finance part of the cost of specific job training as part of an incentive program. The Kentucky Bluegrass State Skills Corporation was created in part to provide limited funds for this purpose. During my administration I increased the amount requested for job training through BSSC. I also funded training commitments made to General Electric, Ford, and Toyota by the previous administration. Actions of the type just described usually are combined with other economic incentives designed to lure new jobs to the state or to prevent the loss of existing jobs. The very fact job training is now an important element in an incentive package shows how much business and industry value it.

The problem with this approach is that it tends to rely too much on "deal making" and doesn't address the training needs of thousands of small and medium-sized businesses in Kentucky that are not at the negotiating table asking for similar assistance. A much more systemic approach has to be developed. We must be just as creative in addressing this problem as we were in restructuring public education. One approach is to give the private sector more direct leverage over the public training system. Rather than put more money directly into the system, I preferred to empower workers and employers to get the system to provide the training they needed. The key idea is to put the purchasing power directly in the hands of employers and workers.

Exploratory discussions were held with representatives of business and labor about the feasibility of creating a Workforce Training Trust Fund to provide private financing for much of the cost of keeping Kentucky workers competitive over the long haul. The idea was to have the state create and manage the fund in a manner similar to the unemployment insurance program. Contributions would be made by business and industry, and the benefits would accrue to each contributor when it came time to train or retrain either new or existing workers. The concept was given serious consideration, but in anticipation of a tax increase in the 1990 legislative session they wanted to put the idea on hold for awhile.

I sought to provide direct help to the worker who had already lost a job through a job training certificate program modeled after the federal GI bill created for veterans of World War II and the Korean conflict. In my first legislative session in 1988, I submitted a bill to create a job training certificate program designed to meet the needs of the experienced but temporarily unemployed worker. The bill was referred to the House Education Committee, where it got bottled up with my education incentive program and became another victim of Rep. Roger Noe's shortsightedness.

Even though I failed to get the legislation or budget appropriation for the program at that time, I did create a pilot program by executive order in March 1989, and funded it with money from the Job Training Partnership Act. Workers who had been laid off due to plant closings, general economic conditions, or natural disasters were eligible to receive a certificate which paid for a part or all of the cost of training for re-employment. The program made training funds available to workers in seven counties in the Louisville area.

Restructuring the Training System

Probably the most important action I took to improve the Kentucky workforce was to restructure the state bureaucracy to bring about greater coordination of the existing public investment in job training. The opportunity to act on the policy assumptions I articulated at Oxford six months earlier was now at hand. In the 1990 session of the General Assembly I submitted a bill to create a Workforce Development Cabinet, the first of its kind in the nation. The legislation passed with little opposition even though it probably represented one of the largest reorganizations in state government in at least a decade.

While public attention was focused on the Task Force for School Reform, Jack Foster quietly initiated a series of discussions with key staff from the agencies which currently had responsibility for some aspect of job training to review various options. It was almost certain the Department of Education was in for a major shakeup, so the time was right to make a decision about where adult and vocational education should be placed. Just before Thanksgiving I received the outline of a reorganization proposal and gave the go ahead on it in early December 1989. Jack was heavily involved in the work of the Task Force on School Reform, so I asked his deputy Sandy Gubser to take responsibility for development and passage of the legislation. She did an excellent job and contributed greatly to the task of getting it through the legislative minefield.

Known as HB 814, the legislation brought under one umbrella agencies from the Department of Education, the Cabinet for Education and Humanities, and the Cabinet for

Human Resources. Various boards and commissions dealing with adult or vocational training also were moved to the new cabinet. I appointed Sandy Gubser as the first secretary of the cabinet with a mandate to do whatever was necessary to get control of the job training bureaucracy, which had become almost a kingdom of its own. All the tools of reorganization were in the legislation such as the re-appointment of staff, compensation, structure, and governance of each element of the policy and training apparatus.

I am very proud of this achievement even though I didn't feel we went as far as we probably should have in streamlining the delivery system. The political influence of vocational education teachers proved to be difficult to over-come. Reorganizations are very difficult to pull off successfully. Usually the agencies brought together find ways to keep their turf protected within the new structure. Still I think we set the stage for many important improvements in the system, and the potential is there to bring about more change in the future.

A year after its creation, I commissioned a study of the reorganization by Dr. Roger Vaughan which was com-pleted just before I left office in 1991. His findings were that the reorganization still had not succeeded in consolidating policy making, lacked a strong internal management informa-tion system to guide policy and support accountability for program success, and left in place funding mechanisms which do not promote and reward efficiency and innovation. He commended Kentucky for taking such a bold step and believed strong action at the time could remediate the problems he identified.

I had hoped to see more change than occurred, but time ran out. It looked to me like we had just changed the address for the vocational education department. To some degree the same thing happened with the department of educa-tion. The reform act wiped out the department, only to see it recreated with many of the same faces. It is very difficult to significantly change government bureacracies.

On the other hand, I am pleased at what we were able to do in just four years to improve the economic environment of the state. Our business recruitment and retention efforts paid off handsomely. The infrastructure improvements we made were a good beginning toward remediating years of neglect by Frankfort. The effort to improve the skills and education of the workforce takes a much longer perspective to evaluate. Only time will tell how much improvement we made in our ability to create and maintain a trained, flexible, productive workforce that can compete on a par with workers anywhere in the world. Certainly the changes we made in public education and in the structure of workforce development positioned the commonwealth to compete aggressively for jobs in the future.

XIII. THE POLITICS
OF CONFRONTATION

Throughout my administration I was variously described as combative, confrontational, abrasive, and uncompromising in my relationship with the General Assembly. One reporter even counted the number of times I used the word "fight" in one of my addresses to the legislature. I came from an environment where people were willing to fight for what they believed in, and they were respected for doing so. Fighting for something didn't mean being brutal, ruthless, or unethical, but it did mean being willing to use every legitimate means available to reach your goal.

Newspaper editors and political columnists constantly chided me for not showing a more cooperative spirit. They argued that my "fighting" attitude was impairing the effectiveness of my administration. Even within my circle of advisors there were some who thought I was at times unnecessarily rough on the legislature. I'm sure many people have wondered if the style I chose to use with the legislature was just the behavior of a stubborn businessman who is used to getting his way, or a deliberate political strategy designed to irritate and motivate an unfriendly legislature. I will put this question to rest right now.

Under most circumstances, my style is to be relaxed, disarming, and persuasive. In fact, I'm known for my friendly "bear hugs" and vigorous handshake. At one point when things were hottest with the General Assembly, Senator Tim Shaughnessy of Louisville told a *Courier-Journal* reporter, "One on one, that man is the most charming person I have ever met in my life, and I just don't know why he just can't take that same type of attitude and work together." What Senator Shaughnessy didn't understand is that confrontation can be an effective political tool in an adversarial relationship such as the one I found between the governor and the General Assembly in Kentucky, especially with a governor who came to office outside the political mainstream.

Given the circumstances I discovered when I arrived in Frankfort, I personally believe my willingness to confront rather than cater to the legislature was both necessary and appropriate. Allan J. Lichtman, a history professor at American University, was quoted in the *Wall Street Journal* in 1992, saying, "The most successful leaders (nationally) have dealt with Congress by bullying them, but essentially going over their heads to the American people, getting solid support for their proposals and then presenting them to Congress. If you try to coddle them, get into the back room with them, then your programs will be nibbled away and you'll fall into the morass."

The Political Relevance of Style

I came into office understanding that I would have to put up a fight for some of the things I wanted. I was not so naive as to think that all I had to do was suggest some ideas to the legislature and it would promptly enact them into law. As a populist governor, I didn't have available the tools of party discipline or long-standing working relationships with legislators. Only a handful of legislators supported me during the primary election campaign. It was obvious I would have to be politically aggressive if I wanted to see my programs enacted into law and funded.

The issue of how hard I was willing to fight for my agenda came up during my first press conference after the November election. Bob Johnson of the *Courier-Journal* asked if I intended to pressure the General Assembly to pass my programs. I responded by saying, "I intend to exercise all the influence that I can to pass our programs." The idea that I would not do everything in my power to pass the programs I had talked about as a candidate was completely foreign to me.

"Wilkinson will have to learn fine art of compromise" was the headline of a political commentary appearing in the Owensboro *Messenger-Inquirer* shortly after the November election in 1987. A portion of the column written by Keith Lawrence is worth sharing here because he accurately summed up the situation I faced.

> *Wilkinson takes pride in being a self-made man. He likes to talk about pulling himself up by his bootstraps from poverty to wealth. He's a take-charge person who is used to doing things himself.*
>
> *But being governor doesn't work that way. Since 1980, the Kentucky General Assembly— particularly the House—has been taking an assertive course. In the old days, a governor could come up with a plan of action and give the orders. The legislature would jump in line and carry out his wishes.*
>
> *Compromise is a fact of life in Frankfort. Being governor requires the ability to share the power and the ideas. These days you handle the House like you would a porcupine. Approach it from the front, don't turn your back on it, and don't get it mad.* [*Messenger-Inquirer*, November 29, 1987]

Lawrence surely was right when he characterized the House as an ill-tempered "porcupine" which fends you off with threats if you challenge it. However, as I will explain in a moment, all this talk about "working with the General Assembly" actually was nonsense.

The Call for Cooperation Was Misguided

I came to the office of governor with an agenda for change. I wanted to see the legislature take action on that agenda. We didn't need to like each other to be able to work together. Government is not about people "getting along." It's about getting on with the people's business. Cooperation is fine, but if it isn't forthcoming, other methods must be used, or you simply have to give up on what you came to do. There are some fundamental reasons why cooperation with the General Assembly at that time was doomed to failure.

When I came to the governorship, there was little indication by legislative leadership that they were prepared to cooperate with the executive branch. There was a lot of public expression of a desire to work together, but little substance behind it. What leadership really wanted was good relations with the governor, meaning no open *hostility* between us. A kind of peaceful coexistence, if you will. The governor was to be seen but not heard. They certainly did *not* mean they expected or wanted the governor and legislature to work amicably together on a common agenda.

Because the *institution* of the governor's office was being increasingly ignored by the legislature, it was politically important to communicate forcefully the level of my commitment to the agenda I put forth as a candidate. There could be no doubt in the minds of legislators about my willingness to "go to the mat" for the things I wanted. Every public statement and action had to convey that message. Furthermore, leadership intended to continue to diminish the power of the executive branch. I knew it would be necessary to put them on notice that I would strenuously resist any further erosion of executive authority.

From a practical standpoint, I really had no other option than to enter into open political warfare with the legislature. As uncomfortable as this political style made some people feel, it was the only effective way to deal with a defiant Kentucky legislature. I was under no illusion that I could somehow intimidate or coerce the legislature into enacting my agenda into law. The legislature had grown independent enough that a governor no longer could directly force it to do anything it didn't want to do. Here are some reason why cooperation between a governor and the legislature was not feasible at this point in Kentucky history.

The Myth of Political Cooperation

History has shown that most attempts at cooperation in government fail miserably, whether it's between agencies or branches of government. Cooperation requires an organization to subject its decisions to the review, consent, or participation of people it cannot control. Such behavior is generally contrary to the self-interest of most organizations. In fact most organizations do everything they can to achieve *independence* so they don't have to negotiate or compromise their decisions. People with power always want to exercise that power without interference from others. They only share power with others when required to do so or it is clearly in their self-interest to do so.

The form of government adopted in the United States is based on a concept of power being balanced among three branches of government. Our forefathers anticipated a power struggle between the branches and tried to contain it by placing constitutional limits on what each branch of government can do without the consent of the others. Sharing power is not optional; it is required by the constitution.

The interdependence of the branches was created by the constitution to force them to work together even when they are under the control of opposing political parties. In reality, however, it hasn't always worked out that way. Unless checked by the electorate or by a sense of what constitutes "good government," one branch from time to time will seek to overpower the other. The continual ebb and flow of power between the branches probably is inevitable, but the constitution eventually should bring it back into balance.

The Quest for Legislative Independence

Historically, Kentucky governors exerted direct control over the legislature. Wendell Ford was the last governor to openly impose his will on the General Assembly, although Julian Carroll did so during the early part of his administration. Committee chairs would wait for a list from the governor's office to learn what bills the governor wanted action on that day and what action he wanted on them. A governor's budget could be passed in just five days without amendment. The General Assembly was a captive of the governor, who appointed the leadership, committee chairs, and approved committee appointments. Certainly one could not consider the General Assembly an equal branch of government under these circumstances.

A book titled *The Sometime Governments* was published by Bantam Books in 1971 which was highly critical of state legislatures. The book reported the results of a national study which essentially declared most state legislatures moribund. The results were reported in the national media and spurred action to strengthen state legislatures throughout the country. The control Kentucky governors had over the General Assembly was considered inconsistent with the constitutional provision for separate but equal branches of government.

Beginning in the mid-1960s the Kentucky General Assembly enacted a series of changes designed to free itself from the direct influence of a governor. In a 1967 memorandum to Legislative Research Commission members detailed in *The Kentucky Legislature: Two Decades of Change* (Jewell and Miller, University of Kentucky Press, 1988), then director Jim Fleming argued that changes could be made in the legislature without constitutional amendments. "The General Assembly has failed to use all of the powers it now has," says Fleming. In his memorandum, Fleming outlined a system with fewer but more powerful committees, the establishment of interim committees, and a decrease in leadership's discretion in assigning bills.

Over the next decade legislative leadership took every available opportunity to distance itself from the governor's office. In 1979 voters approved a constitutional amendment which changed the election of legislators to a different year than election of the governor as a way to curb the alleged political control of legislative races by governors. This change gave the interim committees one year to work before a new governor took office.

Structure was not the only thing to change. There also was a change in the political goals of legislative leadership. In time, equal came to mean independent. In its evolution toward greater freedom from the influence of a governor, the political posture of the legislature has moved from rebellion against the executive branch to a position of dominance and finally to dysfunction.

Cooperation is in reality antithetical to the Kentucky legislature's goal of absolute freedom from the influence of a governor. Legislative leaders have been obsessed with the notion of "independence." Unfortunately, in their pursuit of freedom from domination by a governor, legislative leadership confused independence with autocracy. Given their constitutional authority to write laws and to appropriate money, legislators came to believe they alone could and *should* govern the commonwealth.

The more independent you feel, the more autocratic you tend to behave. Legislative leaders said many times "*we* will decide what is good for the commonwealth." Translated, this meant their intention to take action with or without the governor's participation. It is very frustrating to try to work cooperatively with the leadership of an "independent" General Assembly which equates independence with power and ascendancy. As long as legislative leadership continued to believe they could act alone, I could not be an effective governor. No one could be under these circumstances. If nothing else, I had to stay "in their face" to keep them aware that the governor was someone whom they simply could not ignore or consider irrelevant.

No Mechanisms Exist to Support Cooperation

In my view, working together means sitting down and coming to agreement on what can be done together. I invited leadership to the governor's mansion on various occasions for this very purpose. Perhaps out of fear of domination, leadership carefully avoided any action which might create the perception they were acting under my influence. They politely listened to what I had to say but refused to engage in any discussion that looked to them like negotiations.

In this new era of legislative-executive relations, I quickly learned that a private agreement with leadership carries no assurance that they will (or can) follow through on it afterward. In fact, I learned that an agreement with leadership was not necessarily an agreement at all. What a governor is told is "we will work for it, but the members will ultimately make up their own minds." In other words, you are expected to work with and through leadership if you want something, but then they tell you they cannot promise to deliver anything.

In an attempt to explain why they could not negotiate with me, Senator Rose at one point told me the legislature was past the point where leadership could cut "back room deals" with a governor. Everything had to go through the "process." Well, the process is precisely what stood in the way of cooperation. There was no one who could sit down and say, "All right, here's what we will try to do. I will use whatever means are available to get it done." Instead, what I heard was "it's up to the committees to decide what should be done." If the legislature actually is run by committees, as leadership wanted me to believe, then there is little reason for a governor to meet with leadership or even regard them as important. The governor should meet with committee chairs and bypass leadership entirely.

The whole idea that the legislative process is some kind of self-determining thing is nonsense. Leadership clearly exercises a control over what the committees do. When it came time to take action on succession, the road bonds, education reform, and other issues of importance to me, leadership saw to it that the committees did precisely what leadership wanted. The point I'm making is that the legislative process is structured in such a way that a governor has no clear point of access. Although governors should not be in a position to dictate to the legislature, they should be able to influence the legislative process in some manner. A process must exist through which legislative leaders and a governor can work out their political differences and move forward with the public's business. Such a process doesn't exist in Kentucky.

Cooperation is a Two-Way Street

Cooperation cannot be a solo performance. Both sides must open their doors to participation and discussion. The political behavior of legislative leadership didn't support the kind of open dialogue between the branches required for cooperation. Time after time I tried to work with leadership, but there was no reciprocation. Every meeting I had with leadership was at my invitation. Not once was I ever invited by leadership to meet with them on anything.

In the entire four years, I could rarely get leadership to sit across the table with me to *work together*. The only exceptions were the meeting I had with leadership right after the court decision, a series of meetings I had with the budget chairs to work on the budget numbers for KERA, and the historic meeting in my office when I reluctantly agreed to the sales tax rate increase. With the burden on the governor to initiate and maintain communication, the governor is almost always in a no-win situation. Should leadership determine it is in their interest to initiate communication with the governor, they do so. When it's not, they simply say the governor won't work with them.

I don't believe this avoidance behavior was due to my critical comments about them, as some people might think. Politicians are not that thin-skinned. There was a pattern to leadership behavior going back at least two administrations. Governors invited legislators to their office, but never the other way around. Not much business was ever conducted in these meetings. People talked *to* each other, but not *with* each other. After a while a governor gets the picture. If there is to be a meeting between the governor and the legislature, the governor must initiate the action. That's not exactly how I think cooperation should work.

An Absence of Incentives for Cooperation

At the present time, there is little reason for the General Assembly to try to work with a governor. There is not much governors in Kentucky can offer legislators to encourage or reward their cooperation and help. In the days when governors controlled leadership and legislative committee appointments, a governor could use these tools to secure loyalty to his or her political agenda. Now legislative leaders use these same tools to secure and maintain loyalty to their own political agenda and in some cases opposition to the governor.

Over the previous decade, the legislature systematically took control of most things which bound legislators to a governor. This trend continued throughout my administration as the legislature sought control over roads, economic development, board appointments, and regulations. By the time I was elected, the legislature didn't need a governor to accomplish most of what it wanted. So what price was there to pay for opposition to or defiance of a governor? The only thing legislators still seemed to fear from a governor was opposition at the polls.

A cooperative relationship between the legislature and the governor might be a desirable state in the minds of some people, but it was clear to me that cooperation with the

General Assembly was not feasible. Furthermore, it was time for someone to challenge the leadership of the General Assembly and put an end to any further encroachment on the constitutional authority and responsibilities of the office of the governor and the principle of separate but equal branches of government.

Confrontation is a Legitimate Political Strategy

Confrontation is to stand up to those who oppose you. It means not being afraid to challenge others to clarify their positions, to come out of hiding and be on one side or another of an issue. Being willing to stand up for what you believe, even in the face of fierce opposition, is the essence of political courage. It communicates commitment and strength to ideas and action. In politics one often finds critical issues hanging indefinitely in political suspension because no one wants to "bite the bullet" and make difficult or unpopular decisions. Like it or not, confronting people forces the action, one way or the other.

Confrontation can have its downsides. Pressing people the way I did can polarize them and get them locked into political positions they find difficult to abandon. Most people find confrontation very stressful. The tension wears them down. They would rather wage peace than war, so they seek a compromise to eliminate the tension. Unfortunately, sound decisions generally are not made while in retreat.

It would be nice to say my struggles with the legislature were always over great ideas and historic issues. Unfortunately, this was not the case. Very often I felt like I was in a gang fight over neighborhood turf. Rhetorical battles were fought over specific issues, but the war had more to do with the attitude of leadership than with substantive issues facing the commonwealth. With the possible exception of the best way to restructure education, we agreed for the most part on what had to be done to improve Kentucky. The real struggle was over who would make the decisions about what should be done.

When faced with a hostile, uncooperative legislature, I felt there was no choice but to push my ideas and agenda forcefully.

Confrontation as a Political Strategy

It should have come as no surprise to anyone that the legislature immediately made my aggressive style an issue. They had become very comfortable with challenging governors and getting them to back off. However, it was obvious that Wallace Wilkinson would be a different kind of governor than his predecessors. Predictably, the media seized on the war developing between the branches and made it the political story for most of my term in office. Reporters regularly recounted what each side had to say about the conduct of the other. Unfortunately for me, the editorial writers always seemed to side with the legislature. They regularly lectured me about how the day was past when governors could intimidate the General Assembly.

As was noted elsewhere, I didn't expect the General Assembly to welcome me with open arms. What I hoped to accomplish with my aggressive style was to get across to leadership that I intended to fight for what I wanted. However, my aggressive stance was not intended to mean I would not engage in a reasonable discussion of my proposals. It certainly was not a case of "my way or no way." However, the response of leadership was not discussion, but defiance. My actions were met with an attitude rather than a debate. Their response was "you won't tell us what to do" rather than "let's talk things over and see what we can agree to." Clearly, leadership preferred to stand up to me than to work with me.

After my first legislative session, I tried on various occasions to soften my approach to the legislature. Relations improved somewhat during the months preceding the special session on the lottery legislation. Once the legislature was in session, however, the same defiant attitude surfaced again which confirmed for me there had been no fundamental change in position. While I got most of what I wanted in the lottery legislation, a message was repeatedly sent to me that the legislature would do whatever it wanted with anything I sent to it, both now and in the future. It was like leadership felt it was necessary to continually remind me that they had the final word.

Matters got worse very quickly after the special session in December 1988. With the lottery behind me, I was ready to turn again to education. We had agreed during the summer of 1988 that the target date for a special session was March 1989. The time for that session was growing near, and I had made no headway toward getting agreement with leadership on what to do about education. Leadership continued to be successful in assigning blame to me for the impasse on school reform. Once again I felt I had to go on the offensive in order to keep control of the policy agenda.

To shift the burden of responsibility for inaction on school reform from myself to the legislature, I leveled the charge that leadership didn't know what it wanted, which was essentially true. The package floated at the education forum in February was much too expensive even for their taste. On the other hand, I was ready to act as soon as I had something tangible from the legislature. Leadership began immediately to put something together for me. It is doubtful they would have done so without my having put the ball in their court with my remarks to the media.

A Strategy for Confrontation Emerges

The most confrontational period came midway through my term in office. As the 1990 legislative session approached, it was obvious that I was in a very weak political position. Almost every part of my agenda was under legislative attack. I was told by sources in and out of the legislature that leadership was out to "teach me a lesson" about who is in charge of state government. Leadership was going to accuse me of being responsible for a poor working relationship and use that as an excuse to ignore or oppose anything I wanted. That wasn't big news to me because it had been used before, but this time it seemed to be a calculated move on the part of leadership.

Facing the prospect of being overrun by the legislature, I called my advisors together to plan a strategy for dealing with what I considered an impending crisis in my administration. Every possible scenario was played out along with a possible response on my part. This was our assessment of the situation.

First, a compromise with the legislature seemed highly unlikely now. Leadership was prepared to play an "all or nothing" game against me, believing there was little reason to accommodate me. They thought I was mortally wounded because of my continuous fighting with them and intended to make that the issue.

Second, I concluded that legislators really didn't like confrontation and controversy, and they certainly would not like to spend their time in Frankfort under siege. If I were to ratchet up the attack on them, I believed they would respond at some point to this heavy bombardment by suing for peace to get it to stop.

Third, I could not expect any support from the media, which had been consistently critical of both my administration and of me personally. The practical effect of the media's negative coverage of my efforts was to encourage the legislature to take me on regardless of the merit of any of the things I proposed. The legislature was called upon to save the commonwealth from this antitax "bubba" governor. If I was going to be successful in framing the debate publicly, it would have to be through paid media.

After much discussion the following ideas emerged and became the foundation of my strategy for dealing with this rebellious, head-strong, defiant legislature. The strategy called for a preemptive strike, beginning in December 1989 and continuing through the early weeks of the 1990 legislative session. The battle would be waged with the skillful exploitation of a hostile but responsive free media, and through several paid advertisements to be aired in all the major media markets. The objective was twofold: (1) to keep legislative leadership distracted by the controversy, and (2) to force them into a position where their only effective response was to deal with me in order to "shut me up."

The media campaign against leadership was to be carried out on two fronts. The paid advertisements would be launched as soon as legislators were back in the Capitol. The first paid advertisement would put the legislature in a bad light, but with a relatively soft touch. The intensity of the attack would be ratcheted up with each successive ad. The ads would run in saturation mode, and the time between ads be spaced long enough that we could assess their effect on the legislature. In the meantime, I would play the populist role with the capitol press corp. Every opportunity for free media would be used to characterize leadership as defenders of the status quo and a captive of special interests. I had come to office as an outsider so my position as the champion of populist themes was well-established.

Among those who cautioned me of the risk I was taking was Mark Mellman. Mark and his partner Ed Lazarus had proven their ability to assess the mood of the public during the campaign. I valued their counsel as I thought through my strategy. Mark spoke for everyone involved in helping me make this decision when he cautioned that, if it didn't work, I could end up with a "scorched earth" scenario in which nothing got done, and education would go down the tube with everything else. History would damn me forever.

On the other hand, if I was convinced this was the only way to get anything done and still didn't try it, I could lose everything I had set out to do anyway and be regarded as a political failure. It was a risk with great political danger and had to be carried out with great determination and precision, but I felt I had no other viable alternative. Once I embarked on this approach, there would be no turning back.

The Fight Begins

The first opportunity to use the free media came after leadership suggested they might seek a two-penny increase in the sales tax. I publicly ridiculed their proposal and quipped, "I wonder what they're putting in the whiskey at Flynn's these days," a reference to a favorite watering hole for legislators and lobbyists in Frankfort. The image was perfect—legislators and lobbyists "schmoozing" at a local restaurant and bar trading off the public interest.

What followed was a series of stories in the media where I portrayed leadership as self-serving puppets of the special interests. My attacks were direct, purposeful, and strident. I wanted to create the greatest amount of tension possible. The message to leadership was simple: "I have declared war. Take up your arms." The message to the public was just as simple: "I am waging war against the enemy of the common man, the entrenched interests in Frankfort."

The inclination of leadership to go for a sales tax rate increase was a major concern to me. I anticipated strong resistance from lobbyists to the tobacco and services taxes I proposed, so my rhetoric had to counter their influence on the legislature. I kept hammering away at the theme that the legislature was a captive of special interests to make sure the public eye would be on lobbyist activity. Commenting to the press on the legislature's opposition to my revenue proposal, I said "this fight . . . is between the daddies and the mammas who take their children fishing on Saturday morning and the lobbyists who take the legislators golfing on Wednesday afternoon."

I kept up the pressure in my State of the Commonwealth address. There was little reason for me to make this a "get along" kind of speech, and I didn't. At the request of leadership and as a courtesy to members of the General Assembly, a copy of the speech was distributed in advance. Fully aware of what I intended to say in this address which would be televised statewide by Kentucky Educational Television, legislators orchestrated a visible show of their discontent. Many did not even show up. Those who did, greeted me with only a smattering of polite applause when I entered the House chamber. In contrast, Lieutenant Governor Brereton Jones was given a standing ovation upon his entry into the House chamber, an obvious attempt to embarrass me.

In my address, I continued to link the legislature with special interests and attacked the idea of a sales tax rate increase. I made no apology for my aggressive style.

> *Our agenda for the future may cause a few more disagreements in Frankfort. I hope not. But I was sent here to do a job, and I intend to do just that.*
>
> *I know I could be easier to get along with and you know it too. But I wasn't sent here to get along. I was sent here to get Kentucky moving again.*

I then took on the special interests.

> *It would be easy to go along to get along, to agree to yet another tax increase on those who are already paying too much. What's harder is taking on the special interests who want to raise taxes on the blue jeans and winter coats our families work so hard to buy, but not on the advertising and legal advice the corporations and the special interests make millions from and pay no tax on.*

The response to my speech was predictable. It was no "olive branch" speech. At this point there was little indication that the leadership in either house was prepared to back down. The full court press had to continue for awhile yet.

The Ad Campaign

Sparks really started to fly with the first paid ad. From the beginning of the lottery debate, I had talked about the importance of dedicating lottery proceeds to early childhood education, senior citizen programs, and a one-time bonus for Vietnam veterans. While we had accomplished the bonus, the General Assembly steadfastly refused to earmark the proceeds. I knew this was an issue of public interest. People had often complained to me (and still do) that they expected their "lottery money" would help causes of importance to them. I also knew this was an issue leadership did not want to deal with again in this session.

Speaking directly to the people in the first ad, I said the General Assembly wanted to put lottery proceeds in "their general fund" rather than dedicate them to specific programs. I urged people to call their legislators and gave them the LRC 800 telephone number to call. Other ads were planned to deal with the sales tax versus a tax on services, the needs of education, and perhaps succession. However, I wanted to see what effect this first ad would have before approving others.

I personally thought the lottery ad was not particularly offensive, but it proved to be very effective. The legislature responded immediately with cries of "foul." Leadership said they couldn't understand why I would begin this important legislative session with a public attack on the very body which had to pass my legislation. "Never in all my years have I seen anything like it," one legislator said to the media. I knew their personal pride would not let them just ignore the ads. They would feel compelled to respond.

Leadership had been very successful in using the free media (mainly the Capitol press corp) to respond to me, but the TV spots were something they could not afford to combat in kind. The only medium of response to the ads available to the legislature was to complain to the news media, which of course took their part in the exchange, just as I predicted they would. The editorial writers thought I had turned into a wild man intent on self-destruction.

The most immediate effect was increased solidarity within leadership and a show of support for leadership from the rank-and-file legislators. There was a closing of the ranks against this governor who was out to destroy the legislature. This is exactly what I thought might happen in the short term. However, of greater interest was how leadership would react to being kept "under the gun" for an extended period of time.

After the first ad was broadcast, Greg Stumbo came to my office to discuss the "poor relationship" between myself and the legislature. He questioned the wisdom of running the ads at this particular time. During our discussion I showed him the script for future ads, all of which were much rougher on the legislature. I wanted him to have a clear picture of how much worse it could get. I knew he would carry back to leadership the message that I was not about to back down.

It took only a few weeks until Speaker Bland-ford met with "Smitty" Taylor, my secretary of the cabinet, to seek his help to get me to stop the assault. It was the first sign that the strategy might work. Leadership wanted out from under the pressure. This was the response I was looking for.

About a week later I agreed to stop the ads, at least for the moment. I certainly didn't expect a love feast to follow my pulling the ads, but there was a noticeable increase in contact between my office and leadership. The strategy appeared to be working, but it was important not to overplay my hand. By mid-February I stopped the vitriolic criticism of leadership and focused more on the legislation at hand.

How effective was the confrontation? Critics will argue that the actual result was a stronger legislature because of a series of constitutional amendments they proposed designed to further weaken the executive branch. Although voters later rejected those amendments, the fact my veto of them was overridden by a large margin shows that the war against the executive branch was unabated by my actions. In this regard, my actions probably precipitated an even greater desire to strip the governor of any remaining influence.

On the other hand, objective observers will agree that the 1990 session was a very productive one. We came out of the session with my budget intact, school reform and the money to pay for it, road bonds, and community development bonds. Except for the sales and services tax issues, and perhaps succession, I got everything I wanted. No other governor had done that in recent memory. Of course, I will never know what might have happened had I taken a different approach, but I'm certain no other approach would have produced these results. From my perspective, it was a very successful strategy.

Not All "Fights" Were Planned

I certainly was willing to confront the legislature on behalf of those issues I believed in, but not everything which appeared to be confrontation was intended to be so. Once one gains a reputation for being aggressive, everything that happens gets defined in those terms. Actually, it was not my intent to constantly pick a fight at every opportunity. Sometimes it was simply a matter of misunderstanding. Such was the case when Bob Johnson of the *Courier-Journal* asked if I intended to pressure the General Assembly to pass my programs—a good example of a fight I didn't seek.

After responding that "I intend to exercise all the influence that I can to pass our programs," I was then asked if this meant I was going to abandon the hands-off attitude of Governors Brown and Collins and get involved in the selection of legislative leaders. "Of course not," I responded. When asked if the political action committee I had just created could support challengers to incumbent legislators, I responded "I guess it's *possible*," but not intended.

By the time General Assembly members were asked to respond, the word "possible" had become "likely." The hypothetical became the reality in the span of a few hours. When the story appeared in the newspapers the next day, the political writers reported that I *might* consider running opposition candidates against legislators unless they supported my programs. The fact is that I had never given the subject of legislative elections a thought until Bob Johnson raised it in the press conference.

Nevertheless, right from the start I was accused of poisoning my working relationship with the General Assembly by threatening them with opposition. It was not my intent at that time to pick a fight with the legislature or to threaten them with opposition at the polls. On the other hand, I should have realized that, after a decade of relentless pursuit of independence, legislators would consider even the *hint* that a governor might get involved in legislative races to be a threat to their independence.

What is ironic about this situation is that I had discussed with my advisors on several occasions my intent to be accessible and candid with the press corp in Frankfort. I went to the press conference that day determined that no one would be able to accuse me of avoiding any question or subject. However, one of the first lessons one must learn in public life is not to respond to questions based on purely hypothetical situations. I made the mistake of responding to a "might, should, would, or could" kind of question. I dropped my guard and got burned.

Unfortunately, this kind of situation would be repeated all too many times over the next four years. For example, an explosive situation arose at a critical time in my administration when my former campaign manager Danny Briscoe answered another hypothetical question. Danny was asked following a televised interview if education reform *could* be held hostage for succession. Briscoe replied that he supposed it *could* be, meaning "anything is *possible* but not necessarily *probable*." It took three days, a press conference by Briscoe, and another one by me to get the point across that there never had been, nor was there ever going to be, any consideration of politically linking education and succession.

The point I want to make here is that some of what appeared to be antagonistic behavior was *not* always intentional. Unfortunately, it took me a while to appreciate the parameters the media set for policy debate. My tendency to be blunt in my assessment of situations and people, and my determination to do what I thought needed to be done, was a constant source of trouble for me and fodder for their stories. Even though my confrontational style was deliberate on some occasions, without question there were other times when I unwittingly gave the media a basis for portraying me as confrontational when there was no intent to be.

While I learned to avoid answering the hypothetical questions of "what if" or "would you consider," I never could understand the extent to which some members of the media will go to actually provoke or even create a confrontation. All public officials will tell you that their experiences with the media do little to encourage candor with the press corp. You always have to be on the lookout for the "I gotcha!" for which journalists are well known.

It All Depends on Who Wages the Fight

The truth of the matter is that Wallace Wilkinson was not the only politician in Frankfort who wanted to get his own way. Members of the General Assembly are quite willing to use their positions in government to achieve their political objectives. In fact, legislators are very open about wanting to chair, or at least serve on, certain powerful committees, because it gives them the opportunity to advocate for things they want done and to obstruct things they oppose.

Effectiveness as a political leader requires the skillful use of whatever institutional power is vested in the office. To believe that the use of the power of one's office to achieve political objectives is alien to the democratic process is to ignore the realities of any political system. People elect public officials precisely in the hope they can get something done while in office and certainly expect them to try. Although the public doesn't want politicians to *abuse* their power, they surely expect the people they put into office to use whatever power they have to achieve what they set out to do.

Earlier I made the point that most legislators come to Frankfort to take something back to their districts. Such "trophies" are the most tangible evidence legislators can offer of their effectiveness in representing the interests of their constituents. Little wonder legislators use whatever vehicles are available to them to get what they think their constituents want. Here is just one glaring example of how individuals in the legislature use their position to get their way on an issue.

Senator Michael Moloney has been a powerful member of the Kentucky Senate for many years, largely because of his position as chair of the Senate Appropriations and Revenue Committee. He is a great supporter and friend of higher education, and the University of Kentucky is in his legislative district. He was angered at my funding proposal for higher education in 1988. I had gored his ox," and he was determined to prevent the damage he felt my proposal would inflict on higher education, regardless of the damage his action might inflict somewhere else.

The last step before passage of a budget is a conference committee made up of members of each chamber. Even though the governor is legally required to present a budget early in each regular session, everyone familiar with Frankfort knows that nothing of lasting importance happens until the conference committee meets behind closed doors. The conference committee is where legislators are most able to impose their will on state spending and do their horse trading away from public view. I have often said we have the whole process backward. The weeks of meaningless wrangling over the budget should be held behind closed doors, and the conference committee meeting be opened to the public.

Prior to the conference committee meeting, Rep. Harry Moberly, chair of the education subcommittee of the House A&R Committee, had diverted the money I requested for poor school districts and the incentive program, along with some other funds, to pay for further reductions in class size — something of great importance to the "turks" in the House who had fought hard for the 1986 education reforms. In turn Mike Moloney took this money from elementary and secondary education so he could fund *his* constituents, the universities. Senator Moloney used the conference committee process to increase the higher education appropriation by $30 million and, for good measure, add $4 million more for university and community college building and renovation projects *in addition to* the ones I recommended in my budget. Some of these projects weren't even in the Council on Higher Education's budget request.

The point here is not whether higher education was deserving of more money than I had proposed for it. That is a matter of judgment and availability of revenue. The point is that the legislative process is distorted when one senator can take it upon himself to use the power of his position, away from public view, to not only get his way but to get it at the expense of things considered more important by others. Legislators are just as capable as any governor of fighting for what they want and using whatever political leverage is available to get it. In this instance it was a case of a powerful Senator using his position to in effect tell the governor, "I'll have the last word!" no matter what it costs others.

Unfortunately, the media likes to characterize the give and take that is inherent in the political process as though what is most important is not what gets done but who wins out in the end. It is the public, not the politician, who is the winner or loser. Effective government is not about who can win a political war; it is about how a group of elected officials can go about determining what is best for the people in a civil manner. When winning and losing becomes more important to politicians than achieving the public good, they do a great disservice to those who elect them to office. Such clearly is the case when public officials deny something to other public officials simply to demonstrate that they have the power to do it.

What Lies Ahead?

It is unlikely that future Kentucky governors can expect to see a change in the current state of affairs any time soon. I believe this divisive, contentious, and adversarial relationship between the office of the governor and the General Assembly will continue for some time to come, no matter who fills the chair of governor. Unfortunately, many of those who feel obligated to judge governors on how well they get along with the legislature fail to see that it takes two to tango.

The legislature was just as combative as I, although this fact seemed to be overlooked by my critics. Leadership was always quick to say something critical about my ideas, especially on education. Rude treatment of cabinet officials by committee members, leaks to the media about private conversations, legislation drafted for the purpose of punishing me are examples of the aggressive, confrontational behavior exhibited by leadership. However, not wanting to be perceived as confrontational themselves, leadership seized every opportunity to characterize me as the aggressor and themselves as victims. The media was always ready to carry their message.

My experience in Frankfort was much more contentious than I would have liked. The tension and fighting were no more to my liking than they were to legislators'. Could it have been different? Only if I had been willing to concede to the legislature its claim that governors are essentially irrelevant. I knew there would be a fight on my hands, but I wanted it to be over ideas and public policy. Instead, I got a turf war as intense as anything I could have imagined.

People respect politicians who fight for what they believe in even if they don't agree with their positions. People may not always appreciate the nuances of the debate, but they expect a debate. Nothing happens in politics without it. What they *dis*respect is a standoff between powerful political leaders in which nothing gets done. For good or ill, there needs to be resolution. Often this means there will be winners and losers. What the public particularly resents is to have the institutions of government fighting each other for power at the expense of the public's business.

It's Time to Say "Whoa!"

Sometimes I felt leadership would like it better if Kentucky had a parliamentary form of government in which the legislature directly controls the executive branch. Leadership wants to control all key board appointments, and they are probably only a few sessions away from wanting to approve all cabinet appointments. No doubt they also would like to elect the governor if they could. Every time I stood up to leadership, they threatened to annex more of my territory. The last round of proposed constitutional amendments was a particularly blatant grab for power in the name of keeping a balance between a "weak" legislature and a "powerful" governor.

Kentucky voters want an effective legislature, but I doubt they want the kind of affront to the governor's leadership role that I and other recent Kentucky governors have experienced. We cannot have two governments at work in Kentucky. The leadership in each branch must find effective ways to work together, not against each other. The laws which guide the relationship between the branches must preserve the unique strength of each one. Political gridlock results when either branch is more concerned with who gets the last word than with what constitutes the public interest.

It is the function of *political leaders*, not the branches of government, to define the issues and seek the support of the people for their particular response to those issues. Once elected, the winning party should have a reasonable opportunity to fulfill its promises to the electorate. Difficult times require strong political leadership, unity and a resolve to deal courageously with pressing problems. Perhaps some of the problem in Kentucky can be explained by the fact that we traditionally have had in effect a one-party system. In a two-party system, political leaders debate philosophic differences, but in a one-party system the politics is more personal than philosophic. *Intra*party politics replaces *inter*party politics.

The Democratic Party in Kentucky has a fractious history. The lack of unity within the party means that our political leaders are not elected on a party platform toward which both the governor and legislators of the same party work together to implement. Kentucky governors are elected as individuals based on what *they* declare is their political platform. Most legislators are elected on a slate of local concerns and special interest, rather than a coherent statewide policy agenda. There is no common agenda or political bond based on party affiliation to unify the governor and a majority of legislators.

Legislatures are Unsuited to Direct Public Policy

A strong political leader is needed to set the policy agenda for the state and to oversee its proper implementation. Sound policy must be crafted in a thoughtful manner, taking into account the individual interests which are affected by it but keeping the general public good the priority. I don't believe good policy can be made by a collection of individuals whose political careers are based on how well they serve the narrow interests of the area within a state or region which they represent, rather than on how well they serve the public interest in general.

In recent years the policy leadership role of governors in nearly all the states has been challenged by proactive legislatures. Many legislators now believe policy-making is exclusively their province, and the role of the executive branch is only to carry out the policies determined by the legislature. Most legislatures now have their own staff, hire their own consultants, and basically use executive agencies as sources of data and information when setting policy for the state. Even the budget is considered only a proposal from the governor to be disposed of in any manner the legislature sees fit. The governor is left with only a "bully pulpit" from which to expound great ideas but no real ability to get them enacted into law.

This dramatic shift of power toward the legislative branch has greatly overcompensated for the abuses of executive authority in the past. We need a correction in the trend so that a more workable balance of power can be achieved. I will remind the champions of the balance of power that the Kentucky constitution gives neither the General Assembly nor the governor the right to dictate how the other conducts its business. In fact, it was this very issue which led the legislature to seek independence from the excessive influence of the executive branch. I am greatly concerned about the long term effect of these developments. Kentucky has seriously crippled the ability of governors to lead and affect change.

A War of Attrition

Although the Kentucky constitution gives broad authority to a Governor, most of the specific duties of the office are established through statute by the General Assembly. As the biblical saying goes, the "Lord giveth and the Lord taketh away." What the media gurus of Kentucky politics are missing in their uncritical support of legislative independence is the fact that the legislature fully realizes it is in the driver's seat. Leadership has taken advantage of the one-term governorship and their own longevity to steadily insulate themselves from external influence.

If the legislature in a single action were to strip the governor of all duties, just as it did the office of the superintendent of public instruction in 1990, they would likely precipitate a constitutional crisis. If these same duties are stripped away a few at a time as has occurred over the last decade, the consequences are less dramatic but no less damaging. They have achieved, one action at a time, something which would have caused great alarm if done in one sweeping piece of legislation.

The question I raise is "who can stop this juggernaut?" As far as I can see, nothing stands in the way of the legislature continuing its war on the executive branch and ultimately making it just as subservient to a legislature as the legislature once was to a governor. The difference in this case is significant. To reverse the situation, a governor would have to persuade the legislature to give up power to another branch of government. Given its present mood, that's about as likely as a snowball surviving in hell.

The only thing which can satisfy the thirst for power is more power. It would be foolish to think that the General Assembly will any time soon feel it has enough power or a governor has just the right amount. We may in this decade find the situation to be of sufficient concern that the pendulum will have to be stopped. But don't count on the legislature to stop it voluntarily. At some point a Kentucky governor must draw the line and legally challenge this continuing interference by the legislature in matters which more properly belong to the executive branch.

XIV. SOME OTHER
THINGS ALONG THE WAY

When I pursued the governorship, there were certain things I wanted to accomplish. The goals were clear in my mind. However, as a candidate for a state office you can't always anticipate issues which might arise on your watch. During my term as governor several issues of great importance to Kentucky arose which I had not addressed in my policy agenda as a candidate. Important among these were issues involving state-federal relations. Even if I had anticipated them, they probably would not have been mentioned in the *Kentucky First* plan. Issues of a federal nature have no political appeal in a campaign for state office.

Throughout most of this book I have written about policymaking at the state level. However, there are important areas where federal policy takes primacy and dictates what states are able to do on their own. During my tenure as governor, I became involved in several debates on federal policy, particularly in education, energy, transportation, and Medicaid. Federal policies and programs in these particular areas have a direct impact on Kentucky citizens. It was my responsibility to look out for changes in federal policy which might have a negative effect on Kentucky.

National Education Policy

Under the federal constitution, anything not specifically assigned to the federal government is a responsibility of state governments, which have great latitude to develop policies and programs to address their unique needs. Since the early 1970s the governors of the states and territories have been proactive in trying to influence federal policy, especially in those areas where states are required to perform certain functions according to federal guidelines or mandates.

Education is one policy area which is uniquely the sole responsibility of the states. The federal government's role in education in recent decades has been to ensure equal access. Initially the focus was on eliminating racial segregation, but later Congress enacted an array of programs on behalf of children with various special needs. Large sums of federal money now flow to states to help pay the cost of food programs, early childhood education, and educating handicapped, migrant, economically disadvantaged, and learning-disabled children.

Early in the 1980s President Ronald Reagan convened a national panel to examine the status of education in America. Critics of American education contended the level of educational achievement demonstrated by our students had fallen far behind other industrialized nations. The commission report titled *A Nation at Risk* warned that we had to make dramatic changes in what children are expected to know and be able to do. We also had to significantly reduce the number of graduates entering the job market without even the basic skills needed to function in the modern workplace.

Clearly the federal study had a tremendous impact on state education policy. Governors responded to this challenge with a flurry of education reforms. Kentucky was among a dozen or so states which passed major reform legislation in the mid-1980s. Education was a national political issue by the end of the 1980s. George Bush made it an issue in his 1988 presidential election campaign, the first candidate to do so since the Sputnik era of the 1950s.

In his first year as president, Mr. Bush convened a meeting with the nation's governors at Charlottesville, Virginia, to discuss the federal role in education. The "education summit" seemed to have been an off-the-cuff idea. Much to the surprise of his staff, Mr. Bush stated in a speech to the governors at their annual winter meeting in Washington that he wanted to meet with them to discuss education. Soon after that brief comment, the White House staff contacted the National Governors' Association (NGA) about the logistics of holding a meeting with the nation's governors to discuss the federal role in education.

Out of what appeared to be a spur of the moment thought came a truly an historic event. Only once before in this century had a president convened the governors of the states to help shape a national policy. The letter of invitation stated the president stood ready to help the nation's governors meet the crisis in education, but he acknowledged that education was clearly a responsibility of the states and not the federal government.

Consensus on Restructuring Education

As explained elsewhere, education reform was a high priority on my policy agenda. Having championed the need to restructure public education in Kentucky, I welcomed this opportunity to participate in a national discussion about what the federal government might do to help the states. The president's education summit gave me an opportunity to join other governors in the push for systemic reform of education at the national level.

At the close of the summit, the president and governors issued a joint statement setting forth four things they agreed to do:

1. establish a process for setting national education goals;
2. seek greater flexibility and enhanced accountability in the use of federal resources to meet the goals, through both regulatory and legislative changes;
3. undertake a major state-by-state effort to restructure our education system; and
4. report annually on progress in achieving our goals.

The first and fourth items were to be a joint effort by the president and the governors. The second item dealt with federal programs, and the third item was a strong commitment by the governors to restructure education.

Of most encouragement to me was the consensus I found on the need to restructure the education system and on what was meant by the term "restructure." The joint statement issued by the president and governors said the most successful restructuring efforts seem to have these common characteristics:

1. a system of accountability that focuses on results, rather than on compliance with rules and regulations;
2. decentralization of authority and decision-making responsibility to the school site, so that educators are empowered to determine the means for achieving the goals and are held accountable for accomplishing them;
3. a rigorous program of instruction designed to ensure that every child can acquire the knowledge and skills required in an economy in which our citizens must be able to think for a living;
4. an education system that develops first-rate teachers and creates a professional environment that provides real rewards for success with students, real consequences for failure, and the tools and flexibility required to get the job done; and
5. active, sustained parental and business community involvement.

All of these elements were part of the restructuring program I had advocated in Kentucky for more than two years. At the end of the summit I commented to some newspaper reporters that "Kentucky's agenda was now the nation's agenda."

A Federal Role in Education

My basic philosophy about state-federal relations is that the federal government should only involve itself in those issues which states cannot effectively deal with on their own. This was particularly true in the area of public education. Governors were invited to offer their suggestions for ways the federal government might help states fulfill the responsibility to provide an educational system which meets the security, economic, and social needs of a nation faced with global competition. In an open letter to President Bush, I proposed that the federal government focus on these seven things:

1. ensure educational equity among the states;
2. help end the scourge of drugs in schools;
3. donate either a NASA or military satellite to the states which they could use to electronically share their instructional resources;
4. help develop a national strategy for training and retraining the American workforce;
5. increase federal support for preschool health and educational programs;
6. better coordinate federal day care and preschool education programs administered by the states; and
7. help underwrite the research and development cost to improve our ability to document student learning outcomes.

In my opinion these were areas where participation by the federal government could be very helpful to the states. Beside sharing the letter with fellow governors, I personally pressed the president for action on several of these items.

A Satellite Dedicated to Education

The idea of a public domain satellite dedicated to education I felt was something the president could do with little burden on the federal government, but of great financial help to the states. In my view, the contribution of a satellite would help every state achieve greater equity in educational opportunity through the kind of instructional programming Kentucky was financing through KET. We were spending several million dollars for satellite time just to reach our own Star Channel schools. A dedicated satellite would save money for Kentucky, but it also would make it possible for all states to share their educational resources through the use of telecommunications. The proposal was quickly supported by other governors and seemed to be well received by the president.

At the NGA annual meeting in Washington, D.C., the next February, I raised the issue in person with the president at a White House reception for the governors. President Bush recommended that we work with the National Space Council and his domestic advisor Roger Porter. I subsequently wrote letters to all the governors asking for their support. Several meetings with White House staff followed, but the president failed to follow through on the idea.

Early in 1990, Ms. Shelly Weinstein, president of the EDSAT Institute of Washington, offered to sponsor a research study to document the need for an education satellite and examine the financial, technical, legal, and policy issues which would have to be resolved to make the project feasible. I encouraged the study, but maintained that the president should just dedicate an existing NASA or military satellite for this purpose. The study proved helpful in supporting the idea, but it did not result in any federal action.

Under the leadership of Ms. Weinstein, a National Education Telecommunications Organization (NETO) was created to secure private financing and to establish a management structure for an education satellite. As a member of the NETO board of directors, I encouraged the organization to continue to put pressure on the White House to act on its own to create an education satellite. The general sentiment of other board members was that President Bush was not going to make this a priority. The only practical solution was for the states to work together through NETO to create their own system.

Senator Conrad Burns of Montana submitted a bill to the Congress in 1991 which would provide a federal loan guarantee to any organization which could find private capital to finance a public domain satellite. A federal loan guarantee would make private financing of an education satellite feasible. The Burns bill was fought by the Public Broadcasting System (PBS), which thought it should be the one to control educational broadcasting. PBS was successful in keeping Sen. Conrad's bill from coming to a vote in the Congress.

The position PBS took was a clear case of a special interest in Washington looking out for itself rather than the public interest. PBS was created to serve the educational needs of the states but instead has become a publicly financed arts, information, and entertainment network using the educational television facilities of the states. PBS had asked Congress for money to buy its own satellite, but never purchased it. Furthermore, PBS charged states almost as much for time on its satellite facilities as the private vendors were asking. What was even worse, PBS used public money to lobby the Congress in this case against something which would not have hurt them, but would have provided a way for states to do something to help themselves.

For a brief period of time, NETO was able to secure a small amount of satellite transponder capacity to sell to the consortium of schools which joined the organization. However, as of the date of this book the reality of a satellite dedicated to education is still awaiting fulfillment. I learned from this experience that good ideas are as hard to advance in Washington as in Frankfort for many of the same reasons. Special interests are able to prevent things because they have good connections with congressional staff who are willing to work on their behalf to protect them.

Assessment Research and Development

The Congress several decades ago created a national test called the National Assessment of Progress in Education (NAPE) to measure how we were doing as a nation.

The test is taken by a random sample of students from all the states and is given every two years on alternating subjects. However, states were forbidden by law to use the test, and the results were not broken down by state. At the time the education summit was held, a debate was going on in the Congress over proposed changes in the NAPE, including whether or not it might be changed so that it could be used by states.

Many technical, research, and practical questions were raised about the feasibility, and even the desirability, of using one test to measure progress toward the national education goals which were eventually approved by the governors and President Bush. Probably the most persuasive argument came out of a fear that such a test would lead to a national curriculum and diminish the role of the states in determining what children should know and be able to do in a system of public education. In the end, the governors said they wanted to use their own tests to measure progress rather than wait until an acceptable national test could be developed.

Assessment is an essential part of accountability, but it has to take a better form than the old paper and pencil, fill-in-the-blank kind of test. Although the details were yet to be worked out, I was certain Kentucky would have some type of performance-based test of student learning as part of its reward system. I knew it would be costly to develop and administer a new test of our own. On the other hand, I didn't want the federal government to do anything more than help with the cost of research and development.

Since other states were moving in the same direction as Kentucky, I thought it was appropriate for the federal government to contribute to the cost to research and develop new assessment tools by making large financial grants to states which were embarking into this new area. States could share the results of their research and development activities, especially if the federal government contributed to its cost. In my letter to the president, I proposed that he immediately proceed to make significant grants to those states which were willing to develop and use the new generation of tests. There was sufficient money available in the U.S. Department of Education budget to implement this proposal without special legislation, so availability of money was not a serious obstacle. The President would only have to order Secretary of Education Lauro Cavazos to make the grants.

Action by the president on this proposal would have had a great impact on what Kentucky and other states were doing. As was the case with the proposal for an education satellite, the Bush administration did not follow through on the proposal. For a time we tried to work with the Council of Chief State School Officers to develop a consortium of states which would pool their own money, but this didn't work out either. We eventually had to shell out over $30 million of our own money to develop our own test. Federal help can sometimes bring with it bureaucratic constraints, but perhaps we might have avoided some of the controversy which surrounded the student assessment program in Kentucky if we could have been more successful in involving other states in its research and development.

Equity among the States

For nearly half a century, state governments have tried to minimize differences in the amount of money spent per school child from one school district to another. Constitutional challenges to school funding formulae have been based on allegations of inequitable funding within a state. Of course, it was this issue which led the Supreme Court in Kentucky to declare our entire school system unconstitutional. What often is overlooked is the disparity which exists among the states, which vary widely in resources to provide basic educational opportunities to their citizens. In large part this is due to significant differences in per capita income or property wealth from one state to another. States clearly are unequal in their ability to provide similar financial support for education, even with the same level of tax effort. Recent immigration patterns as well as historical racial and social discrimination leave some states with a greater educational burden than others.

In my view, it was in the national interest to address the issue of interstate disparity in educational opportunity at a summit on education. Obviously, no one has a solution to this issue. The federal government has focused on individual inequities, funding a number of programs for disadvantaged children. Furthermore, it is hard to argue that disparity among the states is a constitutional issue at the federal level. On the other hand, some consideration needed to be given to this issue when examining a national strategy for improving education in the nation as a whole. If education is truly a national security concern, then there must be some role for the federal government in helping smooth out the economic differences among the states.

The issue was raised at several points in our discussions, but it was obvious that I was asking for federal action in an area which some of my fellow governors felt should be reserved to the states. I had no specific proposal of my own to offer, but I thought the issue ought to be on the table for discussion. While admitting that these differences were important, there was a fear among the governors that Congress would simply mandate equity as a condition of participation in federal programs. Such a situation would put the states in an impossible fiscal situation.

Indeed, the following year a bill was introduced in the Congress which would require states to settle their school funding litigation as a condition of receiving future federal school funds. Fortunately, the bill never was given serious consideration, but it reflects the attitude the Congress has toward the states. Obviously, the fiscal condition of the federal government made any direct financial help out of the question, but surely there could be a more sensitive attitude toward the fiscal situation of the states.

National Education Goals

Probably the most substantive thing to come out of the presidential summit was a commitment by the governors to work with the president to set national goals to focus our joint efforts and provide a public measure of our progress in improving American education. In the months which followed, a panel of governors worked with the White House to develop a set of goals which could be jointly announced by President Bush and the governors at the meeting of the National Governors' Association in Mobile, Alabama, in 1990.

The day before the NGA meeting was to open, the Democratic governors met in nearby Pascagula, Mississippi, to discuss their stand on various issues which were to come before the NGA. The issue of the national education goals was brought up. We had no problem with the goals as presented, but I raised questions about how progress toward attainment of the national education goals would be measured. I knew that the Republican governors were supporting a goals panel dominated by federal people. This structure would have the president sitting in judgment on the states with no accountability for the federal government. Governors would have little ability to control how their efforts would be judged.

I strongly objected to this arrangement and appealed to my fellow Democrats to stop the proposal before it got to the floor for a vote. They asked me to prepare an alternative proposal which they would review in Mobile the next morning. Then Governor Bill Clinton was the Democratic co-chair of the NGA goals panel at the time. He said he would do whatever we decided, but warned that the president was in a position to punish those states which opposed the idea. This sounded to me like an idle threat which we could safely challenge.

Upon arriving in Mobile, I discovered that the wheels had been greased already with representatives of the president there, ready to announce his support of the goals and creation of the panel which would devise a way to measure progress. After a brief conference with several of my Demo-

---

cratic colleagues, I quickly asked Governor Carroll Campbell, the Republican co-chair of the NGA education goals committee, for an opportunity to speak to the education committee which was to meet briefly before the plenary session. He reluctantly agreed, perhaps because he had heard of my concerns.

The committee convened expecting to discuss how to handle the press conference announcing the goals and creation of the national education goals panel. When I told the committee members that the Democrat governors opposed the proposed structure of the goals panel, the meeting grew very tense. I was told in effect that a deal had been cut with the White House and it was too late to change it. I said it was never too late, and we would carry our objections to the floor if that was necessary. Gov. Campbell wanted to know what had to be done to avoid an embarrassing confrontation in public. I proposed that the membership of the goals panel be restructured to give the governors at least a one vote majority over the federal bureaucrats.

After a closed door session between the Republican governors and the White House staff, we were able to win our point. However, the discussion had delayed the beginning of the NGA session for more than an hour. It was extremely rare for the conference to go off schedule. As the clock ticked, tension began to rise. The media gathered outside the meeting room smelling a story in the making. When the meeting finally broke up, I was confronted by a wall of reporters who wanted to know what was going on in the closed meeting. I told my side of the story and said we basically got what we wanted and were ready to move ahead.

I was upset personally that the leadership of NGA was going to let the Republicans win this one on a purely partisan basis. It was the only time I ever saw White House staff sitting directly behind the NGA conference table as they were on that occasion. If it had not been for my firm stance in that very important committee meeting, I am certain we would have a much different national education goals panel today.

Kentucky Becomes a National Model

Dr. Frank Newman, president of the Education Commission of the States, an interstate organization based in Denver, Colorado, had been to Kentucky for the first few meetings of the Education Reform Task Force and offered sound advice on how to proceed. Dr. Newman also chaired the final session of the task force when the draft legislation was approved. He followed our debate over restructuring prior to the Supreme Court decision and was very familiar with the struggle that had preceded the creation of the task force.

After passage of our historic legislation in 1990, Dr. Newman asked me to serve as chairman of the policies and priorities committee of the Education Commission of the States. During that year I had the opportunity to speak at several of their meetings about the politics of change and how it came about that Kentucky was able to come up with such a cohesive, forward-thinking piece of legislation in such a short period of time. In my many conversations with governors, legislators, and educators from other states about their experience with restructuring, the story was always the same. They admired what we had done, but they didn't think they could get it done politically without a mandate from the court like we had in Kentucky.

None of the states where there have been court decisions have been successful in enacting the kind of comprehensive legislation Kentucky did. The reason is that most court decisions, unlike Kentucky, addressed only inequity in funding. Thus the debate in those states centered on money and not education. I believe it might have been the same for Kentucky if it were not for the focus on restructuring before the Supreme Court declared the *entire* system unconstitutional.

The politics of change are the same everywhere. The entrenched educational bureaucracy is almost impervious to change unless change is forced upon it. The political control education interests have on state legislatures all across the nation stands in the way of other states following Kentucky's lead.

The State-Federal Partnership

In a federal system of government, the states and the federal government work together to solve problems that are national in scope. National domestic policy for the most part is implemented by state governments. Such an arrangement is almost necessitated because of the diversity which exists in this nation. Consequently, very few programs enacted by the U.S. Congress are administered solely by the federal government. They are carried out as a joint effort between the states and the federal government.

In recent years Americans have increasingly turned to the federal government for help with problems they believe the states are not dealing with in an effective manner. Federal initiatives created in response to calls for action at a national level have multiplied greatly in recent years. Most of these programs are not created at the request of the states, but are initiated by the Congress in response to pressure groups who establish a presence in Washington to lobby for laws or programs that address their special concerns. When Congress decides to act, the states are called upon to implement its decisions.

Although state participation in many of these programs is voluntary, the constituencies which lobbied Congress to create these programs in turn lobby their state politicians to participate in them on the argument that the state stands to lose millions of federal dollars if it doesn't do so. The catch is that, to get these millions of federal dollars, states also must make a financial commitment to the program. It is always appealing to participate in something which brings five dollars into the treasury for every dollar spent. The feeling is that the state can improve or expand services with a relatively low investment by acquiring the federal funds. Most state politicians readily ante up the money required to participate in these programs.

As governor of Kentucky, I found that many policy decisions were being made solely because of the availability of federal funds. Things were being done that would not be done if it were not for the fact that federal funds were there to underwrite a major part of the cost. Obviously, it is attractive to gain access to other funds. I did my share of it, especially when I made my first executive budget. However, there is an opportunity cost to this behavior. We might have spent those matching funds on something quite different if the federal funds were not so enticing.

The budgetary interdependency between the states and the federal government has enormous consequences for states. A large share of expenditures approved by state legislatures each session are either a state match for federal program funds or are direct appropriations of federal funds. Changes in federal budgets or policies roll through state finances like a tide with sometimes devastating consequences. In its desire to have a national policy in a growing number of areas, Congress has gradually pushed the states beyond their fiscal ability to participate as partners. Despite recent successes by the governors to get Congress to ease up on mandates, the legacy of commitments already made means states face some rough times ahead.

During my term in office, I faced two major situations in which actions by the federal government had a very negative impact on the budget of Kentucky and other states. One situation dealt with Medicaid funding and the other with the federal highway trust fund. In both situations, I fought to keep federal funding intact. Although I was somewhat successful in this fight, the political climate indicates that such successes will be fewer in coming years. The two examples I just mentioned illustrate very well what probably is ahead for state governments as we enter the next century. Therefore, I will explain what happened in these instances to show how aggressive action by a governor can make a difference, but also to make the point that we are only seeing the beginning of what future governors must be prepared to do to protect the fiscal integrity of their state finances.

The Medicaid Provider Tax

Administration of the federal Medicare and Medicaid programs is vested in the states as a state-federal partnership, although state administrative responsibility for Medicare is limited. The federal government sets the parameters of the programs and provides a major portion of the money. States establish criteria for eligibility and set reimbursement rates within broad federal guidelines. The amount of federal Medicaid funds a state receives is based on a formula which takes into account the income levels of the population. The ratio of state to federal dollars will vary according to the income level in each state.

Title XIX of the Social Security Act was enacted to assist states in providing medical care to their low income populations. The Medicaid program gives states considerable flexibility in how their programs are structured within the framework of federal guidelines. A series of acts of Congress in the mid-1980s greatly expanded Medicaid coverage. Both Medicaid and Medicare costs borne by the states rapidly escalated during this period and threatened to break state budgets. These expansions increased the Kentucky state match by $50 million in 1990. That figure was projected to rise to $62 million in just two years. Every governor in the nation complained about the impact these mandated expenditures were having on other public services. In order to keep the Medicaid program from "busting the budget," states could alter the reimbursement rate, the eligibility criteria, or both.

The federal Health Care Financing Administration (HCFA) in 1985 changed federal regulations so states could raise more Medicaid fund by either levying a tax on providers or by accepting "donations" from providers. The state could increase the reimbursement rate for the participating hospitals to cover the cost of providing care to a greater number of indigent patients without raising the cost of care to others. The state could call this participation by providers a donation if the money was voluntarily placed in a trust fund restricted to this specific purpose, or the state could simply levy a provider tax and dedicate these funds to the cost of expanded care. In the Omnibus Budget Reconciliation Act of 1990, Congress passed and President Bush signed into law a provision which specifically prohibited HCFA from restricting the use of provider donations as a state's share until after December 31, 1991.

To take advantage of this alternative method of raising Medicaid funds, I developed a program called the Hospital Indigent Care Assistance Program (HICAP), a mechanism created to administer money raised from a tax paid by the participating providers. The General Assembly enacted this program in 1990 after I was able to convince the medical community it would get back every dollar paid into the trust fund set up by the program. In return for their willingness to help the state leverage more federal Medicaid funds, the HICAP program guaranteed the return of all the taxes they paid into the fund or $100,000 each year, whichever was higher. Since states set their own reimbursement rate, contributions made by providers could legally be repaid through higher reimbursements for services.

At that time, Kentucky was getting seven federal dollars for every three it contributed to the Medicare program. After giving the tax money back to the providers, the state still had more than twice that amount with which to increase Medicaid services. We estimated the provider tax of $156 million would leverage $377 million additional federal dollars in FY 1991 alone. We planned to use these additional funds to preserve the Medicaid benefits for some 425,000 Kentuckians and extend inpatient hospital coverage to 350,000 more of the state's so-called working poor.

By 1990 the number of states using provider donations or taxes rose to eighteen states, and at least that many other were considering doing so. Just after we enacted the provider tax, the inspector general for HCFA issued a memorandum challenging the practice of using provider funds as a state match when the funds are returned through higher reimbursement rates. HCFA subsequently circulated a draft regulation prohibiting the practice effective January 1992, the time when the Congressional constraint on such a regulation expired. The federal concern was that states were legitimately able to increase the federal financial participation in Medicaid without actually putting any more money into the program, which distorted the formula for setting the size of the federal contribution, the so-called "Kentucky Plan."

Concern about budget deficits led to the HCFA action. In practice it was true that this method of raising money for the state match to Medicaid funds did not require an increase in general fund appropriations to the Medicaid program. On the other hand, the provider tax did represent a way to increase the *federal* participation. What seemed ironic about this was that states had found a way to shift costs back to the federal government at a time when they were trying to do the same thing to us.

In anticipation of an adverse action by HCFA, the HICAP program was amended in a special session of the General Assembly in February 1991. The changes in the law were based on information coming from HCFA which targeted certain features of the provider tax and donation programs. It was my intent to make the program more acceptable while retaining the main feature of returning the tax to the provider through adjustments in the reimbursement for services provided. In the meantime, I joined with other governors to persuade the Congress to make the practice legal beyond the January 1992 deadline.

At the midyear meeting of the National Governors' Association, I read a prepared statement urging all the governors to unite on this issue. We argued a fundamental states' rights issue. The federal government cannot and should not tell the states who they can tax. "You made the rules," I told HCFA. "Now you want to punish us for taking advantage of them."

In early October 1991, Governor David Walters of Oklahoma and I met with Senators Lloyd Bentson and Henry Waxman to urge their support of legislative intervention to prevent implementation of the ban proposed by HCFA. We were encouraged by what we heard. Several members of the House of Representatives, including then Majority Leader Richard Gephardt, urged in floor speeches, committee hearings, and letters that the administration on its own withhold the regulation. It was clear, however, that the administration was not going to take any action which would contribute to the ballooning federal budget deficit.

Because I was leaving, office I was unable to keep up the debate. In late November 1991, Colorado Governor Roy Roemer and NGA staff negotiated a compromise with Senators Lloyd Bentson and Wendell Ford which Congress passed and President Bush signed into law. The legislation clarified when provider taxes would qualify for federal Medicaid matching. Essentially, the Congress permitted the use of provider taxes but limited the applicability of these revenues to not more than 25 percent of the state contribution. It also limited the amount of Medicaid funds that could be used for what it called "disproportionate" share payments to 12 percent the total Medicaid service expenditures. I felt it was inappropriate for the federal government to tell states how they can raise money, but the final compromise certainly was better than what might have happened otherwise.

Putting "Trust" Back in The Highway Trust Fund

As mentioned earlier, I faced two situations in which actions by the federal government had a very negative impact on the budget of Kentucky. I just discussed the first situation, which dealt with a dispute over the method Kentucky and other states were using to raise funds for Medicaid. In the second instance I worked with other governors to get the federal government to keep its commitment to return to the states the money it collected through dedicated federal highway taxes.

The highway trust fund was created to help equalize the burden of building and maintaining the interstate highway system and to provide money for major transportation projects which states and cities could not afford to finance on their own. The money collected from a federal gasoline tax is placed in a trust fund which is supposed to protect it from use for any purpose other than transportation. The commitment to the states was a partnership in the construction and maintenance of the interstate highway system. Over time the money also was used for other surface transportation projects.

Highway trust funds are allocated among the states according to a formula, but the actual amount a state will receive is a function of federal approval of the state highway plan and a budget cap placed on the amount of money which the U.S. Department of Transportation can release from the trust fund in a given fiscal year. The cap is called an "obligation ceiling," which refers to the amount of money that can be committed for work on projects already approved by U.S. DOT, but not yet started.

During my tenure as vice chair and later as chair of the National Governors' Association Committee on Transportation, Commerce, and Communications, a dispute over highway trust funds arose because of an effort by the Bush administration to use them to help reduce the federal budget deficit. The administration was not returning to the states all the highway tax revenues it collected each year, as is required by federal law and had been promised when the trust fund was originally created. Although the federal government was not actually spending the trust fund money for something else, it was withholding it from states in order to reduce the federal deficit on paper. I made an increase in the distribution of federal highway trust funds a major issue, arguing that it was time to put the "trust" back in the highway trust fund.

When I became a member of the NGA committee the federal cap was $12 billion, but federal gas tax revenues that same year were projected to be at least $15 billion. In effect the federal government was withholding from states $3 billion in new trust fund revenues to help lower the budget deficit. Actually, the new cap proposed by the administration was $240 million less than the previous year, making the situation for the states even worse. The governors agreed that at the very least the federal government should return to the states current revenues and then commit to a plan to spend down the reserve in the fund.

Forty-seven governors signed a letter to then President Bush requesting executive action to raise the obligation limit to $15 billion, the projected tax revenues dedicated to the trust fund for FY 1991. This proposal would increase Kentucky's share by almost $40 million that year alone. States would actually draw down less than the proposed $3 billion increase in the obligation ceiling because it takes several years, as projects go through the construction process, to spend the additional funds.

The federal government actually was making money on the highway funds it held in trust on behalf of the states. The General Accounting Office estimated that interest earned on trust fund reserves would be about $920 million in FY 1991. Not only were the "feds" keeping our money, they were using the interest on it to help reduce the deficits they were running up for other federal programs! The actual cash the states would draw from the trust fund in FY 1991 would be about $470 million of the $3 billion surplus available that fiscal year. The Bush administration could finance the entire allocation from just the interest earned and never touch the $3 billion we requested.

I galvanized the other governors to put a full court press on members of Congress to increase the obligation ceiling when they approved the FY 1991 budget. I personally met with congressman and senators on Capitol Hill and with various administration officials until we got a satisfactory resolution to this matter. When the budget bill was passed by the Congress, the obligation ceiling was raised to $14.5 billion. It was not what we asked for, but $2.3 billion more than we would have received if it had not been for the hardball political pressure put on the administration and members of Congress. From my viewpoint, our partner in state-federal relations was abusing its position of trust by playing budget games with money badly needed by states and taxpayers and rightfully belonging to them.

The Issue of Federal Mandates

Over the years Congress has imposed obligations on states without considering the serious fiscal problems they create for governors and legislatures struggling to balance their budgets. These actions are referred to as "unfunded mandates." Unfunded mandates are federal laws which require states to do certain things, but no funds are provided by the Congress to carry them out. Governors have complained about this for many years with little effect on Congress. Quite frankly, it appears that Congress regards the states as step-children in the federal system. Although we hear a lot about a state-federal partnership, the reality is that states have been sued when federal bureaucrats feel states have not carried out a federal mandate.

As I finish this book, there seems to be a move in Congress to curb the "unfunded mandates" practice, but this will probably only affect future actions. It would be nearly impossible for the Congress to underwrite the cost of every mandate it has passed in the last thirty or forty years. It would take several years of research just to identify them and determine their cost.

Congress has for many years consciously used funding as a vehicle to implement national domestic policy. Congress frequently holds participation in a highly desired federal program contingent to a state complying with some federal mandate, which was the case with federal highway funds during my term as governor. In a release from the National Governors' Association, my committee called attention to this issue:

> *A recently approved federal mandate requires states to suspend the driver's license of all convicted drug offenders or risk losing part of their federal highway funds. States now face 13 different financial penalties under which they can lose from 5 percent to 100 percent of their highway funds for failure to comply with federal requirements ranging from control of junkyards and outdoor advertising to national minimum drinking age laws.*

This is just one of many examples I could site of the Congress using its program funds to enforce federal policies which the states did not help create. The issue here is not the advisability of suspending the driver's license of a convicted drug offender. The issue is the moral right of the federal government to withhold tax revenues held in trust on behalf of states for any purpose other than the one for which the tax was enacted. In this particular case, Congress is by law virtually impounding our money to enforce compliance with a federal policy which has nothing whatever to do with transportation infrastructure.

Not only did Congress make highway funds contingent on compliance with these new laws, it provided no

money with which to implement these new federal requirements. At the time the law I mentioned above was enacted,
only one state (New Jersey) currently had a state law that met
the requirements. States were given at best four years to
comply without losing funds retroactively.

A more recent example of an unfunded mandate
is the requirement that states provide citizens an opportunity to
register to vote when they apply for new or renewed drivers'
licenses—the "motor voter law," as it is called. Congress
imposed this action on the states, but provided no funds to
implement it. The merits of the law aside, it is just another
example of something the Congress imposed on states without
providing money to carry it out.

There are literally hundreds of these federal
laws which over the years steadily increased the burden of tax
payers at the state and local level. The collateral costs of
complying with federal mandates are seldom considered when
these laws are passed, but they usually involve a cost to
someone. No one knows, I suppose, just how much states
spend to satisfy federal mandates, but it has to be in the hundred millions of dollars for a state like Kentucky.

States usually have no option but to meet the
mandate or forego participation in critical federal programs
like transportation construction funds. The fiscal interdependence of this federal-state "partnership" makes it virtually
impossible for states to opt out of most of the voluntary programs, so state policymakers continue to accommodate the
federal demands placed on states rather than take the financial
loss of federal funds. Consequently, a significant portion of a
state budget is beyond the control of state policymakers due to
federal mandates over which they have no control.

Some costly state-federal programs are called
"entitlements" because expenditures are mandated if people
meet the criteria for receiving the benefits provided by the
program. Federal programs like Social Security and its two
health care components, Medicare and Medicaid, are examples

of large entitlement programs. When Congress decides to expand one of these programs, state expenditures must grow in order to remain a participant in a program. Much of the growth in state spending for human services in the last fifty years can be directly attributed to expansion of these programs.

A Painful Road Lies Ahead

In recent years the cost of federal domestic programs has exceeded funds available in the federal treasury by billions of dollars. Congress says it wants to curb federal spending, but it hasn't as yet been able to curb its appetite for expanding existing programs and even creating new ones which it cannot afford to support. As it struggles with debt reduction, Congress is trying to shift more of the cost of expensive programs to the states. While these actions reduce federal spending, they do not reduce the cost to the taxpayer. It only shifts the tax burden from the federal government to the states. The growing national debt threatens to destabilize the state-federal relationship and is placing great fiscal stress on the states.

It's very hard to back away from a federal program once a state has agreed to participate. While the public seems to want to cut government, it doesn't want to give up anything in the process. Every federal program has a politically astute constituency ready to defend it on the steps of the statehouse. As pressure mounts on Congress to cut back domestic spending, pressure on state politicians will intensify with demands that they fight to keep Congress from reducing federal funding for particular programs. If that effort fails, the beneficiaries of these programs will carry their fight to the state legislatures seeking money to continue these programs with state funds.

Governors and state legislators are being placed in a very difficult position. No politician wants to be in the position of denying something which in many cases people have come to take for granted. On the other hand, continued participation in costly federal programs is having a very negative effect on the ability of state and local governments to provide other vital services for which there is no federal help.

The fiscal interdependence of which I spoke earlier will surely mean painful days are ahead for state governments as Congress and the president try to reduce the commitments the federal government has made to millions of Americans. The amount of pain for state politicians will depend on whether Congress is willing just to cut off programs or instead tries to push the cost of these programs down to the states.

Working with Other Governors

Collective action is effective as every lobby organization fully understands. As the relationship between the states and the federal government becomes more adversarial, interstate organizations like the National Governors' Association grow in importance. In my brief experience with such organizations, I saw both their potential and their weakness. In situations like the ones I described above, governors are able to pull together and put enough pressure on the federal government to cause changes in federal policy or regulations. In other situations, partisan politics has kept the governors from acting in what might be the best interest of the states, as happened when the Republican governors tried to give President Bush the education goals panel structure he wanted.

The failure of the Democratic governors to counter the blatantly partisan posturing of the Republican governors in the National Governors' Association meeting in Mobile was a great disappointment to me. By calling the education summit in Charlottesville, President Bush was able to look like he was doing more for education than he actually was prepared to do. As I indicated earlier, I was particularly chagrined at the reluctance of my fellow Democratic governors to get into a battle with this Republican administration over the federal role in education.

In the Pascagula meeting of the Democratic governors prior to the summer meeting of the NGA in 1990, we talked about political strategy. A number of governors voiced objections to various parts of the national goals initiative. Some of them wanted an opportunity to express some of their concerns during the conference in Mobile. Governors Ray Mabus of Mississippi and Doug Wilder of Virginia and I were particularly outspoken on the structure of the national goals panel as framed by the White House and the Republican governors. Since Democratic governors held the majority, we felt like we were in a strong position to challenge certain aspects of the goals.

Bill Clinton, then governor of Arkansas, was the Democratic co-chair of the education goals task force. Clinton had committed a great deal of time and effort to the development of the goals, so he was concerned that we not derail the project at this late date. After we assured him that we would support the education goals when it was time to vote, he agreed to make sure we would have an opportunity to speak briefly about our concerns before the roll was called.

When the time came for the education goals to be approved, the NGA chair called on Governor Carroll Campbell, the Republican co-chair, to give a brief report and call for passage of a resolution supporting the education goals and the creation of the goals panel to evaluate progress toward them. At this point, Governor Clinton was supposed to be given the floor to give us a chance to express our concerns before a vote was taken on the resolution. Instead, much to my amazement, NGA chair Governor Terry Brandstad (R-Iowa) took the podium and called for the question. The vote was taken and the resolution was adopted without discussion. In a matter of fifteen seconds, the Republicans had squelched the rebellion with the help of Bill Clinton.

Wondering what happened, I looked around the room and saw Governor Clinton with his back to the podium having a chat with Governor Jim Thompson of Illinois. Later that day I had a brief talk with Clinton. I came away from that discussion with the clear impression that he had promised to support the president on this issue and really could not do what he had earlier indicated he would do. I think he was concerned that the White House would retaliate against him personally by trying to defeat him in his bid for re-election if he failed to support their agenda vigorously at this late date. He clearly didn't care what the cargo was so long as the train got to the station on time. Although he didn't say it, I also knew he needed the national exposure the education goals panel would give him to help him build a foundation for his run for president. His response says a lot about why Democrats have such a tough time holding together on an issue.

While there are times for national action, sometimes all the nation's governors cannot work collectively on an issue because their interests are not mutual. For example, during the oil embargo a decade ago the northeastern states suffered severe shortages of fuel oil and high prices for the oil that was available. The energy producing states in the south experienced economic growth during this era as the economy of the northeastern states suffered. The governors of the northeastern states created the Coalition of Northeast Governors to lobby the Congress for action to deal with fuel oil shortages and escalating prices, which were hurting their citizens and killing off their industrial growth as one company after another moved to the southern states in search of cheaper energy.

The governors of the southern states maintained that the economic growth in the south was not occurring at the expense of the northeast. Rather it was the result of many years of cultivating the "sunbelt" as a good environment for business for many reasons including its abundant supply of relatively cheap energy. In fact, the Southern Growth Policies Board, an interstate organization created to promote economic growth in the southeastern states, launched a study of the reasons for the industrial growth in the south during that period and concluded the southern states were still far behind most midwestern and northeastern states in per capita income and other indicators of economic well-being. The point of all this is to say that sometimes federal policy (or perhaps the absence of it) can divide rather than unite the states.

Energy Policy is Still Divisive

Federal decisions affecting energy use and production are still causing divisions among the governors. One example occurred during my tenure as governor when Congress amended the Clean Air Act to deal with the alleged "acid rain" problem, which primarily affected the timber and paper industries in the northeastern states. The economy of the energy-producing states in the south were severely threatened by the stringent emission standards imposed by Title IV of the Clean Air Act. This act was amended by Congress in 1990 in response to claims by northeastern governors that acid rain was depleting their forests, killing their agriculture, and threatening the health of their citizens.

The Clean Air Act amendment imposed severe emission standards on coal, particularly coal with a high sulfur content such as is found in west Kentucky. The impact on coal-producing states like Kentucky was potentially great if not devastating. In an open letter to the Kentucky congressional delegation, I asked that implementation of Title IV be deferred for three years. In that letter I contended that the short timeline given to industry to meet the new standards was unjustified. A crisis sufficient to demand such immediate and drastic action simply did not exist.

Congress had commissioned a ten-year, $500 million study to assess the acid rain issue. The National Acid Precipitation Assessment program, hailed for its scientific quality and objectivity, concluded that acid rain is a long-term problem requiring emission reductions, but it also concluded that an environmental crisis requiring immediate action did not exist. Furthermore, the EPA found that substantial reductions in offending sulfur dioxide emissions had already occurred over the previous decade—a reduction of some 25 percent from 1980 to 1989—which proved the stringent rules put in place by the Clean Air Amendments approved in 1990 were unnecessary and too restrictive.

I took the position that we were well on the way to solving the problem of acid rain through advanced technologies, so why place such a heavy burden on the coal industry at this time? In fact, the U.S. Department of Energy was currently testing newer technologies which would more effectively reduce sulfur and carbon dioxide emission. To rush industry into buying scrubbers or other lower technologies at this time would result in retrofitting their power plants later with the newer technology. Such investments are an inefficient use of scarce capital at a time when we must do everything we can to be more competitive in the world economy.

My concern about the economic impact of Title IV was shared by other governors in the region. During my tenure as chair of the Southern Governors' Association, the southern governors adopted resolutions which strongly supported the position of the United States in the International Negotiating Committee for a Framework Convention on Climate Change and firmly rejected "carbon taxes" and other broad-based energy taxes as being unjustified and demonstrably harmful to the well-being of the United States and its citizens.

A Tussle with TVA

My concerns about the impact of Title IV of the Clean Air Act amendment were quickly affirmed when the Tennessee Valley Authority (TVA) approached me about a financial contribution toward the cost of installing scrubbers. To Kentucky's benefit, TVA purchased millions of tons of coal every year from west Kentucky coal companies. However, this coal is high in sulfur and contributed heavily to TVA's power plant emissions of sulfur dioxide. TVA advised me they would need state financial assistance with the purchase of scrubbers which would remove the offending emissions or they would have to purchase lower sulfur coal from the Powder River basin in Wyoming. The deal was this: give us money or we will take our business elsewhere.

All through the summer of 1991, I deliberated while TVA kept putting the heat on (no pun intended). It was a stare-down if ever I saw one, each side waiting to see who would blink first. TVA clearly thought the threat of losing thousands of coal related jobs in that part of Kentucky would be unthinkable to me. On the other hand, I didn't believe TVA could realistically import coal from the western states and save enough money to make it more economical than to install the scrubbers. Having been in the coal business myself at one time, the numbers just didn't add up.

This was no ordinary economic development request. A quasi-governmental agency like TVA is different from a private energy company. TVA was created with a statutory mission to help the economy of the region it serves. I felt strongly it was wrong for TVA to hold Kentucky jobs hostage to its corporate economic interests. The request was not appropriate, and I told them so. The pressure on me was great. Many of the coal operators in the region urged me to give TVA what they wanted. To their personal credit, there were two men who put the public interest first, however. Bob Anderson, then president of Andalex, and Bud Ogden, who was chairman of Island Creek at the time, both said that I should not give in to TVA even though the purchase of the expensive scrubbers would have benefited their respective companies.

Finally, in early fall I called their bluff and raised the stakes for Kentucky at the same time. I told them that financial help from Kentucky was out of the question and furthermore I expected them to continue to buy Kentucky coal. I also told them that, if they carried out the threat to buy western coal, I would immediately ask the General Assembly to put TVA under the jurisdiction of the Public Service Commission and regulate it like a private energy company. Senator Wendell Ford, a resident of west Kentucky, backed up my position by notifying TVA he was prepared to introduce federal legislation that would make them subject to regulation in Kentucky. TVA quickly backed off and their request for a financial subsidy from Kentucky was never raised again.

Although we won that one, it proved that I was not crying "wolf" when I said Title IV of the Clean Air Act could have serious economic consequences for Kentucky. It seems like I was fighting the battle both in Washington and at home, with the odds against me in both places. On the other hand, I owed it to Kentucky taxpayers not to allow one of the biggest purchasers of Kentucky coal to extort money from the state treasury. TVA has been a good citizen over the years and will continue to be in the future, but its action in this situation was not appropriate.

I have written a good bit about my work in Washington. I should say here that having a state office in Washington proved to be very helpful. The assistance given to me by Linda Breathitt, my director of the Washington office, was immeasurable. A Washington presence is more than just having a place to drop your hat and coat when in town. Contacts are made, information is gathered, logistics are arranged, and hearing are attended—all things which simply could not be done from Frankfort. As she had done for governors before me, Linda astutely and tirelessly watched over Kentucky's interests in Washington. I greatly appreciated the help all the Washington staff provided to me throughout my term as governor.

So far I have talked about actions at the national and regional level which affected Kentucky. There are times when states can use their own good offices to solve mutual problems. It has been done at other times in other places, but I worked with three other states to help solve a problem we all faced—what to do with toxic waste.

An Interstate Agreement on Toxic Waste

Federal regulations for the "superfund" created by Congress to help clean up large toxic waste dumps require all states to document that they have adequate capacity to treat and dispose of all the hazardous waste the states are projected to generate for the next twenty years. This capacity has to be updated on a regular basis. Toxic waste takes many forms, and each form requires special facilities and treatment procedures. The governors of Tennessee, Alabama, and South Carolina and I saw the advantage of each state specializing in processing certain types of toxic waste and then shipping its waste to the state best prepared to process it. Using this approach, each state could avoid the excessive cost of maintaining and regulating facilities to treat all toxic waste generated within its own borders.

Much of the environmental debate at the time centered on the importation of out-of-state waste. Hardly an evening went by that the television news didn't picture mountains of garbage collected in the metropolitan areas of the east coast being shipped to some far-off landfill. At one point the nation's attention was focused on a barge ladden with garbage floating off the coast of New York with nowhere to go.

Even though the interstate compact would actually *reduce* the amount of toxic waste coming into Kentucky compared to the waste it would *export* to other states, environmental groups opposed it on the argument that Kentucky should not be importing *any* toxic waste. I had a difficult time getting them to understand that by *not* entering into the compact, Kentucky would have to dispose of its own waste within the state, an amount far greater than we were ever going to import under the compact.

In November 1989 the four governors signed an interstate agreement in which we agreed to exchange various forms of toxic waste. (At one point the governor of North Carolina asked to be part of the interstate agreement, but withdrew before it was signed because he couldn't get his legislature to agree to build the facilities to hold up his part of the deal.) Without being specific as to the kind of waste each state would accept from the others, it was understood that each state would accept the kind of waste for which it already had the best facilities.

An interstate agreement like this one could save the participating states costly duplication of expensive facilities. Here was an excellent example of ways governors can work together to solve mutual problems without a formal organizational structure to facilitate it. They just need to show an interest and take the initiative to move ahead on it.

Some Unfinished Business

Although the 1990 legislative session was historic for many reasons, there were still some important items left off the agenda. Among them were the contentious issues of solid waste management and the new federal law regarding the suspension of drivers' licenses of drug offenders. I supported a stronger Driving Under the Influence (DUI) law in the 1990 session, but it was defeated largely due to the lobbying by lawyer/legislators who saw their legal practice threatened by it. I called a special session of the General Assembly for January 14, 1991, to deal with what turned out to be an extensive agenda of fourteen items.

The Solid Waste Issue

One of the really difficult aspects of the solid waste disposal issue was the lack of reliable information on which to evaluate the magnitude of the problem and how best to approach it with a comprehensive, statewide management plan. Landfills had become an emotional issue that tended to be driven by extreme views and the high media visibility given to the perceived threat of out-of-state garbage.

In an attempt to get useful information, I asked the University of Kentucky to prepare an analysis of

Kentucky's present landfill capacity and long-term needs. Unfortunately, what I received was a three inch thick report that answered none of the fundamental questions that had to be addressed. After patiently sitting through a two-hour briefing on the contents of the report, I said, "Is this what we've waited three months for?" I was so disappointed in the study I refused payment of the bill the University sent me for the cost to prepare it.

Subsequently we did some research of our own and hired two consultants who advised the NGA and the state of Georgia to help prepare our legislation. I remember personally reading stacks of documents and various drafts of the bill to understand thoroughly both the facts and the proposed law. Quite frankly, it was the most boring stuff I had read in a long time, but the issue was too important for me not to know what impact the law would have on the environment, local governments, and landfill operators. The legislation would be attacked from all sides. It had to be scientifically sound, environmentally safe, and affordable.

Opposition to the bill came from local officials and landfill operators who were fearful of too much regulation and higher costs. We were proposing mandatory solid waste pickup county-wide, which some rural county officials didn't think was feasible. Environmentalists wanted local control of the siting of landfills while we were devising a a statewide plan for management of solid waste. Then there was concern about out-of-state and out-of-area garbage, as it was called. The lobbyists from all sides crawled all over the Capitol trying to get the bill altered one way or another. I remember in particular an encounter I had with Dan Walton and Jack Underwood, who were very aggressive lobbyists representing the commercial landfill operators on this issue.

Time was running out on the session, and I was frustrated over the lack of action on the bill by the legislature. Walton and Underwood had successfully bottled up the legislation for weeks. I knew that at some point I would have to ask them to get out of the way. I frequently ate lunch in the cafeteria located in the Capitol Annex, especially when the General Assembly was in session. As I made my way to the lunch line, my legislative liaison Tom Dorman pointed out Walton and Underwood having lunch. "Good!" I said. "I'd like to talk to them."

Apparently they surmised I was looking for them because in the few minutes it took me to say a brief hello to some people and get through the lunch line these two gentlemen had disappeared. Tom later told me he saw them go into the men's room in the rear of the cafeteria. I got up from the table and went to the restroom and, sure enough, there they were huddled in the corner enjoying a quiet conversation and a glass of iced tea. They were surprised to see me, to say the least. "Gentlemen," I said. "you have a choice. You can let my bill pass, or you can kill it and I will regulate you by executive order. I promise that you will like the bill better than the executive order I'll write." They got the message, and the legislation passed the next day.

The DUI Issue

I had tried and failed during the 1990 regular legislative session to pass significant drunk driving legislation. We enacted legislation to improve school bus safety but failed to get the strongest measures I wanted in the DUI bill that was passed in 1990. I came back again with a new bill in the 1991 special session with more success. As noted earlier, the federal government threatened the states with a loss of highway construction funds unless they suspended the drivers' licenses of convicted drug offenders. It was important that we not place our highway funds in jeopardy. Furthermore, the Carrollton church bus crash had made this a national story.

The most contentious part of the DUI bill was what is known as "illegal *per se,*" which means one is deemed to be legally drunk based on a specific level of alcohol found in the driver's blood. No other proof is required such as demonstrated impairment of body functions like being unable to count backwards, walk a straight line, or see a pencil placed in front of the nose. Illegal *per se* eliminates the discretion involved in determining if someone should be charged with driving under the influence of alcohol or any other chemical substance.

Trial lawyers argued that this was a violation of civil rights, but it also meant that there was less of an opportunity for an attorney to defend the drunken driver. The legal profession is well represented in the General Assembly, so lawyer/legislators lobbied their own cause with their fellow legislators. Some legislators had been arrested for DUI under existing law and had successfully beaten the rap. They didn't want to see the law changed either.

The law was passed this time with some additional provisions which aided us in our effort to deal with illegal drugs. For example, the law contained a provision allowing the state to seize property proven to be acquired through illegal drug or drug-related transactions. This element of the law has been very helpful in the war on drugs in Kentucky.

There is a myth in Kentucky that governors are lame ducks after the mid-term legislative session. Clearly an interim legislative session of limited duration is needed to deal with special issues which do not make it through the regular session. The legislature now must approve so many board appointments, it seems one needs a special session or two just to fill vacancies on critical state boards. I know there was some mumbling among House leadership that I was just doing this for political reasons, but I was not about to be a lame duck governor.

I opened this chapter with the observation that many things arise during a term in office which are not on anyone's agenda when a governor takes the oath of office. The intergovernmental aspects of public policy requires the Chief

Executive Officer to be alert and very aggressive in the defense of the state's financial well-being and policy integrity. Perhaps in the years to come we will see a less proactive and aggressive Congress as our national leaders begin to see the limitations to what the federal government can realistically accomplish. On the other hand, the job of governor could get dramatically more difficult as the pressure to downsize federal programs and commitments falls more and more on state and local governments.

XV. REFLECTIONS

In this book I have tried to provide insight into the major issues and events in my administration, and to explain some of the things I tried to do. I have written about both my successes and failures, strengths and weaknesses. In these closing pages I just want to share some of the lighter moments Martha and I experienced along with a few closing thoughts.

Reaching Out to the People

I made a decision during my campaign that I would not become a prisoner of Frankfort. In fact, the insular nature of Frankfort was one of the aspects of state government that I found most troubling. In an age when transportation and communication have reduced time and distance, it is ironic that Kentuckians, particularly in rural areas, continue to feel distanced from the Capitol. Surveys consistently show a "they don't care about us" attitude. There are a lot of reasons for this attitude, and they are not unique to Kentucky, but I wanted to do something about it.

Few Kentuckians ever make it to the Capitol to meet with a governor. I wanted to minimize the isolation people felt, so I made a great effort to reach out to them. When the administration ended I had logged over 121,000 air miles, virtually all of it in-state. That's eighty-four miles for every day in office. Excluding the days leading up to and during legislative sessions when I rarely left Frankfort, I was somewhere in Kentucky other than Frankfort for about half of my administration.

The ability to remain close to the people you represent and have a sense for how your decisions affect them in their daily lives is one of the most appealing aspects of being governor. For me that meant being as many places as I could be to bring the "people's government" to them in person. It involved difficult logistical efforts like our Capitol to the Counties program. It meant dropping everything to attend to crisis management during emergencies. It meant being a cheerleader when someone needed a pat on the back and a friend when they needed someone to lean on. It meant being a "good guy" one minute and a "bad guy" the next.

Even though it is relatively easy for a governor to get around to meet people, the terrain and size of the state make helicopter the preferred method of travel. Flying was something I took seriously and made sure conditions were acceptable before taking to the air. The Kentucky State Police and the state aircraft pilots went about their work in such a professional and efficient manner I always felt safe, except for the rare occasions when things didn't go according to plan.

There was one occasion which took us all by surprise. To find a place to land the aircraft, and to have transportation there to pick us up at just the right time, was no small task. Even when the destination was an area familiar to them, the pilots often relied on someone on the ground to communicate and identify a landing site for them. Even when you are used to landing in parking lots, football fields, and open fields, things never look the same from the air.

As we arrived for the opening of the new state prison in Morgan County one afternoon, it was obvious that the pilots were having some difficulty recognizing the designated landing area. There wasn't a lot of flat land around the prison anyway, so the options were limited. Finally they selected what I must agree looked like the most obvious choice. It was the largest open area we could see, and a number of people were standing in the general vicinity with some cars close by.

As we closed in on touch down, we could see that most of our welcoming party had rifles. I didn't think that much about it, since it was after all a prison. Only when we could finally see the shocked look in their eyes did I look out the opposite window and see the targets. We had landed in the middle of the firing range during practice!

Some Things Didn't Work Out

No reader of this book would feel it was complete if I didn't address two controversies which drew a lot of attention: Martha's decision to run for governor and my self-appointment to the University of Kentucky Board of Trustees. Both decisions were made with the best of intentions. Both were considered by my critics to be the most audacious decisions ever made by people in our positions. Given the speculation which still surrounds these two things, I will briefly discuss each one. And let me say right up front, neither of us have any regrets about either decision.

Martha's Run for Governor

Four years is a very short time in which to do everything we wanted to accomplish. I was feeling the time pressure and no doubt communicated my concern to Martha. She understood what was at stake in the failure to get succession. As the 1990 session moved along, Martha began to talk more about the importance of sustaining what we had started once I left office. She even suggested that she just might run for governor herself, a notion I didn't take very seriously at the time.

Once the 1990 session was over, I was feeling good about what we had accomplished, even though now there was no possibility that I could succeed myself in office. We celebrated the signing of the KERA legislation and began preparing for Derby Day, always an important event for the governor and family. As Derby Day drew closer, Martha grew more concerned about what might happen to our initiatives once I left office. We had only about eighteen months left, not much time to consolidate the gains we had made.

We were having coffee on the Sunday morning after the Kentucky Derby when Martha told me she had just decided that she wanted to be a candidate for governor in 1991. I was taken by surprise. Martha and I have been partners in everything we have done over the years. We built our businesses together. We planned my run for the governorship together. However, we had not discussed this as was our custom before important decisions are made.

Martha told me about the many people who urged her to run for governor if the General Assembly denied me the opportunity of succession. She was encouraged by their support, but she did not want to run as my puppet. Martha wanted to have her own agenda and positions. Obviously, she was prepared to defend the things we had begun, but she wanted to be more than an echo of my administration. I can tell you honestly: Martha is her own person.

Of course I would support her decision if this was what she truly wanted, but there were serious obstacles to overcome. Not the least of these would be me! Although we do things together, she has her own views of what should be done. In my mind there was no doubt she would be governor in her own right and I would be the spouse in the mansion. However, I knew it would be very difficult for Martha to establish herself as something other than a surrogate for me, given the intensive media attention to my desire to succeed myself. She would have to convince the public and the media that she would not be just a ceremonial governor while I continued to run state government.

On the other hand, there was no doubt in my mind she would be an effective campaigner. Martha was an energetic, vibrant contributor to my campaign. She made speeches, worked with campaign staff and volunteers, and was involved in every aspect of the campaign. She had become a veteran political campaigner even though she had never run for public office in her own right. I felt her down-to-earth, common sense approach to things would resonate positively with voters. I felt it was worth a shot if she was prepared to take the abuse she would get from the media and other candidates.

Martha's campaign was a great experience. Once again we had the opportunity to feel the excitement of reaching out to voters and asking for their support, but this time for Martha and not for me. She crisscrossed the state, giving speech after speech, just as we had done together four years earlier. There was a solid vote out there for her candidacy in the primary election, but the media refused to regard her as a serious candidate. Most damaging was the continued perception that she would be governor in name only. It clearly was an uphill battle.

In March 1991, right in the middle of the primary election campaign, I found a lump in my right arm which was diagnosed as lymphoma. It frightened both of us. Over the two weeks or so it took to confirm the diagnosis and determine what it meant, Martha said she began to think ahead. "What if Wallace has to undergo extensive treatments or, even worse, be seriously ill for months? Would I want to be in the governor's office in Frankfort at a time like that?" she thought. My treatment was a serious diversion at a critical time in her campaign.

Given her inability to differentiate herself as a candidate in her own right and the uncertainty about the future of my health, Martha decided what she thought was best for herself and her family. In May 1991, almost one year after she made the decision to run for governor, Martha announced she was withdrawing from the race. It was a sad day for both of us. Martha feels to this day she never received a fair assessment of what she could do for the Commonwealth if she were governor. No doubt being my spouse was a liability she just could not overcome. On the other hand, neither of us have any regrets about having launched the campaign. I think her views on this decision were made very clear in her withdrawal speech.

When I began this race, I said it was more than just a campaign; it was a crusade. A campaign is just about winning an election. But a crusade is about a whole lot more. It has become obvious that I will not win the campaign to become Kentucky's next governor. But we didn't set out merely to win an office. We set out to change Kentucky; to try to help all the hard working, tax paying families who do it all for Kentucky. And in that crusade, we have been successful.

For four years, now, Wallace and I have served that crusade in the Governor's Mansion. For 13 months now we have taken that crusade to the counties and communities; the creeks and the "hollers" and the branches and the knobs that make up our Commonwealth. We have carried to those places a record of hope and opportunity: 65,000 new jobs; 50,000 adults who earned a high school equivalency diploma; a Kentucky lottery, which no one thought we could bring; fundamental education reform; hundreds of miles of new roads; and countless hopes and dreams that have been given new life. And nothing can ever take away from the pride we take in what we've done, or the appreciation that we have for the people who have given us the highest honor in this Commonwealth.

But our record is one to build on, not one to sit on. That's why I've also carried a message of change—to put state government back on the side of the do-it-alls. Cracking down on deadbeat dads; competency testing for teachers; social reforms that value work over welfare; and a world-

class system of public education for our world-class children.

But somewhere along the way, the campaign got in the way of the crusade. Issues got blurred, or ignored, in the rush to criticize, analyze and scrutinize. And I want to make something very clear. I take full responsibility for that. I have come to the conclusion that my very presence in this race has distracted attention from the very issues I have tried to advance and the very people for whom Wallace and I have always cared.

I am withdrawing from this campaign, but I will not withdraw from the issues I believe in and the people I care about—the people who have opened their hearts and their homes to Wallace and me for these four years. . . .

Finally, I want to say to all the people of this great Commonwealth who have bestowed on us their highest honor; whose faith and strength have been an inspiration to us every day; and whose cause remains our crusade, you have our deepest appreciation, affection, and admiration. You believed in us, and that means more than you'll ever know.

My Foray into Higher Education

As I have made clear throughout this book, education was a major issue with me. Higher education was no exception. It was my hope that I might have some influence on certain higher education issues which I felt were of public concern. From time to time I expressed my views only to be told to mind my own business. Given the importance of higher education and the enormous resources it commands, I felt it was proper for a public official to speak out on the concerns held by taxpayers who foot the bill. The response from my critics in higher education was pointedly to "butt out."

My relationship with most university presidents was at least respectful. It would be an understatement, however, to say that my relationship with David Roselle, then president of the University of Kentucky, was less than cordial. Roselle typified for me the arrogance and insensitivity of many in the university community. He was particularly incensed when I publicly suggested that a lengthy and expensive investigation into the U.K. athletics program ought to be made public. For my part, I had no patience whatsoever with the way Dr. Roselle handled his candidacy for the presidency of the University of Delaware. It was my opinion that he was just trying to extort a higher budget from us under the threat that he would leave the university if it wasn't forthcoming.

Despite the overwhelming need for reform in higher education, no one has successfully managed to penetrate the ivory tower. At least one governor told me not to even try. "Just give them what they want, and leave them alone," was his advice. Indeed, I got off to a bad start when I called the university presidents "cry babies" during budget meetings in 1988. Despite the lift my 1990 budget had given them, the largest single increase in history, I knew fiscal problems loomed ahead. With all the other issues I had taken on during the administration, there was precious little time to challenge perhaps the most revered of sacred cows. In my mind, however, it remained unfinished business.

Whenever possible I tried to take steps that would get some kind of higher education reform started. I had done all I could do to affect change through the budget process. I tried to appoint people who understood the need for change to be trustees of the various universities. Having successfully led the community colleges through a period of unprecedented growth, I had high hopes that Charles Wethington could be an effective agent of change. As a candidate for president of U.K., Charles certainly sounded like someone who recognized what needed to be done to make the university more responsive and responsible. Like so many others, however, Charles as president of the university was so determined to appease the faculty which opposed his appointment that any thoughts that he might address reform went out the window.

After much thought about how to be most effective in moving forward an agenda for reform in higher education, I decided the only approach was to become part of the process. Appointing myself to the policy body of the flagship university would make me a legitimate part of that process. There were several issue of great importance to students and the public I wanted discussed. If I could just have the opportunity to present the issues and discuss them extensively, I felt the other board members would address them in a responsible way.

In my last remarks as a member of the U.K. Board of Trustees, I outlined the issues I thought the board needed to address and offered some recommendations. Here is the essence of my concerns as expressed in a document I distributed at that meeting:

1. <u>Improve Completion Rates:</u> We need to better understand why some of our customers don't come back. A report on why students aren't re-enrolling, with appropriate demographic data, will enable the university to develop and maintain programs to reduce attrition in enrollment.

2. <u>Improve Accountability for Effectiveness:</u> We need to develop new and better ways to account for university activities. One way to do that is to provide comprehensive data on classroom activities and degree requirements. The university ought to develop a "truth in education" report as a tool in evaluating our success against stated goals. I suggested various items of information which might be included in such a report.

3. <u>Contain the Rapid Growth in the Cost of Higher Education:</u> It is tempting to simply try to find ways for the university to reduce costs, but that misses the point. Our

goal is to better understand why higher education costs what it does. One of higher education's greatest failings has been its inability to find effective methods of allocating costs. The various methods that have been tried do not take into account the unique needs of each particular institution or situation, but instead are generic to all institutions and circumstances. To meet this challenge, perhaps our most difficult, we have to find new ways to account for and evaluate productivity and quality in teaching, research, and public service.

While the cost of higher education has risen faster than inflation over the last decade, we still lack a clear understanding of what a higher education should cost at any of our universities. Given the increasing pressure on state budgets and the expectation that tuition and costs will continue to rise, the taxpayers of Kentucky in general, and the parents and students of the University of Kentucky in particular, deserve better information relating to how their higher education dollar is being spent.

4. A Lack of Emphasis on the Importance of Teaching: Much of the focus in this area has been on reducing the student-faculty ratio. However, simply lowering the number of students per class without giving attention to the availability of tenured senior faculty to undergraduates ignores a vital part of this effort. Analysis of statistical data illustrates the need to make a determined effort to examine our priorities and determine whether or not we are applying our resources in a way that is consistent with our goals.

Information compiled by the president's office indicates that 72 percent of our faculty are full-time tenured professors. Of that 72 percent, two-thirds are teaching two or fewer courses. Simply put, as our faculty rise up the professional ladder, most of them drift farther and farther from the classroom. This is not to suggest that I think all research is irrelevant or that public service is not an important part of this institution's mission. It does, however, graphically illustrate the need to re-examine our priorities and determine whether or not our undergraduates have appropriate access to senior and tenured faculty.

Asking that higher education place a greater emphasis on teaching is not an assault on research, unless it is research that does not contribute to our educational mission and the priorities set by the university. Until we can adequately account for the use of our financial and human resources, we have no way of knowing whether or not we are indeed accomplishing what it is we are supposed to be accomplishing.

I concluded my agenda for reforming higher education with these observations:

> *We have long passed the point at which fundamental reforms in higher education are needed in order to justify and account for the ever increasing cost of a college degree. Increasing pressures on national and state budgets are going to mandate changes. Rather than wait for the inevitable, we can seize the opportunity to begin now to prepare for the future.*
>
> *Some states have already established minimum teaching requirements. Major institutions like Yale University have undertaken evaluations of institutional priorities and goals. The number of people inside and outside academia calling for reform in higher education is growing. Almost without exception, all point to a failure to adequately emphasize the importance of teaching in promotion policies and tenure decisions as a principal reason for a need to re-evaluate our goals and priorities.*
>
> *The people of this Commonwealth have always looked to the University of Kentucky for leadership in higher education and for good reason. I am asking that this Board step forward now and*

*provide the leadership necessary to address criti-
cal issues in higher education today.*

Nobody except the university faculty seriously challenged the
need to address these issues. Most of these issues remain
important today, and some have recently been addressed by the
Council on Higher Education, although not very effectively in
my view.

The appointment of myself to the University of
Kentucky Board of Trustees was perhaps the most controversial action taken during my tenure in office. It was unprecedented, although governors used to sit *ex officio* on all university boards. My critics said it was the most egoistic act of my
entire administration. Once again I heard the familiar refrain
"you can't do that, Governor." I knew my action would stir up
a storm of protest from the university faculty, but I thought the
controversy would subside with time. On several occasions I
appointed previous governors to university boards, all of whom
made positive contributions. Surely over time I could demonstrate to my critics I also had the ability to work "within the
system" as well as outside it.

Unfortunately, I didn't have the chance to stay
on the board long enough to see these issues given a fair
hearing. All university boards were restructured by action of
the next General Assembly, which saw my removal as the
ultimate *coup de grace*. I have regretted not challenging the
new law which I believe was unconstitutional. On the other
hand, a law suit would only have led to more controversy and
further inhibited my ability to serve in a constructive capacity.

The "Itty-Bitty Journal" fiasco

At the close of my first board meeting, I was
confronted by a faculty member as I entered the elevator. He
took issue with my criticism of the emphasis on research. I
replied that the tenure system penalizes teaching but rewards
professors who publish obscure research articles in "itty-bitty

journals." Although the rhetoric may have been cute, when it appeared in print it gave a caustic edge to what had been an animated but sincere discussion between us. Once again I saw people focus on some off-hand comment rather than on the issues I raised.

The media immediately used this remark to characterize me as hostile and disrespectful of the university and its faculty. I again found myself as the issue rather than the problems I wanted addressed. Nonetheless, I have no regrets over the decision to appoint myself to the board. Unfortunately, my action probably resulted in the General Assembly unnecessarily creating a very cumbersome and decidedly more political and less accountable process for appointing future board members.

Some Days You Ought to Just Stay in Bed

Of all the responsibilities a governor has, none takes up more time or is more important than his or her relationship with the media. Why this is the case and whether it ought to be so is probably a subject better discussed elsewhere. On the other hand, the media played a significant role in how my administration was perceived by the public.

The "fourth estate," as it has been called, is in reality a fourth branch of government, the members of which view events as insiders to the process. They are as entrenched as any of the special interests. They are disdainful of those they believe have failed to pay proper dues in rising to prominence and demand that homage be paid to them once you get there. I could not have been an easier target, providing them with an endless array of subjects on which to disagree with me: an outsider, proposing what seemed to some of them as radical ideas, particularly about education reform, who had never held elective office.

Where it is pertinent in this book, I have tried to keep the media's role and influence in perspective as it related to the specific issues or events under discussion. Earlier in this book I discussed in some detail my trials and tribulations dealing with them during the campaign. Since then, some have been open and honest in admitting that they completely missed my campaign. Others were embarrassed to have missed the voter mood and were determined to be hostile from the outset.

Some of that is understandable, given the competitive and confrontational nature of the news media today. Most of it, however, was often petty and irrelevant. Just how much so was illustrated to me in early 1990 at a bicentennial celebration sponsored by the General Assembly at the Old State Capitol. Billed as an occasion to recognize the contributions of legislatures from decades past, keynote speaker John Ed Pearce, who is considered by many to be the dean of print journalists in Kentucky, chose instead to launch a rambling diatribe at me on issues he obviously knew little about.

So ridiculous was the personal attack on me that even some of my staunchest critics in the General Assembly apologized to me afterward. Like players in a game who think they got a bad call from the referee, you just have to walk away from it lest you make a bad situation worse by trying to respond to it. I learned to accept the media's role and how to deal with reporters, but there are times when they just don't make good sense.

Many Good Memories

Much of what I have written might leave the reader with the impression that being governor is just a lot of hard work. Actually, there are many memories which make it all worthwhile. Some of them show that even a governor has a human side.

The Chocolate Lover

During the early days of my administration, I was asked by a reporter if I had any particular personal likes and dislikes. Since everyone has them, I thought the question was pretty silly. I will never be convinced that the general public wants to know such personal things about public officials. Nonetheless, I responded that I enjoyed chocolate. I have been sorry ever since that I didn't suggest that I enjoyed something more valuable and less fattening. From that point on, I never went anywhere that someone didn't make sure I was amply supplied with chocolate candy, chocolate bars, chocolate brownies, and an infinite variety of other chocolate confections. People even mailed chocolate to the office. Come to think of it, my staff ate most of it and probably kept telling people I liked chocolate to satisfy their own appetites.

The Silver Service

As a visitor to the Mansion prior to taking up residence there, I often admired the gift of silver Kentucky made to the first *U.S.S. Kentucky* when it was commissioned in 1898. It has long been a custom of the United States Navy to name ships after states, and the states reciprocated by presenting something of value to the ship. When the ship was decommissioned in the 1920s, the silver service was returned to the state of Kentucky.

Having seen the beautiful silver in the Mansion, I was surprised it was not on display when I moved in. Since thousands of people visit the Executive Mansion every year, I thought such an interesting and valuable set should be on display there. Upon inquiring about the service, I was informed that it now permanently resided at the Military History Museum and would not be available for display at the Mansion. Perhaps naively, I thought that a governor had the authority to have it placed in the Mansion if it was requested. When I asked for it, I was told it could not be moved.

After several requests failed to get the silver moved, I finally called Adjutant General Michael Davidson of Military Affairs to embark on a rescue mission. To our chagrin, Mike also was rebuffed on his first attempt to recover the silver. Finally, General Davidson took a more direct approach. "Have the silver packed and ready," he told the officials at the Military Museum. "I'm coming over for it and I'm prepared to come in a tank." The silver was delivered as requested.

A Zealous Worker and Over-Zealous Woodsman

Kentucky has one of the most beautiful Capitol buildings in America. I took particular pride in the appearance of the grounds as well as the buildings. Funding and restoration of the state reception room and repairs to several of the statues in the Rotunda of the Capitol were undertaken during my tenure in office. I also had funded a restoration of the Berry Hill Mansion as well as a new roof for the Old Capitol building before leaving.

Anyone who has ever visited the Capitol Building knows that the floors are marble and always polished to a bright shine. Kenny McClease has cleaned the governor's office and much of the first floor of the Capitol building for the past decade. It's easy to see why the Capitol is so beautifully maintained by watching Kenny work.

Night after night, as I left the office, I would see Kenny buffing the floors, restoring the shine after the day's traffic. At the end of one particularly long night at the office, Kenny and I sat down on the steps of the Capitol. As Kenny told me about his family, I was telling him how much I appreciated the effort he put into his work. "Kenny," I finally said before walking off into the night air, "if everyone did their jobs as well as you do yours, we'd have the best government in America."

I generally made it a point to know what was going on regarding the physical environment of the Capitol. One morning I was awakened to the sound of a power saw in the garden of the Executive Mansion. I threw on my robe and went to the front window to see what was going on. As I looked out, I saw a man preparing to cut down a large pine tree beside the Mansion. Going outside I inquired, "What are you doing?" "We're taking down this pine," the man replied. "But it looks perfectly fine to me," I said. "Why are we doing this?" "Because it's going to die," he said in a matter of fact manner. "Then don't you think it would be better to let it die first?" I said. As far as I know the tree still stands today, but only because of my quick action to save it from an early death.

A Memorable Gift

One of my cherished memories involves someone I never even met. Martha and our sons commissioned a handmade desk for my office. My good friend Dick Faulkner and his craftsmen at Stanford Wood Products constructed a beautiful mahogany treasure that is truly a work of art. Centered on the top of the desk is the Great Seal of the Commonwealth of Kentucky inlaid in natural Kentucky woods. The extraordinary handiwork on the Seal was done by an 84-year-old craftsman named O. B. Schuler. Soon after the desk was delivered, I invited all the people who had worked on it to the governor's office for coffee. The day before they were scheduled to be in Frankfort, Mr. Schuller died. I never got to thank him in person for the beautiful work he had crafted.

Some encounters are just plain strange. On one trip to Harlan, I met an angry man who asked if I could "do something about the State Police." I replied that I had funded three classes of new recruits, boosted retirement, bought them new cars, and raised starting salaries. "Just what is it you think I need to do?" I asked. "Well, they're okay to have around when we have a parade or ball game or something like that. But every time we have a little killin' they're crawling all over the place. We can take care of our own affairs," he said.

And there was the day when an obviously agitated man approached me on the street in Russellville as I prepared to speak to the local Rotarians. He got right in my face and said, "I have just one thing to say to you, Governor!" I thought to myself, "Just what have I done to this man?" Slightly more colorfully, he blurted out, "Screw the *Courier-Journal*!" and walked off.

I am sure that to the casual observer it seemed like there were times when everybody was mad about something. I was *there* and it certainly seemed like it to me! While I never went looking for a fight, neither did I shy away from one if I thought it was necessary to get something done. The battle was intense at times, yet I felt throughout my tenure in office that there was no other place I would rather be. As I told the media at my last news conference, we could all agree on at least one thing: "It was never boring." There is much for which I am proud, and I look back with no regrets. Everything was done with a sincere belief that Kentucky would be better for it.

The Best Job in the World

There remains only one final question to be answered: was it worth it? I approached being governor pretty much like I did my business career, determined to out-work the competition. It did take its toll on my family and me. Martha often reminds me that I had never spent a day in a hospital until I was governor. There is no way to know whether my health problems were mere coincidences or the result of stress and fatigue, but there is no getting around the fact that the job can take a heavy toll on you if you let it.

Anything you work hard at can take a toll on you, of course. In few other jobs, however, are there so many obstacles in the way of getting something done. Perhaps that is one of the reasons fewer and fewer people want the job of governor, and those who do spend most of their time trying to avoid controversy.

My public service career began just as our two boys were at a point in their lives when their personal privacy meant much to them. Although being part of the commonwealth's "first family" brought with it certain amenities and a learning experience for our boys, one of them was not protection from public scrutiny. The job of governor is very demanding and severely limits family time. Martha was determined to give Glenn and Andrew the private family life they deserved.

Glenn had a particularly difficult time when he entered Lexington Community College and spent time on the University of Kentucky campus during my term in office. It was common for faculty members and an occasional student to pull him aside and confront him with their objections to my policies. As it turned out, although both boys would have preferred to attend college in Kentucky, they both left the state so they could lead normal college lives.

Of course there are many good moments for the first family, and one in particular I got to share with Glenn. I can thank former Governor Doug Wilder for this one, which becomes more treasured with the passing of time. I had the opportunity to attend several inaugural ceremonies as governor, including President George Bush's in 1989. The one I remember most fondly, however, was Governor Wilder's. Following the ceremony, Doug invited Glenn and me to join his other guests for lunch at the Governor's Mansion. To my surprise, he immediately ushered us to the front of the buffet line.

"I want you to be the first people served in this Mansion as guests of this country's first elected African-American governor," he said. With that statement, he served Glenn the first plate. I was certainly mindful of the history being made that day, but it was Doug's gesture of hospitality and the unexpected opportunity to be a small part of that history, which will forever make the day special to me.

Although one pays a personal price to enter public life, it has its rewards as well. For me, it was the personal nature of being governor which made the job so special. One can deal with issues and people directly. Governors come in contact with thousands of people, some with problems, some with praise, some with complaints, and some with suggestions. Some just want to meet the governor. Most of the people I met simply want to work at their jobs, raise their families, and educate their children with minimal interference from government. They simply want to do their part to make Kentucky a better place.

Sometimes serious, sometimes poignant, sometimes heartbreaking, sometimes lighthearted, the memories of people and places come back in flashes of recognition and recollection. I will never forget the pain and a feeling of helplessness after the Carrollton bus crash, the desire to do something when nothing could be done. I will never forget the strength of Kentucky's families and communities every time I saw them face tragedy and disaster. Nor will I forget their determination and competitive spirit when faced with new challenges and opportunities.

On a day-to-day basis no group has more frequent contact with a governor than the executive security detail. They see you in every kind of situation and every kind of mood. After awhile it's hard not to think of them as part of the family. I was blessed with the best group of Kentucky State Troopers any governor could possibly have. I'm proud that each one has remained a friend since we left Frankfort.

Throughout this book I have mentioned many of those who served so well in my administration. It is impractical to publicly acknowledge them all in a book like this. Without intending to diminish the contribution of any one of them, I want to mention one who served me well in a most critical area of government service—Dr. Harry Cowherd. His quiet demeanor often belied the strength of will and his dedication to public service. Much like the family physician he was in private practice, Harry served as secretary of the Cabinet for Human Resources with distinction. Perhaps more than anyone he appreciated the enormous capacity of government to affect people's lives in a positive way. He also keenly felt the enormous frustration that goes with trying to make a huge bureaucracy responsive to people's needs. As a teacher, healer, and friend, we lost him far too soon.

Perhaps my critical attitude toward the General Assembly might leave the impression that I had no respect for any legislator. As I said early in this book, as governor I developed personal friendships with many legislators. I came especially to respect and admire one legislator in particular who I thought best demonstrated the kind of public service desired from a citizen legislator—State Representative Paul Mason. Like many of his colleagues, Paul doesn't get the credit he deserves for making our government of and for the people. We need many more like him. He was and is my dear friend.

I realize there is much more that could be said about people I met and about the many whom I never had the opportunity to meet who gave me encouragement and support, even when things looked the darkest. Dozens of other anecdotes could be told, some funny and some sad, all real stories about real people and places and things that happened. These I will save for another time.

As I finish this book, there is one more story I want to share which expresses better than any other how I felt about being the governor of Kentucky. The last few days of the administration were filled with as much activity as any other day. I remember preparing for one last trip to west Kentucky that week. After working late the night before, I slowly walked over to the Mansion. Martha had spent the day with movers. Everything personal was gone but our clothing. As I walked upstairs to our living quarters, the reality that it was all coming to an end began to set in. Martha and I sat on a sofa and began to talk.

"I'm moving your things to Greenbriar tomorrow," she said. "The troopers will take you there when you get back tomorrow night." I just stared at her. Emotion welled up in both of us. Finally, I said "Martha, I can't leave here tomorrow. I'm not finished yet." I suppose all people with a vision never feel their work is done. On that night it seemed like it had only begun.

December 9, 1991

Governor Jones,

Tho the winds of change sweep through the commonwealth time and time again, the strength of Kentucky remains constant. Every day of the next four years your spirit will be renewed by the boundless energy, courage, and determination of your fellow Kentuckians.

In good times and bad, Kentuckians have always looked to their governors for support and leadership. That is a heavy weight that few are chosen to bear. Martha and my prayers will be with you and Libby as you accept that challenge.

Best wishes and God speed.

Wallace G. Wilkinson

Personal letter from Governor Wilkinson to his successor Governor Brereton Jones and left in the governor's desk according to tradition .

—A—

accountability, school, 50, 172, 174, 182, 191, 329, 330, 334
acid rain study, 355
Advocates for Higher Education, 157, 165
agenda, control of the, 126, 149, 153-154, 176-180, 306-309, 323
Alexander, Doug, 22, 28, 46, 143,
Alexander, Kern, 217
Allen, David, 169
Allen, Ron, 270-271
Anderson, Bob, 357
Armstrong v. Collins, 128
Augenblick, John, 204, 218, 220, 222
Avian Farms, 275

—B—

Barrows, Joe, 107, 158, 216
Bayh, Evan, 282
Beatinest Boy, 291
Bell, Robert, 157
benchmark schools, 147, 148
Bentson, Lloyd, 345
Berry Hill Mansion, 380
Beshear, Steve, 25, 29- 43
Bevis, Harold, 270
Bishop, Bill, 243
Blandford, Donald, 104-106, 189-190, 199, 201, 204, 249- 252, 315
Bluegrass State Poll, 41
Bluegrass State Skills Corporation, 292
Brandstad, Terry, 353
Breathitt, Linda, 358

Briscoe, Danny, 23, 28, 110, 318
Brock, John, 138, 156, 175, 177, 178-179, 181, 185, 199, 202, 217
Brown v. L.R.C., 115-116
Brown, John Y., 15- 17, 23, 25, 29-43, 47, 100, 114, 128, 265
Bryant, Milo, 275, 279
budget, 9-10, 12, 52, 54, 55, 67-93, 96-97, 120, 122, 138, 158, 161, 162, 163, 165, 186, 209, 220, 225, 226, 228, 229, 230, 237, 239, 241-245, 251, 258, 263, 277, 282, 290, 293, 302, 305, 316, 320, 324, 341-342, 346, 350, 372
budget memorandum, 124, 127-130
Burns, Conrad, 332
Bush, George, 328, 383

—C—

Campbell, Carroll, 338, 353
Campbellsville College, 8
Capital Plaza Hotel, 26, 266
Capitol to the Counties program, 170, 171, 172, 366
carbon taxes, 356
Carroll, John, 175
Carroll, Julian, 32, 34, 302
Carson, Ron, 241, 243
Carville, James, 1, 24-25, 28, 30, 35, 46
Casey County, 1- 4, 7, 257, 277
Cavazos, Lauro, 335
Chamber of Commerce, 188
Chandler, A. B. "Happy", 3, 277
Chellgren, Mark, 266, 277
Chief State School Officers, Council of, 335

Faulkner, Dick, 381
federal mandates, 328, 341, 348-350
finance & administration cabinet, 9
Fleming, Denis, 270
Fleming, Jim, 302
fly arounds, 34
Flynn's Restaurant, 245, 312
Fogle, Avon, 280
Ford Motor Company, 292
Ford, Wendell, 302, 345, 358
Forgy, Larry, 217
Foster, Jack, 51, 134, 135, 143, 155,
    158, 159, 175-176, 181, 182, 204,
    217, 219, 294
Fruit of the Loom, 289

—G—

Gant, William M., 198
General Educational Development
    (GED), 286-291
General Electric, 292
General Tire, 267-268
Gere, Richard, 24
great compromise", "the *See*
    compromise, the great
Gephardt, Richard, 345
Gill, George, 263
golden triangle, 21, 22, 262
Governor's School Improvement
    Act, 161
Governor's School Improvement
    Program, 141
Grass Roots Coalition, 177
Greater Louisville Downtown
    Economic Development
    Foundation, 263
Grunwald, Mandy, 33
Gubser, Sandra, 175, 216, 295

—H—

Hable, Kevin, 188
Hackbart, Merl, 219, 241
Hamilton, Sally, 276
Harper, John, 40, 41
Hayes, Larry, 47
Hazelwood Hospital, 265
HB6, 47
HB19, 81
HB44, 30
HB217, 80
HB544, 115
HB630, 107
HB814, 294
HB855, 115
HB940, 223-224
HB963, 81
HB1022, 107
Health Care Financing
    Administration, (HCFA), 343
Herald-Leader, Lexington, 20, 26,
    51-52, 59, 71, 175, 274, 280-281
Heritage Days, Louisville, 37
higher education reform, 371-377
highway trust fund, 341, 346-348
Hintze, Bill, 241, 243
hold harmless provision in SEEK,
    222-223
Hoover, Herbert, 2
Hornbeck, David, 204, 205-206
Hospital Indigent Care Assistance
    Program, (HICAP) 343-344
Huddleston, Walter Dee, 17
Human Resources Cabinet, 294, 385
Humana Hospital, 264

—I—

incentives, school financial, 50, 139
Institute for Educational Leadership, 148
Institutional Investor, 260
International Roundtable on Education Reform, 284
"itty-bitty journals", 376-377

—J—

Japan, International Bank of, 259
Japanese yen bond issue, *see Yen Bond*
Jennings, Waylon, 289-290
Jernigan, Jerome, 41
Jesse Stuart Foundation, 291
Job Training Certificate Program, 74
Job Training Partnership Act, 294
Johnson, Bob, 298, 316-317
Johnstone, Ken, 155
Jones, Brereton, 123, 313
Jones, Tom, 158
Jordan, Jim, 20

—K—

KARE health care insurance program, 170
Karem, David, 131, 160
Keller, David, 174
KEA, *See Kentucky Education Association*
KEA Political Action Committee (KEPAC), 169
Kentucky Court of Appeals, 234
Kentucky Derby, 23, 32, 33, 368
Kentucky Development Finance Authority, 117

Kentucky Education Association, 93, 94, 163, 168-173, 201, 223, 249
Kentucky Education Reform Act, (KERA) 138, 148, 191, 206, 220, 224, 305, 367
Kentucky Educational Television, 287, 288, 289, 290, 331
Kentucky Firefighters Assoc., 25
Kentucky First, 61, 62-67, 73, 74, 89, 141, 275, 327
Kentucky Infrastructure Authority (KDFA), 81, 118
Kentucky Integrated Delivery System (KIDS), 138
Kentucky Legislature: Two Decades of Change, 302
Kentucky Lottery, 16, 27-29, 30, 32, 34, 41, 56, 69, 73, 77, 82-86, 100, 104, 107, 138, 178, 308, 309, 314, 370
Kentucky Lottery Commission, 82, 84
Kentucky Pollution Abatement and Water Resources Finance Authority, 80
Kentucky Post, Covington, 41, 42, 170
Kentucky Public Works Act, 80
Kentucky Standard, Bardstown, 280
Kentucky Supreme Court, 54, 57, 115, 116, 128, 165, 182, 189-192, 199-200, 207, 215, 218, 224-225, 335, 339
KET Star Channel, 332
Kimbrough, Randy, 176
Kring, Ray, 270

—L—

Lawrence, Keith, 299
Lazarus, Ed, 30, 38, 39, 311
League of Women Voters, 28, 249
Lear, Bill, 107, 119
legislative independence, 11, 12, 60, 103
legislative offices, 122-123
Legislative Research Commission (LRC), 27, 47, 115, 117, 159, 167, 197, 216, 220, 302, 314
Lexington Community College, 383
Liberty, Kentucky, 3, 4, 22, 36
Lichtman, Allan J., 298
Literacy Commission, 138, 291
Local Government, Dept of, 276-277
Loftus, Tom, 187
Lomicka, Bill, 264
London Interbank Borrowing Rate (LIBOR), 268
Lottery Yes Committee, 83
Lowery, Steve, 280

—M—

Mabus, Ray, 353
Malloy, Pat, 264
Martha's Army, 287-291
Mason, Paul, 385
McBrayer, Terry, 17
McClease, Kenny, 380
McDonald, Alice, 47
Medicaid, 350
Medicaid Provider Tax, 342-345
Medicare, 350
Meiners, Terry, 36
Mellman, Mark, 30, 38, 39, 311
Melton, James, 216, 217

Messenger-Inquirer, Owensboro, 269
Meyer, Danny, 107
Meyer, Joe, 107
Miller, John Winn, 143
Miller, Scott, 33
minimum foundation program, 74, 95, 167, 214, 219
Moberly, Harry, 158, 320
Moloney, Michael, 49, 53, 123, 188, 219, 220, 246, 253, 260, 319-320
Moody's, 79
Mountz, Wade, 177, 178

—N—

Natcher, William H., 279-280, 282
Nation at Risk, A, 328
National Alliance of Business, 260
National Assessment of Progress in Education (NAPE), 333
National Conference of State Legislatures (NCSL), 204
National Education Telecommunications Organization (NETO), 332-333
National Governors' Association (NGA), 329, 345, 346, 349, 352
Newman, Frank, 339
Nichols, J.D., 181
Noe, Roger, 49, 107, 158, 160-161, 290, 293
Noel, Jeff, 262
Nomura Securities, 259
North American Stainless, 275

Toyota Motor Company, 26-27, 79, 117, 231, 261, 262, 265-267, 286, 292

Troutwine, Lee, 275-276

"two Kentuckys", 7, 262

—U—

U.S.S. Kentucky, 379

Underwood, Jack, 361

United Airlines, 271-274

University of Kentucky, 8, 226, 275, 319, 360, 383

University of Kentucky Board of Trustees, 367, 371-376

University of Louisville Hospital, 264

—V—

Valeria, Louis, 274

Vance, Roy N., 197

Vaughan, Roger, 295

venture capital fund, 62, 63, 81

—W—

Wallace, Cliff, 176

Walters, David, 345

Walton, Dan, 361

Watson, Sylvia, 217

Waxman, Henry, 345

Weinstein, Shelly, 332

Wells, L. Rogers, 231, 242, 259, 270-271

Wethington, Charles, 372

WHAS, 35-36

Wilder, Doug, 353, 383

Wilkinson, Andrew, 383

Wilkinson, Glenn, 383

Wilkinson, Martha, 15, 16, 18-19, 28, 287-291, 365, 367-371, 381, 382-383, 385-386

Williams, Terry, 170

Willis, Tom, 220

Wills, Garry, 45

Wiseman, Jim, 179-180

Wolf, Stephen, 272

workforce development, 256, 284, 292, 296

Workforce Development Cabinet, 138, 294

workforce training trust fund, 293

World Coal Center, 43

Wright, Joe, 83, 101, 103, 106, 160, 252

Wyatt, Wilson, Sr., 240

—Y—

yen bond issue, 257, 259-260